To Michael
With all our love,
Katherine, Bob, Sam & Kit
Christmas 1992.

My Secret Planet

Also by Denis Healey

The Time of My Life
When Shrimps Learn to Whistle

MY SECRET PLANET

Denis Healey

MICHAEL JOSEPH
London

To Jenny, Tim and Cressida,
who have kept me young for nearly half a century.

MICHAEL JOSEPH LTD

Published by the Penguin Group
Penguin Books Ltd, 27 Wrights Lane, London W8 5TZ, England
Penguin Books USA Inc., 375 Hudson Street, New York, New York 10014, USA
Penguin Books Australia Ltd, Ringwood, Victoria, Australia
Penguin Books Canada Ltd, 10 Alcorn Avenue, Toronto, Ontario, Canada M4V 3B2
Penguin Books (NZ) Ltd, 182–190 Wairau Road, Auckland 10, New Zealand

Penguin Books Ltd, Registered Offices: Harmondsworth, Middlesex, England

First published in Great Britain 1992

Typeset by DatIX International Limited, Bungay, Suffolk
Set in 11½ on 13 pt Monophoto Bembo
Printed in England by Clays Ltd, St Ives plc

A CIP catalogue record for this book is available from the British Library

ISBN 0 7181 3667 5

CONTENTS

INTRODUCTION

The original quality in any man of imagination is imagery. It is a thing like the landscape of his dreams; the sort of world he would wish to make or in which he would wish to wander; the strange flora and fauna of his own secret planet; the sort of thing he likes to think about.

G.K. Chesterton

This book is my secret planet. It is an attempt to describe some of the furniture of my mind – writings which have influenced me at various periods of my life or which illustrate aspects of my world which are important to me. Towards the end of his life Yeats wrote:

> I must lie down where all the ladders start,
> In the foul rag-and-bone shop of the heart.

By contrast, this book is a lumber room under the roof over which I play my torch, discovering things long forgotten, some of which I did not realize I possessed.

I described the external events of my life in my memoir *The Time of My Life*. In *When Shrimps Learn to Whistle* I tried to show, through a collection of my writings and speeches, how my political ideas had developed since the war. Here I am engaged in a more difficult and dangerous enterprise – to explore my inner life over seventy-four years, through writings which have planted seeds to germinate in my mind.

Although I describe here how my approach to politics was shaped when I was a student, and include a chapter of writings about politics, I am not concerned to discuss political issues in this book. My purpose here is to illuminate the nature of political activity compared, say, with writing poetry or painting pictures. You may be as surprised as I was to discover that there are often as many similarities as differences.

Among my favourite writers Wordsworth, Heine, Yeats and Auden were all at times directly engaged in politics. Virginia Woolf, however, was interested in nothing but the personal life; she found politics and history equally 'spectral'. Traherne lived through the English Civil War, and Emily Dickinson through the even bloodier American Civil War, without even mentioning them. Yet all these writers have had an equally profound influence on me.

Where the writers are comparatively little known – the works of Traherne, Dickinson, and Hopkins were not even published until long after their deaths – I have to tried to sketch enough of their lives to make it easier to understand their poetry. In most cases I have set my quotations in their historical context, as I think it is difficult fully to appreciate creative writing without understanding something of the time in which it was produced.

Since we all develop as we move through life, I thought it best to describe my reading from my childhood onwards. However, as in my memoirs, I have had to group the more important aspects of my adult life under separate themes, such as art, nature, human relations and the spirit; inevitably there is a good deal of overlapping between these themes.

Shortage of space prevents me from including very lengthy pieces, or I would print, for example, whole novels by Tolstoy, Dostoevsky, Flaubert and Stendhal. That is why I have used more poetry than prose. Poetry can concentrate its meaning far more intensely; it makes its point through images, sounds and symbols rather than through sentences. Emily Dickinson, for example, can pack more meaning into forty words than some writers get into forty pages.

I have often included quotations from writers whose general attitude to life I do not share. You can enjoy much of D.H.

Lawrence without supporting phallocracy, and find insights in much of Nietzsche without believing in his Superman.

The Time of My Life compelled me to reflect on the lessons of my political experience for the first time since the war. Here I describe the conclusions I have reached about other subjects which are no less important to me, such as philosophy and the arts. I have reached these conclusions by thinking hard about what men and women far greater than myself have written about their consuming passion – for example Kant on the limitations of knowledge, Hopkins on poetry, Berlioz on music, Van Gogh on painting, Blake and Dickinson on the life of the spirit.

More than ever, I came to realize how my years at university before the war shaped my approach to everything that followed. My study of philosophy convinced me that scientific reason, however mighty its achievements in helping us to understand and control the physical world, can throw little light on those questions which by definition matter most to all of us as human beings – questions of value, which require us to use words like 'good' and 'beautiful'.

Similarly I learned that it is not possible to understand politics, particularly in a world which is changing as fast as ours after the end of the Cold War, without knowing something of history. We need also to understand something of the culture of other peoples; here the poets and novelists can teach us more than the so-called political scientists. However, this book is not intended to instruct; I want above all to let you share in the pleasure I have had from reading throughout my life.

The months I spent in writing this book have given me immense delight. I have been able to enjoy again, at leisure, books which the pressure of my political work compelled me to put at the back of my mind. If I succeed in communicating some of my own excitement to you, I shall be content. I hope you may want to read more of some of the authors I have quoted, so I have added a short postscript which may help you to follow them up.

1

BOYHOOD

When that I was and a little tiny boy,
  With hey, ho, the wind and the rain;
A foolish thing was but a toy,
  For the rain it raineth every day.
    – *Twelfth Night*, William Shakespeare

I had a happy childhood, which I now recognize as a blessing beyond price. Indeed I was reluctant to leave my childhood behind. During my teens my friends often accused me of being childish. I much preferred that to being called adolescent, and would remind them that 'unless ye be as little children ye enter not into the kingdom of heaven'. Even today I retain some childish habits, like making horrible faces or using a funny voice on the telephone. I suppose this accounts for my pleasure in making a fool of myself on television with Edna Everage or Victoria Wood.

Young children, however, cannot at the time describe what it is to be a child, nor do they particularly want to read about themselves. The great books about children are written by grown-ups and are best read by adults. Even Kenneth Grahame's *Dream Days* and *The Golden Age* seemed rather sentimental when I first read them as a boy. An exception was Richard Jefferies' *Bevis* which describes the adventures of a boy in the country who builds an encampment on an island in the local reservoir. I enjoyed that book enormously when I was no older than Bevis himself.

The essence of childhood is the capacity for wonder and joy.

Two of my favourite writers, Thomas Traherne and Dylan Thomas, saw their childhood as the happiest time of their life, and wrote their best work about it. I did not come across either until after the war, but they hold a special place in my pantheon. They were very different characters.

Thomas Traherne was born in 1637, the son of a shoemaker in Hereford. After taking a degree at Oxford he spent thirteen years as rector of a little parish near Hereford called Credenhill; for the five years before his death in 1674 he also acted as chaplain to the Lord Keeper of the Great Seal at Teddington outside London.

He cared so little about posterity that he did not sign any of his manuscripts. In fact, except for two undistinguished theses on religion, none of his works was published until two-and-a-half centuries after his death. A bundle of manuscripts was bought for a few pence in 1896; they were discovered to be by Traherne through astonishing detective work by Bertram Dobell, who published them in 1903.

I first came across Traherne at Oxford through a small selection of his poetry and prose chosen by Quiller-Couch. Since then I have returned to him again and again for inspiration. He describes the wonder of his childhood in one of his *Meditations*:

> The corn was Orient and Immortal Wheat, which never should be reaped, nor was ever sown. I thought it had stood from everlasting to everlasting. The Dust and Stones of the Street were as precious as GOLD: the Gates were at first the End of the World. The Green Trees, when I saw them first through one of the Gates Transported and Ravished me, their sweetness and unusual Beauty made my Heart to leap, and almost mad with ecstasie there were such strange and wonderful Things: The Men! O, what Venerable and Reverend Creatures did the Aged seem! Immortal Cherubims and young men Glittering and Sparkling; Angels, and Maids strange Seraphic Pieces of Life and Beauty. Boys and Girles Tumbling in the street and playing, were moving Jewels. I knew not that they were Born, or should Die; But all things abided Eternally as they were in their Proper Places.

Like most of us, he let his memory cast too rosy a glow on his childhood. Later in the same work he wrote:

> Once I remember (I think I was about 4 years old) when I thus reasoned with myself, sitting in a little Obscure Room in my

father's poor House: If there be a God, certainly He must be infinite in Goodness; and that I was prompted to by a real Whispering Instinct of Nature. And if He be infinite in goodness and a Perfect Being in Wisdom and Love, certainly He must do most Glorious Things, and give us infinite riches; how comes it to pass therefore that I am so poor? Of so Scanty and Narrow a fortune, enjoying few and obscure comforts? I thought I could not believe Him a GOD to me unless all his power were employed to Glorify me. I knew not then my Soul or Body, nor did I think of the Heavens and the Earth, the Rivers and the Stars, the Sun or the Seas; all those were lost or absent from me.

Dylan Thomas was born, just after the First World War broke out, in Swansea, another provincial town surrounded by lovely country, with the sea at its foot. I had read his early work as a student, and was impressed, but not over-excited. Then, as I was waiting to be demobilized in October 1945, I read 'Fern Hill' in the magazine, *Horizon*, and was bowled over. Its evocation of Thomas' childhood has glowed in my mind ever since:

Now as I was young and easy under the apple boughs
About the lilting house and happy as the grass was green,
   The night above the dingle starry,
     Time let me hail and climb
    Golden in the heydays of his eyes,
And honoured among wagons I was prince of the apple towns
And once below a time I lordly had the trees and leaves
     Trail with daisies and barley
    Down the rivers of the windfall light.

And as I was green and carefree, famous among the barns
About the happy yard and singing as the farm was home,
   In the sun that is young once only,
     Time let me play and be
    Golden in the mercy of his means,
And green and golden I was huntsman and herdsman, the calves
Sang to my horn, the foxes on the hills barked clear and cold,
     And the sabbath rang slowly
    In the pebbles of the holy streams.

All the sun long it was running, it was lovely, the hay
Fields high as the house, the tunes from the chimneys, it was air
    And playing, lovely and watery
     And fire green as grass.

And nightly under the simple stars
As I rode to sleep the owls were bearing the farm away,
All the moon long I heard, blessed among stables, the nightjars
   Flying with the ricks, and the horses
    Flashing into the dark.

And then to awake, and the farm, like a wanderer white
With the dew, come back, the cock on his shoulder: it was all
   Shining, it was Adam and maiden
    The sky gathered again
   And the sun grew round that very day.
So it must have been after the birth of the simple light
In the first, spinning place, the spellbound horses walking warm
   Out of the whinnying green stable
    On to the fields of praise.

And honoured among foxes and pheasants by the gay house
Under the new made clouds and happy as the heart was long,
   In the sun born over and over,
    I ran my heedless ways,
   My wishes raced through the horse high hay
And nothing I cared, at my sky blue trades, that time allows
In all his tuneful turning so few and such morning songs
   Before the children green and golden
    Follow him out of grace,

Nothing I cared, in the lamb white days, that time would take me
Up to the swallow thronged loft by the shadow of my hand,
   In the moon that is always rising.
    Nor that riding to sleep
   I should hear him fly with the high fields
And wake to the farm forever fled from the childless land.
Oh as I was young and easy in the mercy of his means,
    Time held me green and dying
   Though I sang in my chains like the sea.

Thomas was always at his best in writing of his childhood – 'Poem in October' is another of my favourites. His early success, however, went to his head. He was lionized by the literary set which frequented the Fitzroy Tavern in Soho. His friend Louis MacNeice describes him as 'Gwilym' in 'Autumn Sequel':

    A bulbous Taliessin, a spruce and small
    Bow-tied Silenus roistering his way
    Through lands of fruit and fable, well aware

That even Dionysus has his day
And cannot take it with him. Debonair
He leant against the bar till his cigarette
Became one stream of ash sustained in air
Through which he puffed his talk.

Alas, he looked more often like an unmade bed than this implies. In his later years he wrote some superb scripts for the BBC, including *Under Milk Wood*, before he drank himself to death on the American lecture-circuit, a hazard that earlier poets did not have to face. Shortly before he died at the age of thirty-nine, he wrote another magnificent evocation of his schoolboy days, which started as a radio script, *A Child's Christmas in Wales*:

Years and years and years ago, when I was a boy, when there were wolves in Wales, and birds the colour of red-flannel petticoats whisked past the harp-shaped hills, when we sang and wallowed all night and day in caves that smelt like Sunday afternoons in damp front farmhouse parlours and we chased, with the jawbones of deacons, the English and the bears, before the motor-car, before the wheel, before the duchess-faced horse, when we rode the daft and happy hills bareback, it snowed and it snowed. But here a small boy says: 'It snowed last year, too. I made a snowman and my brother knocked it down and I knocked my brother down and then we had tea.'

'But that was not the same snow,' I say. 'Our snow was not only shaken from whitewash buckets down the sky, it came shawling out of the ground and swam and drifted out of the arms and hands and bodies of the trees; snow grew overnight on the roofs of the houses like a pure and grandfather moss, minutely white-ivied the walls and settled on the postman, opening the gate, like a dumb, numb thunderstorm of white, torn Christmas cards.'

'Were there postmen then, too?'

'With sprinkling eyes and wind-cherried noses, on spread, frozen feet they crunched up to the doors and mittened on them manfully. But all that the children could hear was a ringing of bells.'

'You mean that the postman went rat-a-tat-tat and the doors rang?'

'I mean that the bells that the children could hear were inside them.'

'I only hear thunder sometimes, never bells.'

'There were church bells, too.'

'Inside them?'

'No, no, no, in the bat-black, snow-white belfries, tugged by bishops and storks. And they rang their tidings over the bandaged town, over the frozen foam of the powder and ice-cream hills, over the crackling sea. It seemed that all the churches boomed for joy under my window; and the weathercocks crew for Christmas, on our fence.'

'Get back to the postmen.'

'They were just ordinary postmen, fond of walking and dogs and Christmas and the snow. They knocked on the doors with blue knuckles . . .'

'Ours has got a black knocker . . .'

'And then they stood on the white Welcome mat in the little, drifted porches and huffed and puffed, making ghosts with their breath, and jogged from foot to foot like small boys wanting to go out.'

'And then the Presents?'

'And then the Presents, after the Christmas box. And the cold postman, with a rose on his button-nose, tingled down the tea-tray-slithered run of the chilly glinting hill. He went in his ice-bound boots like a man on fishmonger's slabs. He wagged his bag like a frozen camel's hump, dizzily turned the corner on one foot, and, by God, he was gone.'

'Get back to the Presents.'

'There were the Useful Presents: engulfing mufflers of the old coach days, and mittens made for giant sloths; zebra scarfs of a substance like silky gum that could be tug-of-warred down to the galoshes: blinding tam-o'-shanters like patchwork tea cosies and bunny-suited busbies and balaclavas for victims of head-shrinking tribes; from aunts who always wore wool next to the skin there were moustached and rasping vests that made you wonder why the aunts had any skin left at all; and once I had a little crocheted nose bag from an aunt now, alas, no longer whinnying with us. And pictureless books in which small boys, though warned with quotations not to, *would* skate on Farmer Giles' pond and did and drowned; and books that told me everything about the wasp, except why.'

'Go on to the Useless Presents.'

Bags of moist and many-coloured jelly babies and a folded flag and a false nose and a tram-conductor's cap and a machine that punched tickets and rang a bell; never a catapult; once, by mistake that no one could explain, a little hatchet; and a celluloid duck that made, when you pressed it, a most unducklike sound, a mewing moo that an ambitious cat might make who wished to be a cow; and a painting book in which I could make the grass, the trees, the sea and the animals any colour I pleased, and still the dazzling sky-blue sheep are grazing in the red field under the rainbow-billed and pea-green birds.

'Hardboileds, toffee, fudge and allsorts, crunches, cracknels, humbugs, glaciers, marzipan, and butterwelsh for the Welsh. And troops of bright tin soldiers who, if they could not fight, could always run. And Snakes-and-Families and Happy Ladders. And Easy Hobbi-Games for Little Engineers, complete with instructions.

'Oh, easy for Leonardo! And a whistle to make the dogs bark to wake up the old man next door to make him beat on the wall with his stick to shake our picture off the wall.

'And a packet of cigarettes; you put one in your mouth and you stood at the corner of the street and you waited for hours, in vain, for an old lady to scold you for smoking a cigarette, and then with a smirk you ate it.'

I enjoyed my boyhood as much as did Traherne and Thomas, partly, I think, because like them I lived in a small town surrounded by beautiful countryside. But my childhood does not stand out for me as the happiest time of my life. I have always been happy, even if occasionally my happiness was tempered by concern about my work as a soldier or politician. School, of course, had its pains as well as its pleasures; however, unlike Shakespeare's schoolboy, despite my satchel and my shining morning face, I did not creep like snail, unwillingly to school.

I could identify more easily with John Clare's schoolboys when I first read him after the war. Clare was born in 1793 to a family of poor agricultural labourers near Peterborough; he worked as a herder at the age of seven. When he was twenty-seven his first book of poems on rural life and scenery brought him a short-lived celebrity in London; his later works earned little money, and he had to return to working on the land. Poverty and drink gave him delusions which led to him spending his last twenty-seven years in an asylum for the insane, though he continued writing great poetry until his death in 1864. Much of his verse is inspired by his childhood and youth. His descriptions of schoolboys remind me of my own return from school after I left the bus from Bradford and walked up Granby Lane to my home in Riddlesden.

> Hark to that happy shout! – the school-house door
>   Is open thrown, and out the younkers teem;
> Some run to leap-frog on the rushy moor,

And others dabble in the shallow stream,
Catching young fish, and turning pebbles o'er
   For mussel-clams. Look in that mellow gleam,
Where the retiring sun, that rests the while,
   Streams through the broken hedge! How happy seem
Those friendly schoolboys leaning o'er the stile,
   Both reading in one book! – Anon a dream,
Rich with new joys, doth their young hearts beguile,
   And the book's pocketed right hastily.
Ah, happy boys! well may ye turn and smile,
   When joys are yours that never cost a sigh.

*

The schoolboys still their morning rambles take
To neighbouring village school with playing speed,
Loitering with pastime's leisure till they quake,
Oft looking up the wild-geese droves to heed,
Watching the letters which their journeys make;
Or plucking haws on which the fieldfares feed,
And hips, and sloes; and on each shallow lake
Making glib slides, where they like shadows go
Till some fresh pastimes in their minds awake.
Then off they start anew and hasty blow
Their numbed and clumpsing fingers till they glow;
Then races with their shadows wildly run
That stride huge giants o'er the shining snow
In the pale splendour of the winter sun.

For me, the Great Strike of 1926 meant at first just having to ride the nine miles to school on my bicycle instead of going by bus. Then one of my favourite teachers, a good-looking young man called Captain Benn, who had served in the war, explained how poverty had driven the strikers into industrial action. This made me much more conscious that all children were not as lucky as I. The Great Slump which started a few years later brought massive unemployment to Yorkshire and especially to Todmorden, where my Auntie Maggie worked in a mill. We began giving a penny a week from our pocket money to buy 'Boots for the Bairns'. I began to realize that 'The Chimney Sweeper', in William Blake's poem had his modern parallels:

> When my mother died I was very young,
> And my father sold me while yet my tongue

Could scarcely cry, ''weep! 'weep! 'weep! 'weep!'
So your chimneys I sweep, and in soot I sleep.

There's little Tom Dacre, who cried when his head,
That curl'd like a lamb's back, was shav'd: so I said
'Hush, Tom! never mind it, for when your head's bare
You know that the soot cannot spoil your white hair.'

And so he was quiet, and that very night,
As Tom was a-sleeping, he had such a sight! –
That thousands of sweepers, Dick, Joe, Ned, and Jack,
Were all of them lock'd up in coffins of black.

And by came an Angel who had a bright key,
And he open'd the coffins and set them all free;
Then down a green plain leaping, laughing, they run,
And wash in a river, and shine in the sun.

Then naked and white, all their bags left behind,
They rise upon clouds and sport in the wind;
And the Angel told Tom, if he'd be a good boy,
He'd have God for his father, and never want joy.

And so Tom awoke: and we rose in the dark,
And got with our bags and our brushes to work.
Tho' the morning was cold, Tom was happy and warm:
So if all do their duty they need not fear harm.

My feelings at that time are well expressed in a poem I read in
recent years by Charles Causley, a schoolmaster in Cornwall,
about a boy in his class:

Timothy Winters comes to school
With eyes as wide as a football pool,
Ears like bombs and teeth like splinters:
A blitz of a boy is Timothy Winters.

His belly is white, his neck is dark,
And his hair is an exclamation mark.
His clothes are enough to scare a crow
And through his britches the blue winds blow.

When teacher talks he won't hear a word
And he shoots down dead the arithmetic-bird,
He licks the patterns off his plate
And he's not even heard of the Welfare State.

Timothy Winters has bloody feet
And he lives in a house on Suez Street,
He sleeps in a sack on the kitchen floor
And they say there aren't boys like him any more.

Old Man Winters likes his beer
And his missus ran off with a bombardier,
Grandma sits in the grate with a gin
And Timothy's dosed with an aspirin.

The Welfare Worker lies awake
But the law's as tricky as a ten-foot snake,
So Timothy Winters drinks his cup
And slowly goes on growing up.

At Morning Prayers the Master helves
For children less fortunate than ourselves,
And the loudest response in the room is when
Timothy Winters roars 'Amen!'

So come one angel, come on ten:
Timothy Winters says 'Amen
Amen amen amen amen.'
Timothy Winters, Lord.

                                        Amen.

I suppose that was when 'shades of the prison house' began to close
on me. Nevertheless, I could still share the confidence with which
William Wordsworth described his 'Intimations of Immortality':

Our birth is but a sleep and a forgetting:
The Soul that rises with us, our life's Star,
        Hath had elsewhere its setting,
            And cometh from afar:
        Not in entire forgetfulness,
        And not in utter nakedness,
But trailing clouds of glory do we come
        From God, who is our home:
Heaven lies about us in our infancy!
Shades of the prison-house begin to close
        Upon the growing Boy,
                But He
Beholds the light, and whence it flows,
        He sees it in his joy;

O joy! that in our embers
Is something that doth live,
That nature yet remembers
What was so fugitive!
The thought of our past years in me doth breed
Perpetual benediction: not indeed
For that which is most worthy to be blest –
Delight and liberty, the simple creed
Of Childhood, whether busy or at rest,
With new-fledged hope still fluttering in his breast: –
Not for these I raise
The song of thanks and praise;
But for those obstinate questionings
Of sense and outward things,
Fallings from us, vanishings;
Blank misgivings of a Creature
Moving about in worlds not realized,
High instincts before which our mortal Nature
Did tremble like a guilty Thing surprised:
But for those first affections,
Those shadowy recollections,

Which, be they what they may,
Are yet the fountain light of all our day,
Are yet a master light of all our seeing;
Uphold us, cherish, and have power to make
Our noisy years seem moments in the being
Of the eternal Silence: truths that wake,
To perish never;
Which neither listlessness, nor mad endeavour,
Nor Man nor Boy,
Nor all that is at enmity with joy,
Can utterly abolish or destroy!
Hence in a season of calm weather
Though inland far we be,
Our Souls have sight of that immortal sea
Which brought us hither,
Can in a moment travel thither,
And see the Children sport upon the shore,
And hear the mighty waters rolling evermore.

Then sing, ye Birds, sing, sing a joyous song!
And let the young Lambs bound
As to the tabor's sound!
We in thought will join your throng,

> Ye that pipe and ye that play,
> Ye that through your hearts to-day
> Feel the gladness of the May!
> What though the radiance which was once so bright
> Be now for ever taken from my sight,
> Though nothing can bring back the hour
> Of splendour in the grass, of glory in the flower:

Wordsworth also spoke for me when he wrote that 'the child is father to the man'. Many exasperated parents go further, claiming that insanity is hereditary, because you get it from your children.

I was always much closer to my mother than to my father. It was she who saw that I did my homework and encouraged my interest in the arts, which she herself was studying in the Workers' Education Association. I saw much less of my father, because the evening classes at his Technical College took him away from our home before I got back from school. As a child I found my father curiously sentimental and sometimes very cantankerous. It is in any case impossible for a child to see either of his parents as they really are, or even as they appear to their contemporaries. Mark Twain put it well:

> When I was a boy of fourteen, my father was so ignorant I could hardly stand to have the old man around. But when I got to be twenty-one, I was astonished at how much the old man had learned in seven years.

The mystery of growing up is explored in one of William Butler Yeats' greatest poems, 'Among Schoolchildren' (the woman referred to in verses II to IV is Maude Gonne, for whom he cherished a hopeless passion most of his life):

> I walk through the long schoolroom questioning;
> A kind old nun in a white hood replies;
> The children learn to cipher and to sing,
> To study reading-books and histories,
> To cut and sew, be neat in everything
> In the best modern way – the children's eyes
> In momentary wonder stare upon
> A sixty-year-old smiling public man.

II

I dream of a Ledaean body, bent
Above a sinking fire, a tale that she
Told of a harsh reproof, or trivial event
That changed some childish day to tragedy –
Told, and it seemed that our two natures blent
Into a sphere from youthful sympathy,
Or else, to alter Plato's parable,
Into the yolk and white of the one shell.

III

And thinking of that fit of grief or rage
I look upon one child or t'other there
And wonder if she stood so at that age –
For even daughters of the swan can share
Something of every paddler's heritage –
And had that colour upon cheek or hair,
And thereupon my heart is driven wild:
She stands before me as a living child.

IV

Her present image floats into the mind –
Did Quattrocento finger fashion it
Hollow of cheek as though it drank the wind
And took a mess of shadows for its meat?
And I though never of Ledaean kind
Had pretty plumage once – enough of that,
Better to smile on all that smile, and show
There is a comfortable kind of old scarecrow.

V

What youthful mother, a shape upon her lap
Honey of generation had betrayed,
And that must sleep, shriek, struggle to escape
As recollection or the drug decide,
Would think her son, did she but see that shape
With sixty or more winters on its head,
A compensation for the pang of his birth,
Or the uncertainty of his setting forth?

VI

Plato thought nature but a spume that plays
Upon a ghostly paradigm of things;
Soldier Aristotle played the taws
Upon the bottom of a king of kings;
World-famous golden-thighed Pythagoras

Fingered upon a fiddle-stick or strings
What a star sang and careless Muses heard:
Old clothes upon old sticks to scare a bird.

VII

Both nuns and mothers worship images,
But those the candles light are not as those
That animate a mother's reveries,
But keep a marble or a bronze repose.
And yet they too break hearts – O Presences
That passion, piety or affection knows,
And that all heavenly glory symbolise –
O self-born mockers of man's enterprise;

VIII

Labour is blossoming or dancing where
The body is not bruised to pleasure soul,
Nor beauty born out of its own despair,
Nor blear-eyed wisdom out of midnight oil.
O chestnut-tree, great-rooted blossomer,
Are you the leaf, the blossom or the bole?
O body swayed to music, O brightening glance,
How can we know the dancer from the dance?

I had no sisters, so in my early schooldays I had to rely on books to tell me what girls were like. The *William* books, all of which I read more than once, did not paint an encouraging picture. Violet Elizabeth, with her constant threat to 'thcream and thcream' till she's sick, seemed all too credible, though it was late in my life when I first came across the type in reality – and then in Downing Street.

In childhood the war of the sexes can take unexpected shapes. Daisy Ashford wrote *The Young Visiters* when she was only nine years old; it gives an unfiltered view of the adult world as seen by a child. A year earlier she had dictated *Love and Marriage* to her father. It was less complimentary to males of her own age, as is shown by her description of the wedding breakfast:

For the wedding breakfast they had several cups of Bouillon Fleet and eight of Bovril. They had six Vanilla cream puddings and strawberry ices by the score; but they kept the blinds drawn down in case vulgar little boys should loom in and say 'give us a slice', while the leg of pork was being cut.

Mark Twain went some way towards confirming Daisy Ashford's prejudice when he has Tom Sawyer say:

> There's plenty of boys that will come hankering and gruvvelling around when you've got an apple, and beg the core off you; but when *they've* got one, and you beg for the core and remind them how you give them a core one time, they make a mouth at you and say thank you 'most to death, but there ain't-a-going to be no core.

YORKSHIRE

My family had moved from Woolwich to Yorkshire when I was five. So for most of my boyhood I lived in Riddlesden, a village on the edge of Ilkley Moor looking over Keighley to Haworth, where the Brontë sisters had lived a century before. Yorkshire and Yorkshire folk had changed little in that hundred years. Mrs Gaskell begins her *Life of Charlotte Brontë* with an accurate description of the land and the people:

> In a town one does not look for vivid colouring; what there may be of this is furnished by the wares in the shops, not by foliage or atmospheric effects; but in the country some brilliancy and vividness seems to be instinctively expected, and there is consequently a slight feeling of disappointment at the grey neutral tint of every object, near or far off, on the way from Keighley to Haworth. The distance is about four miles; and, as I have said, what with villas, great worsted factories, rows of workmen's houses, with here and there an old-fashioned farm-house and outbuildings, it can hardly be called 'country' any part of the way. For two miles the road passes over tolerably level ground, distant hills on the left, a 'beck' flowing through meadows on the right, and furnishing water power, at certain points, to the factories built on its banks. The air is dim and lightless with the smoke from all these habitations and places of business. The soil in the valley (or 'bottom', to use the local term) is rich; but, as the road begins to ascend, the vegetation becomes poorer; it does not flourish, it merely exists; and, instead of trees, there are only bushes and shrubs about the dwellings. Stone dykes are everywhere used in place of hedges; and what crops there are, on the patches of arable land, consist of pale, hungry-looking, grey green oats. Right before the traveller on this road rises Haworth village; he can see it for two miles before he

arrives, for it is situated on the side of a pretty steep hill, with a back-ground of dun and purple moors, rising and sweeping away yet higher than the church, which is built at the very summit of the long narrow street. All round the horizon there is this same line of sinuous wave-like hills; the scoops into which they fall only reveal-ing other hills beyond, of similar colour and shape, crowned with wild, bleak moors – grand, from the ideas of solitude and loneliness which they suggest, or oppressive from the feeling which they give of being pent-up by some monotonous and illimitable barrier, according to the mood of mind in which the spectator may be.

Even an inhabitant of the neighbouring county of Lancaster is struck by the peculiar force of character which the Yorkshiremen display. This makes them interesting as a race; while, at the same time, as individuals, the remarkable degree of self-sufficiency they possess gives them an air of independence rather apt to repel a stranger. I use this expression 'self-sufficiency' in the largest sense. Conscious of the strong sagacity and the dogged power of will which seem almost the birthright of the natives of the West Riding, each man relies upon himself, and seeks no help at the hands of his neighbour. From rarely requiring the assistance of others, he comes to doubt the power of bestowing it: from the general success of his efforts, he grows to depend upon them, and to over-esteem his own energy and power. He belongs to that keen, yet short-sighted class, who consider suspicion of all whose honesty is not proved as a sign of wisdom. The practical qualities of a man are held in great respect; but the want of faith in strangers and untried modes of action, extends itself even to the manner in which the virtues are regarded; and if they produce no immediate and tangible result, they are rather put aside as unfit for this busy, striving world; especially if they are more of a passive than an active character. The affections are strong and their foundations lie deep: but they are not – such affections seldom are – wide-spreading; nor do they show themselves on the surface. Indeed, there is little display of any of the amenities of life among this wild, rough population. Their accost is curt; their accent and tone of speech blunt and harsh. Something of this may, probably, be attributed to the freedom of mountain air and of isolated hill-side life; something be derived from their rough Norse ancestry. They have a quick perception of character, and a keen sense of humour; the dwellers among them must be prepared for certain uncomplimentary, though most likely true, observations, pithily expressed. Their feelings are not easily roused, but their duration is lasting. Hence there is much close friendship and faithful service; and for a correct exemplification of the form in which the latter frequently appears, I need only refer the reader of 'Wuthering Heights' to the character of 'Joseph.'

From the same cause come also enduring grudges, in some cases amounting to hatred, which occasionally has been bequeathed from generation to generation. I remember Miss Brontë once telling me that it was a saying round about Haworth, 'Keep a stone in thy pocket seven year; turn it, and keep it seven year longer, that it may be ever ready to thine hand when thine enemy draws near.'

The West Riding men are sleuth-hounds in pursuit of money. Miss Brontë related to my husband a curious instance illustrative of this eager desire for riches. A man that she knew, who was a small manufacturer, had engaged in many local speculations which had always turned out well, and thereby rendered him a person of some wealth. He was rather past middle age, when he bethought him of insuring his life; and he had only just taken out his policy, when he fell ill of an acute disease which was certain to end fatally in a very few days. The doctor, half-hesitatingly, revealed to him his hopeless state. 'By jingo!' cried he, rousing up at once into the old energy, 'I shall *do* the insurance company. I always was a lucky fellow!'

These men are keen and shrewd; faithful and persevering in following out a good purpose, fell in tracking an evil one. They are not emotional; they are not easily made into either friends or enemies; but once lovers or haters, it is difficult to change their feeling. They are a powerful race both in mind and body, both for good and for evil.

Yorkshire people tend, of course, to put it more pithily: 'Where there's muck, there's brass'; and 'If thee does owt for nowt, do it for thissen'.

I was half Yorkshire myself, since my father came from Todmorden. But he was half Irish. So I have always seen the Brontës as kinsfolk, and Yorkshire-Irish as a potent mixture. I was delighted in later life to discover that Yeats' family came originally from Yorkshire.

Patrick Brontë, the father of Charlotte and Emily, was born in Ireland, where his name was Pronty or Brunty. Somehow or other he managed to get from a small thatched cabin near the mountains of Mourne in County Down to St John's College Cambridge with a scholarship. Later he was proud of having served in the college militia with Lord Palmerston. I was equally proud of the fact that while he was Parson of Haworth he lectured at the Mechanics

Institute in Keighley, where my father was later to work as Principal of the Technical College. Patrick published two volumes of poetry, two prose tales, and three pamphlets, so his daughters in fact came from a literary household. Southerners too often forget that from the eighteenth century onwards intellectual life in the British provinces was often as stimulating as in London.

Nothing, however, can explain how this small household on the Yorkshire moors could produce two of Britain's greatest novelists, one of whom was also a great poet. Jane Eyre, like all of Charlotte's heroines, was modelled on herself. She was Yorkshire through and through, reminding me of some of my own Yorkshire friends, like Alice Bacon and Betty Boothroyd. No later feminist has rivalled the chutzpah with which Charlotte starts the concluding chapter of *Jane Eyre*: 'Reader, I married him'.

My own favourite has always been Emily. *Wuthering Heights* can be regarded as the only great Russian novel written in English. But it also breathes the very air of Yorkshire, above all in its last words:

> I sought, and soon discovered, the three head-stones on the slope next the moor: the middle one grey, and half buried in heath: Edgar Linton's only harmonized by the turf and moss creeping up its foot: Heathchiff's still bare.
>
> I lingered round them, under that benign sky; watched the moths fluttering among the heath and harebells, listened to the soft wind breathing through the grass, and wondered how any one could ever imagine unquiet slumbers for the sleepers in that quiet earth.

The happiest days of my boyhood were spent in the Yorkshire moors and dales. I find their essence best captured in some of Emily Brontë's poetry:

> For the moors, for the moors where the short grass
> Like velvet beneath us should lie!
> For the moors, for the moors where each high pass
> Rose sunny against the clear sky!

> For the moors, where the linnet was trilling
> Its song on the old granite stone –
> Where the lark – the wild sky-lark was filling
> Every breast with delight like its own.

*

'Twas one of those dark, cloudy days
That sometimes come in summer's blaze.
When heaven drops not, when earth is still.
And deeper green is on the hill.

*

A little and a lone green lane
That opened on a common wide
A distant, dreamy, dim blue chain
Of mountains circling every side –

A heaven so clear, an earth so calm,
So sweet, so soft, so hushed an air
And, deepening still the dream-like charm,
Wild moor-sheep feeding everywhere.

*

Often rebuked, yet always back returning
To those first feelings that were born with me,
And leaving busy chase of wealth and learning
For idle dreams of things which cannot be,

I'll walk where my own nature would be leading:
It vexes me to choose another guide:
Where the grey flocks in ferny glens are feeding,
Where the wild wind blows on the mountain side.

When I finally decided not to stand for East Leeds again in the General Election of 1992 I was determined to maintain contact with the Yorkshire I had known and loved since childhood. So I became President of the National Trust's Appeal for the Yorkshire Moors and Dales and am able to visit them several times a year. Once I get off the crowded little roads up the bottom of the valleys, I am back in lovely solitudes which have scarcely changed in the century-and-a-half since the Brontës knew them. It is now my agreeable duty to see that they remain unchanged.

So far, nearly all that I have quoted comes from something I have read in later life, which seems to crystallize feelings I had as a child too young to put them into words myself, or indeed to understand them. Yet as a boy I read voraciously for my own pleasure. There was of course no television in those days, still less the computer games on which my grandchildren spend so much time. Much of where what I read was of no more lasting value than what they watch today; indeed some of the modern television films for children are at least as good as anything I read, and are as likely to sow permanent seeds in their imagination. None the less I think that the older I grew, the more I benefited from the amount of time I spent on books. Life is short, and time spent in front of the television set or computer screen is lost for ever.

I started, of course, with the fairy stories of Grimm and Andersen, to which I still occasionally return. I worked my way steadily through some of the great stories of the past in short editions 'Told to the Children'. My mother, as a former school-teacher, had two large volumes of *Classic Myth and Legend* and *Celtic Myth and Legend*. The latter fed my curiosity about Ireland and made Cuchulain my hero for life, though it was many years before I discovered how to pronounce his name. The former stocked my imagination, like that of millions of others over the last three thousand years, with the imperishable symbols of Greek mythology. Even Bertrand Russell, the quintessential rationalist, when confronted with the ultimate horror of the atomic bomb, had to go back to the legend of Prometheus, and describe it as 'cosmic impiety'.

I got many of my books from the school library and later the public library once I was old enough. I discovered at Woolworths the wonders of sixpenny editions of the classics, printed on poor paper and bound in flimsy maroon cardboard. So I began to read Sir Walter Scott — *Ivanhoe* and *The Talisman* — and Charles Dickens — *Oliver Twist* and *The Tale of Two Cities* — well before I was really ready for them. I fear many of us have been put off some great writers for life by reading them too young.

By the age of twelve I was immersed in the adventures of the clubland heroes of Sapper and John Buchan who pursued the dastardly Hun everywhere from Godalming or the Scottish borders to the Middle East. I thrilled to the generosity with which Richard Hannay could say of his opponent 'and in his own foul way, he too was a patriot'. There is a superb passage in *Greenmantle* where the head of the Secret Service gives Hannay a dangerous mission:

Sir Walter shook hands with me and his eyes blinked a little.
  'I may be sending you to your death, Hannay — Good God, what a damned task-mistress duty is! — If so, I shall be haunted with regrets, but *you* will never repent. Have no fear of that. You have

chosen the roughest road, but it goes straight to the hill-tops.'

He handed me the half-sheet of notepaper. On it were written three words – '*Kasredin*', '*cancer*' and '*v.I*'.

'That is the only clue we possess,' he said. 'I cannot construe it, but I can tell you the story. We have had our agents working in Persia and Mesopotamia for years – mostly young officers of the Indian Army. They carry their lives in their hands, and now and then one disappears, and the sewers of Bagdad might tell a tale. But they find out many things, and they count the game worth the candle. They have told us of the star rising in the West, but they could give us no details. All but one – the best of them. He had been working between Mosul and the Persian frontier as a muleteer, and had been south, into the Bakhtiari hills. He found out something, but his enemies knew that he knew and he was pursued. Three months ago, just before Kut, he staggered into Delamain's camp with ten bullet-holes in him and a knife slash on his forehead. He mumbled his name, but beyond that and the fact that there was a Something coming from the West he told them nothing. He died in ten minutes. They found this paper on him, and since he cried out the word 'Kasredin' in his last moments, it must have had something to do with his quest. It is for you to find out if it has any meaning.'

I folded it up and placed it in my pocket-book.

'What a great fellow! What was his name?' I asked.

Sir Walter did not answer at once. He was looking out of the window. 'His name,' he said at last, 'was Harry Bullivant. He was my son. God rest his brave soul!'

I was equally inspired by Henry Newbolt's poem, 'Vitai Lampada', though it was years before I found out that the title meant 'The Torch of Life':

> There's a breathless hush in the Close to-night –
>   Ten to make and the match to win –
> A bumping pitch and a blinding light,
>   An hour to play and the last man in.
> And it's not for the sake of a ribboned coat,
>   Or the selfish hope of a season's fame,
> But his Captain's hand on his shoulder smote –
> 'Play up! play up! and play the game!'
>
> The sand of the desert is sodden red, –
>   Red with the wreck of a square that broke; –
> The Gatling's jammed and the Colonel dead,

And the regiment blind with dust and smoke.
The river of death has brimmed his banks,
    And England's far, and Honour a name,
But the voice of a schoolboy rallies the ranks:
'Play up! play up! and play the game!'

This is the word that year by year,
    While in her place the School is set,
Every one of her sons must hear,
    And none that hears it dare forget.
This they all with a joyful mind
    Bear through life like a torch in flame,
And falling fling to the host behind –
'Play up! play up! and play the game!'

My love for the sentimental patriotism of Buchan and Newbolt
was a natural legacy of the First World War, and was fed by the
boys' magazines I read – above all by the enormous *Chums*
annuals, which carried long serials about the dastardly Huns; it was
much the same for many years after the Second World War with,
for example, the Biggles books. Although Frank Richards' stories
in *The Magnet* were set in an imaginary public school called
Greyfriars, they were also immensely popular with boys like me at
day-schools.

By the time I reached my teens my taste was improving and I
fell in love with G.K. Chesterton's novels, particularly *The Man
who was Thursday*, and *The Napoleon of Notting Hill*. I thrilled to
the romantic bravura of his poems, like 'Lepanto':

Don John pounding from the slaughter-painted poop,
Purpling all the ocean like a bloody pirate's sloop,
Scarlet running over on the silvers and the golds,
Breaking of the hatches up and bursting of the holds,
Thronging of the thousands up that labour under sea
White for bliss and blind for sun and stunned for liberty.
Vivat Hispania!
Domino Gloria!
Don John of Austria
Has set his people free!

Cervantes on his galley sets the sword back in the sheath
(Don John of Austria rides homewards with a wreath.)
And he sees across a weary land a straggling road in Spain.
Up which a lean and foolish knight forever rides in vain.

> And he smiles, but not as Sultans smile, and settles back the
>   blade . . .
> (But Don John of Austria rides home from the Crusade.)

John Masefield taught me to enjoy a more sober romanticism in
his novels, *Sard Harker* and *Odtaa* about a young man's adventures
in South America; *Odtaa* stood for 'one damn thing after another',
an audacious title for those days. However, I enjoyed even more
his story about witches and magic, *The Midnight Folk*. I still like
stories about magic, such as the novels of Angela Carter. I later
badgered my own children to read *The Midnight Folk* so persistently that it has become a family symbol of my obsessions. In
recent years its sequel, *The Box of Delights*, was made into a
successful children's serial on television.

Masefield in his youth was apprenticed aboard a windjammer
and sailed round Cape Horn. His first book, *Salt Water Ballads*,
was a great success in 1902; it included a poem which I loved as a
boy and still enjoy, 'Cargoes':

> Quinquireme of Nineveh from distant Ophir
> Rowing home to haven in sunny Palestine,
> With a cargo of ivory,
> And apes and peacocks,
> Sandalwood, cedarwood, and sweet white wine.
>
> Stately Spanish galleon coming from the Isthmus,
> Dipping through the Tropics by the palm-green shores,
> With a cargo of diamonds,
> Emeralds, amethysts,
> Topazes, and cinnamon, and gold moidores.
>
> Dirty British coaster with a salt-caked smoke stack
> Butting through the channel in the mad March days,
> With a cargo of Tyne coal,
> Road-rail, pig-lead,
> Firewood, iron-ware, and cheap tin trays.

His unique blend of romance and realism led to Masefield becoming Poet Laureate when Robert Bridges died in 1930. It appeals
strongly to something in my own character.

Though I read Dickens and Thackeray at school, I found them
less attractive than the Brontës, and less again than Tolstoy and
Dostoevsky, who had a spiritual dimension lacking in the more
prosaic English writers. In later life Edna has persuaded me to read

Dickens again, and I now get great pleasure from his vast amphitheatre of characters and caricatures. But I still miss in Dickens the depth of the great Russian or French novelists.

Then, when I was sixteen, a young teacher arrived at Bradford straight from Cambridge, where he had studied English under F.R. Leavis. We called him 'Giggling Gus', but his real name was Leslie Shepherd. He introduced us to the 'highbrow' novelists and poets who were writing in the thirties – D.H. Lawrence, E.M. Forster, Virginia Woolf, the later Yeats, Auden, Spender, MacNeice and Day Lewis. More important, he taught us to examine what we read and test it for sincerity of feeling and accuracy of expression.

Our textbook was *Reading and Discrimination* by Denys Thompson, which made us compare writings on the same theme by different poets or novelists – Gerard Manley Hopkins' 'Binsey Poplars' with Cowper's 'The Poplar Field', for example; Herrick with Donne, Marvell with Shelley, Vaughan with Tom Moore. Its sympathy was always for what it saw as moral significance, and for astringency against sentimentality. I later discovered that there was a sheet of comments at the back of the book which should have been detached before it was used in school. Typical of its approach was this comment on poems by Quiller-Couch and George Herbert; 'The unction of A is disgusting; B has exquisite tact, the humility is genuine.' I fear it shared the prejudice of so many literary people against public figures; on extracts from speeches by Ramsay MacDonald and Sir Montague Norman it commented: 'The helplessness of I, the floundering optimism of K, are indices of the fuddled mind, prevalent in politics.'

Nevertheless the critical standards of the Leavisites, so preferable to the arid mumbo-jumbo of many modern schools of criticism, had a lasting effect on my taste.

Of the writers they picked out for praise, Virginia Woolf had the greatest effect on me. I won a school prize with an essay on *To the Lighthouse*. The main characters are based on Virginia's own parents – her mother, Julia, whom she adored, and her father. Leslie Stephen, an austere Victorian intellectual, who edited the *Dictionary of National Biography*. The novel opens by describing them both:

'Yes, of course, if it's fine to-morrow,' said Mrs Ramsay. 'But you'll have to be up with the lark,' she added.

To her son these words conveyed an extraordinary joy, as if it were settled the expedition were bound to take place, and the wonder to which he had looked forward, for years and years it seemed, was, after a night's darkness and a day's sail, within touch. Since he belonged, even at the age of six, to that great clan which cannot keep this feeling separate from that, but must let future prospects, with their joys and sorrows, cloud what is actually at hand, since to such people even in earliest childhood any turn in the wheel of sensation has the power to crystallize and transfix the moment upon which its gloom or radiance rests, James Ramsay, sitting on the floor cutting out pictures from the illustrated catalogue of the Army and Navy Stores, endowed the picture of a refrigerator as his mother spoke with heavenly bliss. It was fringed with joy. The wheelbarrow, the lawn-mower, the sound of poplar trees, leaves whitening before rain, rooks cawing, brooms knocking, dresses rustling – all these were so coloured and distinguished in his mind that he had already his private code, his secret language, though he appeared the image of stark and uncompromising severity, with his high forehead and his fierce blue eyes, impeccably candid and pure, frowning slightly at the sight of human frailty, so that his mother, watching him guide his scissors neatly round the refrigerator, imagined him all red and ermine on the Bench or directing a stern and momentous enterprise in some crisis of public affairs.

'But,' said his father, stopping in front of the drawing-room window, 'it won't be fine.'

Had there been an axe handy, a poker, or any weapon that would have gashed a hole in his father's breast and killed him, there and then, James would have seized it. Such were the extremes of emotion that Mr Ramsay excited in his children's breasts by his mere presence; standing, as now, lean as a knife, narrow as the blade of one, grinning sarcastically, not only with the pleasure of disillusioning his son and casting ridicule upon his wife, who was ten thousand times better in every way than he was (James thought), but also with some secret conceit at his own accuracy of judgement. What he said was true. It was always true. He was incapable of untruth; never tampered with a fact; never altered a disagreeable word to suit the pleasure or convenience of any mortal being, least of all of his own children, who, sprung from his loins, should be aware from childhood that life is difficult; facts uncompromising; and the passage to that fabled land where our brightest hopes are extinguished, our frail barks founder in darkness (here Mr Ramsay would straighten his back and narrow his little blue eyes upon the horizon), one that needs, above all, courage, truth, and the power to endure.

I still find the death of Mrs Ramsay unutterably moving:

> The nights now are full of wind and destruction; the trees plunge
> and bend and their leaves fly helter skelter until the lawn is
> plastered with them and they lie packed in gutters and choke rain
> pipes and scatter damp paths. Also the sea tosses itself and breaks
> itself, and should any sleeper fancying that he might find on the
> beach an answer to his doubts, a sharer of his solitude, throw off his
> bedclothes and go down by himself to walk on the sand, no image
> with semblance of serving and divine promptitude comes readily to
> hand bringing the night to order and making the world reflect the
> compass of the soul. The hand dwindles in his hand; the voice
> bellows in his ear. Almost it would appear that it is useless in such
> confusion to ask the night those questions as to what, and why, and
> wherefore, which tempt the sleeper from his bed to seek an answer.
>
> [Mr Ramsay stumbling along a passage stretched his arms out
> one dark morning, but, Mrs Ramsay having died rather suddenly
> the night before, he stretched his arms out. They remained empty.]

Virginia Woolf has remained a seminal influence on my thinking
ever since; she was also adored by my mother, who studied her at
WEA classes, and learned more about her from Harold Nicolson's
BBC talks on contemporary literature. Nowadays I find her
diaries, letters, and essays even more exciting than her novels. We
live at Alfriston, a couple of miles from Charleston farmhouse,
where Virginia's sister Vanessa lived with her husband, Clive Bell,
and lover, Duncan Grant. Monk's House at Rodmell, where
Virginia lived with her husband, Leonard, is only a little further
away. So we cannot escape her spell.

I never met her myself; she took her own life in 1941. But I
have known many of her friends. Harold Nicolson's son Nigel,
who helped to edit her letters, went up to Balliol the same day as I,
and we still meet from time to time at his home in Sissinghurst. I
worked closely with Virginia's husband, Leonard, after the war,
when I was the Labour Party's International Secretary and he was
Chairman of the Fabian International Bureau. Quentin Bell,
Virginia's nephew and biographer, lives very near to us with his
wife, Olivier, who has edited Virginia's diaries. Though now
eighty-five and physically frail, Quentin still writes as well as ever;
and last year I opened an exhibition of his recent pottery at
Charleston.

Virginia combined a powerful and sensitive intelligence with an incomparable ability to express herself in words and images. Scarcely a page of the many thousands she produced is without a penetrating insight into the people or work she is describing, with a felicity of image which makes me despair of my own clumsiness. In many respects her values are far from mine; I do not admire the fusty and selfish incestuousness of the Bloomsbury Set, and find Virginia herself disturbingly snobbish on occasion. But no writer in English this century can match her for accuracy of observation and beauty of style.

At the other extreme from Virginia Woolf stand James Joyce and his one-time amanuensis, Samuel Beckett. I first knew Joyce at school through his *Portrait of the Artist as a Young Man*, which gave little clue to his later work, but echoed parts of my own boyhood:

The fellows were practising long shies and bowling lobs and slow twisters. In the soft grey silence he could hear the bump of the balls: and from here and there through the quiet air the sound of the cricket bats: pick, pack, pock, puck: like drops of water in a fountain falling softly in the brimming bowl.

Ulysses was still banned in Britain, but I managed to get hold of the Faber paperbacks which printed extracts of *Finnegans Wake* — then called *Work in Progress*. I was most impressed by *Anna Livia Plurabelle*, which was Joyce's name for the River Liffey, and ends with this wonderful evocation of nightfall:

Can't hear with the waters of. The chittering waters of. Flittering bats, fieldmice bawk talk. Ho! Are you not gone ahome? What Thom Malone? Can't hear with bawk of bats, all thim liffeying waters of Ho, talk save us! My foos won't moos. I feel as old as yonder elm. A tale of Shaun or Shem? All Livia's daughter-sons. Dark hawks hear us. Night! Night! My ho head halls. I feel as heavy as yonder stone. Tell me of John or Shaun? Who were Shem and Shaun the living sons or daughters of? Night now! Tell me, tell me, tell me, elm! Night night! Telmetale of stem or stone. Beside the rivering waters of, hitherandthithering waters of. Night!

There is now a good modern bronze statue of a lady representing the River Liffey opposite the Post Office in Dublin. She lies reclining in a stone trough while water trickles over her head and body. The local taxi drivers, no doubt under the influence of Joyce, describe the statue as 'The Floosie in the Jacuzzi', or less kindly 'The Hoor in the Sewer'

Samuel Beckett wrote his first great novel *Murphy*, while I was still at school, though I did not read it till it was published in 1938, my second year at Oxford. It burst like a firework in the sky of my brain, and its stars are still falling to earth. Murphy is a seedy Irish solipsist living alone in London. He never wore a waistcoat because it made him feel like a woman, and never wore a hat, 'the memories it awoke of the caul were too poignant, especially when he had to take it off.' He eats a packet of assorted biscuits in Hyde Park every day, and drinks tea, of which he manages to get almost two cups for the price of one:

The seedy solipsist then, having said his silent grace and savoured his infamy in advance, drew up his chair briskly to the table, seized the cup of tea and half emptied it at one gulp. No sooner had this gone to the right place than he began to splutter, eructate and complain, as though he had been duped into swallowing a saturated solution of powdered glass. In this way he attracted to himself the attention not only of every customer in the saloon but actually of the waitress Vera, who came running to get a good view of the accident, as she supposed. Murphy continued for a little to make sounds as of a flushing-box taxed beyond its powers and then said, in an egg and scorpion voice:

'I ask for China and you give me Indian.'

Though disappointed that it was nothing more interesting, Vera made no bones about making good her mistake. She was a willing little bit of sweated labour, incapable of betraying the slogan of her slavers, that since the customer or sucker was paying for his gutrot ten times what it cost to produce and five times what it cost to fling in his face, it was only reasonable to defer to his complaints up to but not exceeding fifty per cent of his exploitation.

With the fresh cup of tea Murphy adopted quite a new technique. He drank not more than a third of it and then waited till Vera happened to be passing.

'I am most fearfully sorry,' he said, 'Vera, to give you all this trouble, but do you think it would be possible to have this filled with hot?'

Vera showing signs of bridling, Murphy uttered winningly the sesame.

'I know I am a great nuisance, but they have been too generous with the cowjuice.'

Generous and cowjuice were the keywords here. No waitress could hold out against their mingled overtones of gratitude and mammary organs. And Vera was essentially a waitress.

That is the end of how Murphy defrauded a vested interest every day for his lunch, to the honourable extent of paying for one cup of tea and consuming 1.83 cups approximately.

Try it sometime, gentle skimmer.

Murphy has a passion for word games:

'Why did the barmaid champagne?' he said. 'Do you give it up?'

'Yes,' said Celia.

'Because the stout porter bitter,' said Murphy.

This was a joke that did not amuse Celia, at the best of times and places it could not have amused her. That did not matter. So far from being adapted to her, it was not addressed to her. It amused Murphy, that was all that mattered. He always found it most funny, more than most funny, clonic, it and one other concerning a bottle of stout and a card party. These were the Gilmigrim jokes, so called from the Lilliputian wine. He staggered about on the floor in his bare feet, one time amateur theological student's shirt, dicky and lemon bow, overcome by the toxins of this simple little joke. He sank down on the dream of Descartes linoleum, choking and writhing like a chicken with the gapes, seeing the scene. On the one hand the barmaid, fresh from the country, a horse's head on a cow's body, her crape bodice more a W than a V, her legs more an X than an O, her eyes closed for the sweet pain, leaning out through the hatch of the bar parlour. On the other the stout porter, mounting the footrail, his canines gleaming behind a pad of frothy whisker. Then the nip, and Tintoretto's *Origin of the Milky Way*.

The fit was so much more like one of epilepsy than of laughter that Celia felt alarm.

Politics did not interest me very much at school. Although I had lived through the Great Strike of 1926 and the slump of the early thirties, my interest in the Labour Movement was first aroused by John Dos Passos' *Nineteen Nineteen*, which mixes the techniques of cinema newsreel, newspaper headlines, popular journalism and short story to give a brilliant account of the United States after the Great War. I came across it when I was about eighteen in the library of Keighley Technical College, which was kept in my father's office; the same source gave me my first chance to read Ernest Hemingway. Dos Passos, who moved later to the far right of American politics, was then a left-wing radical. Here is his picture of the labour union organizer, Joe Hill:

A young Swede named Hillstrom went to sea, got himself calloused hands on sailingships and tramps, learned English in the focastle of the steamers that make the run from Stockholm to Hull, dreamed the Swede's dream of the west; when he got to America they gave him a job polishing cuspidors in a Bowery saloon.

He moved west to Chicago and worked in a machine-shop.

He moved west and followed the harvest, hung around employment agencies, paid out many a dollar for a job in a construction camp, walked out many a mile when the grub was too bum, or the boss too tough, or too many bugs in the bunkhouse; read Marx and the I.W.W. Preamble and dreamed about forming the structure of the new society within the shell of the old.

He was in California for the S.P. strike (*Casey Jones, two locomotives, Casey Jones*), used to play the concertina outside the bunkhouse door, after supper, evenings, (*Longhaired preachers come out every night*), had a knack for setting rebel words to tunes, (*And the union makes us strong*).

Along the coast in cookshacks, flophouses, jungles, wobblies hoboes bindlestiffs began singing Joe Hill's songs. They sang 'em in the county jails of the State of Washington, Oregon, California, Nevada, Idaho, in the bullpens in Montana and Arizona, sang 'em in Walla Walla, San Quentin and Leavenworth, forming the structure of the new society within the jails of the old.

At Bingham, Utah, Joe Hill organized the workers of the Utah Construction Company in the One Big Union, won a new wage-scale, shorter hours, better grub. (The angel Moroni didn't like labour-organizers any better than the Southern Pacific did.)

The angel Moroni moved the hearts of the Mormons to decide it was Joe Hill shot a grocer named Morrison. The Swedish consul and President Wilson tried to get him a new trial but the angel Moroni moved the hearts of the supreme court of the State of Utah to sustain the verdict of guilty. He was in jail a year, went on making up songs. In November 1915 he was stood up against the wall in the jail yard in Salt Lake City.

'Don't mourn for me organize,' was the last word he sent out to the workingstiffs of the I.W.W. Joe Hill stood up against the wall of the jail yard, looked into the muzzles of the guns and gave the word to fire.

They put him in a black suit, put a stiff collar around his neck and a bow tie, shipped him to Chicago for a bangup funeral, and photographed his handsome stony mask staring into the future.

The first of May they scattered his ashes to the wind.

Dashiell Hammett, though a Communist, did not betray his political allegiance in his superb crime thrillers. However, he developed Dos Passos' view of America in his early novel, *Red Harvest*, about corruption and racketeering in a mining town. Here he sets the scene:

I first heard Personville called Poisonville by a red-haired mucker named Hickey Dewey in the Big Ship in Butte. He also called his shirt a shoit. I didn't think anything of what he had done to the city's name. Later I heard men who could manage their r's give it the same pronunciation. I still didn't see anything in it but the meaningless sort of humor that used to make richardsnary the thieves' word for dictionary. A few years later I went to Personville and learned better.

The city wasn't pretty. Most of its builders had gone in for gaudiness. Maybe they had been successful at first. Since then the smelters whose brick stacks stuck up tall against a gloomy mountain to the south had yellow-smoked everything into uniform dinginess. The result was an ugly city of forty thousand people, set in an ugly notch between two ugly mountains that had been all dirtied up by mining. Spread over this was a grimy sky that looked as if it had come out of the smelters' stacks.

The first policeman I saw needed a shave. The second had a couple of buttons off his shabby uniform. The third stood in the center of the city's main intersection – Broadway and Union Street – directing traffic, with a cigar in one corner of his mouth. After that I stopped checking them up.

My moral indignation was aroused by this sort of writing. But the United States was too far away for it to spur me into political action. However, I did become a pacifist in the sixth form at Bradford. I was greatly affected by the writers of the First World War such as Robert Graves, Richard Aldington, Siegfried Sassoon, and Wilfred Owen. I was particularly moved by Owen's 'Dulce et Decorum est':

Bent double, like old beggars under sacks,
Knock-kneed, coughing like hags, we cursed through sludge,
Till on the haunting flares we turned our backs,

And towards our distant rest began to trudge.
Men marched asleep. Many had lost their boots,
But limped on, blood-shod. All went lame, all blind;
Drunk with fatigue; deaf even to the hoots
Of gas-shells dropping softly behind.

Gas! Gas! Quick, boys! – An ecstasy of fumbling,
Fitting the clumsy helmets just in time,
But someone still was yelling out and stumbling
And floundering like a man in fire or lime. –
Dim through the misty panes and thick green light,
As under a green sea, I saw him drowning.
In all my dreams, before my helpless sight,
He plunges at me, guttering, choking, drowning.

If in some smothering dreams, you too could pace
Behind the wagon that we flung him in,
And watch the white eyes writhing in his face,
His hanging face, like a devil's sick of sin;
If you could hear, at every jolt, the blood
Come gargling from the froth-corrupted lungs,
Obscene as cancer, bitter as the cud
Of vile, incurable sores on innocent tongues, –
My friend, you would not tell with such high zest
To children ardent for some desperate glory,
The old Lie: Dulce et decorum est
Pro patria mori.

Finally I won my scholarship to Balliol College, Oxford and
prepared to take my first step into the adult world. Then I found it
was no longer possible to avoid politics – or war.

2

Oxford

Only connect
– E.M. Forster

If you are lucky enough to get there, your years at a university give you a unique opportunity to reflect on the fundamentals of life, before you have to earn a living. You can develop your own personality by meeting others of similar tastes from a wide variety of backgrounds. My four years at Balliol left me with friends for life in all parts of the world.

As a scholarship boy from a northern grammar school which had never sent a boy to Balliol in my lifetime, I was more than a little nervous during my first few weeks in Oxford. The sound of confident public-school voices in the quad sometimes gave me an inferiority complex. Fortunately this soon passed. Before long I felt more like an earlier grammar school boy from northern England. William Wordsworth in the original version of 'The Prelude' gave a picture of his first reactions to Cambridge in 1787 with which I could easily identify:

> My spirit was up, my thoughts were full of hope;
> Some Friends I had, acquaintances who there
> Seem'd Friends, poor simple Schoolboys, now hung round
> With honour and importance; in a world
> Of welcome faces up and down I rov'd;

Questions, directions, counsel and advice
Flow'd in upon me from all sides, fresh day
Of pride and pleasure! to myself I seem'd
A man of business and expense, and went
From shop to shop about my own affairs,
To Tutors or to Tailors, as befel,
From Street to Street with loose and careless heart.

I was the Dreamer, they the Dream; I roam'd
Delighted, through the motley spectacle;
Gowns grave or gaudy, Doctors, Students, Streets,
Lamps, Gateways, Flocks of Churches, Courts and Towers:
Strange transformation for a mountain Youth,
A northern Villager. As if by word
Of magic or some Fairy's power, at once
Behold me rich in monies, and attir'd
In spendid clothes, with hose of silk, and hair
Glittering like rimy trees when frost is keen.
My lordly Dressing-gown I pass it by,
With other signs of manhood which supplied
The lack of beard. – The weeks went roundly on,
With invitations, suppers, wine, and fruit,
Smooth housekeeping within, and all without
Liberal and suiting Gentleman's array!

Of College labours, of the Lecturer's Room,
All studded round, as thick as chairs could stand,
With loyal Students, faithful to their books,
Half-and-half Idlers, hardy Recusants,
And honest Dunces; – of important Days,
Examinations, when the Man was weigh'd
As in the balance! – of excessive hopes,
Tremblings withal, and commendable fears,
Small jealousies, and triumphs good or bad
I make short mention; things they were which then
I did not love, nor do I love them now.

. . . Oft did I leave
My Comrades, and the Crowd, Buildings and Groves,
And walked along the fields, the level fields,
With Heaven's blue concave rear'd above my head;
And now it was, that, from such change entire
And this first absence from those shapes sublime
Wherewith I had been conversant, my mind
Seem'd busier in itself than heretofore;

At least, I more directly recognised
My powers and habits: let me dare to speak
A higher language, say that now I felt
The strength and consolation which were mine.
As if awaken'd, summon'd, rous'd, constrain'd,
I look'd for universal things; perused
The common countenance of earth and heaven;
And, turning the mind in upon itself,
Pored, watch'd, expected, listen'd; spread my thoughts
And spread them with a wider creeping; felt
Incumbences more awful, visitings
Of the Upholder of the tranquil Soul.

Oxford itself is a beautiful city in beautiful country. The very stones breathe history and culture – an atmosphere exactly caught by Gerard Manley Hopkins in his poem, 'Duns Scotus' Oxford':

Towery city and branchy between towers;
Cuckoo-echoing, bell-swarmèd, lark-charmèd, rook-racked, river-
    rounded;
The dapple-eared lily below thee; that country and town did
Once encounter in, here coped and poisèd powers;

Thou hast a base and brickish skirt there, sours
That neighbour-nature thy grey beauty is grounded
Best in; graceless growth, thou hast confounded
Rural rural keeping – folk, flocks, and flowers.

Yet ah! this air I gather and I release
He lived on; these weeds and waters, these walls are what
He haunted who of all men most sways my spirits to peace;

Of realty the rarest-veinèd unraveller; a not
Rivalled insight, be rival Italy or Greece;
Who fired France for Mary without spot.

Hopkins, like me, took a Double First at Balliol in Latin and Greek, Philosophy and Ancient history. He went up in 1863 with an Exhibition from Highgate Grammar School, where his brilliance as a student did not save him from brutal floggings by the headmaster. He was popular with his schoolmates; his friends remembered him as 'full of fun, rippling over with jokes and chaff, facile with pencil and pen, with rhyming jibe or cartoon'. In fact at that time he hoped to make his living as a painter; his younger brothers both became professional artists.

Though he continued to draw sketches in the style of Ruskin for the rest of his life, at Oxford he realized he must express himself above all in poetry. Religion, however, came to dominate his personality, and in 1866 he was received into the Catholic Church by Newman. The following year, after taking his degree, he decided to become a Jesuit priest. This led him to burn most of the poems he had already written, and to write no more until his superiors asked him to start again in 1875, when he produced one of the greatest poems in our language, 'The Wreck of the Deutschland'. He continued to write great poetry until he died of typhoid fever at the age of forty-four.

None of this poetry was published during his life, though he sent copies to a handful of his friends – particularly to Robert Bridges, who was at Balliol with him. Bridges did not publish the first edition of Hopkins' poems until 1918, nearly thirty years after Hopkins' death, when, as Poet Laureate, he was in a position to defend and explain them. Thus when the young Yeats was introduced to him in 1886, Hopkins made so little impression that Yeats could not remember the occasion later; why should he remember a casual meeting with an unremarkable middle-aged priest who happened to know his father?

It is an odd coincidence that three of the poets who have influenced me most went unpublished in their lifetime – Thomas Traherne, Gerard Manley Hopkins, and Emily Dickinson. Dickinson, as we shall see later, did not want 'to invest her snow'. As a poor country parson, Traherne, perhaps, simply lacked the opportunity. Hopkins, however, may have felt that he had put more of his secret self into his poetry than was proper for a Jesuit priest. Apart from the terrible final sonnets in which he wrestled with his God, much of his writing betrays an almost pagan joy in the natural world which sometimes verges on sensuality.

From the time when he fell in love with Digby Dolben, a fellow-undergraduate at Balliol, he was tortured by a sexual guilt which must have been harder to bear in those days because his feelings were directed at his own sex and at himself. One force which drove him into the Jesuit order was a masochistic need for discipline which he could sometimes satisfy only by whipping himself. We can perhaps say of his poetry what Yeats wrote about his own towards the end of his life:

Those masterful images because complete
Grew in pure mind, but out of what began?
A mound of refuse or the sweepings of a street,
Old kettles, old bottles, and a broken can,
Old iron, old bones, old rags, that raving slut
Who keeps the till. Now that my ladder's gone,
I must lie down where all the ladders start,
In the foul rag-and-bone shop of the heart.

Eleven years after taking his degree Hopkins returned to Oxford to help the parish priest. It was then that he wrote 'Duns Scotus' Oxford' and his exquisite description of Binsey Poplars, which illustrates a very modern concern for the environment:

My aspens dear, whose airy cages quelled,
Quelled or quenched in leaves the leaping sun,
All felled, felled, are all felled;
   Of a fresh and following folded rank
      Not spared, not one
      That dandled a sandalled
    Shadow that swam or sank
On meadow and river and wind-wandering
    weed-winding bank.
  O if we but knew what we do
     When we delve or hew –
   Hack and rack the growing green!
    Since country is so tender
   To touch, her being só slender,
   That, like this sleek and seeing ball
   But a prick will make no eye at all,
   Where we, even where we mean
     To mend her we end her,
   When we hew or delve:
After-comers cannot guess the beauty been.
  Ten or twelve, only ten or twelve
   Strokes of havoc únselve
    The sweet especial scene,
  Rural scene, a rural scene,
  Sweet especial rural scene.

On the back of the sheet of paper on which he wrote this poem Hopkins scribbled one of his only poems about the sort of men he knew at Oxford:

Denis, whose motionable, alert, most vaulting wit
Caps occasion with an intellectual fit.
Yet Arthur is a Bowman: his three-heeled timber'll hit
The bald and bóld blínking gold when áll's dóne
Right rooting in the bare butt's wincing navel in the sight of the sun.

I saw myself at Oxford more like Hopkins' Arthur than his Denis. In any case, by the time I was there, poplars had grown again at Binsey.

    Meanwhile in the 1920s another young man had gone up to Balliol from Highgate Grammar School, where he had been taught English by T.S. Eliot. John Betjeman described aspects of Oxford in the inter-war period which are immensely evocative of my time there:

MAY-DAY SONG FOR NORTH OXFORD
(*Annie Laurie Tune*)

Belbroughton Road is bonny, and pinkly bursts the spray
Of prunus and forsythia across the public way,
For a full spring-tide of blossom seethed and departed hence,
Leaving land-locked pools of jonquils by sunny garden fence.

And a constant sound of flushing runneth from windows where
The toothbrush too is airing in this new North Oxford air
From Summerfields to Lynam's, the thirsty tarmac dries,
And a Cherwell mist dissolveth on elm-discovering skies.

Oh! well-bound Wells and Bridges! Oh! earnest ethical search
For the wide high-table λoyos of St C.S. Lewis's Church.
This diamond-eyed Spring morning my soul soars up the slope
Of a right good rough-cast buttress on the housewall of my hope.

And open-necked and freckled, where once there grazed the cows,
Emancipated children swing on old apple boughs,
And pastel-shaded book rooms bring New Ideas to birth
As the whitening hawthorn only hears the heart beat of the earth.

MYFANWY AT OXFORD

Pink may, double may, dead laburnum
    Shedding an Anglo-Jackson shade,
Shall we ever, my staunch Myfanwy,
    Bicycle down to North Parade?
Kant on the handle-bars, Marx in the saddlebag.
    Light my touch on your shoulder-blade.

Sancta Hilda, Myfanwyatia
  Evansensis – I hold your heart,
Willowy banks of a willowy Cherwell a
  Willowy figure with lips apart,
Strong and willowy, strong to pillow me,
  Gold Myfanwy, kisses and art.

Tubular bells of tall St Barnabas,
  Single clatter above St Paul,
Chasuble, acolyte, incense-offering,
  Spectacled faces held in thrall.
There in the nimbus and Comper tracery
  Gold Myfanwy blesses us all.

Gleam of gas upon Oxford station,
  Gleam of gas on her straight gold hair,
Hair flung back with an ostentation,
  Waiting alone for a girl friend there.
Second in Mods and a Third in Theology
  Come to breathe again Oxford air.

Her Myfanwy as in Cadena days,
  Her Myfanwy, a schoolgirl voice,
Tentative brush of a cheek in a cocoa crush,
  Coffee and Ulysses, Tennyson, Joyce,
Alpha-minded and other dimensional,
  Freud or Calvary? Take your choice.

Her Myfanwy? *My* Myfanwy.
  Bicycle bells in a Boar's Hill Pine,
Stedman Triple from All Saints' steeple,
  Tom and his hundred and one at nine,
Bells of Butterfield, caught in Keble,
  Sally and backstroke answer '*Mine!*'

I spent many entrancing hours reading through sixteenth and seventeenth-century poetry in the Balliol College Library, where I developed a lasting love for the metaphysical poets from Donne to Herbert. One poem by Francis Beaumont may serve to immortalize the Balliol Buttery:

THE GOOD FELLOW

When shall we meet againe to have a taste
Of that transcendent ale we dranke of last?
What wild ingredient did the woman chuse

To make her drinke withall? It made me lose
My wit before I quencht my thirst; there came
Such whimsies in my braine, and such a flame
Of fiery drunkennesse had sing'd my nose,
My bearde shrunk in for feare; there were of those
That took me for a comet, some afar
Distant remote, thought me a blazing star:
The Earth, methought, just as it was, it went
Round in a wheeling course of merriment;
My head was ever drooping, and my nose
Offering to be a suitor to my toes;
My pock-hole face, they say, appear'd to some
Just like a dry and burning honey combe;
My tongue did swim in ale, and joy'd to boast
It selfe a greater seaman than the toast,
My mouth was grown awry, as if it were
Lab'ring to reach the whisper in mine eare;
My guts were mines of sulphur, and my set
Of parched teeth struck fire as they met:
Nay, when I pist, my urine was so hot
It burnt a hole right through the chamber-pot
Each brewer that I met I kiss'd, and made
Suit to be bound apprentice to the trade:
One did approve the motion when he saw,
That my own legs could my indentures draw
Well, sir, I grew starke mad, as you may see
By this adventure upon poetry.
You easily may guesse, I am not quite
Grown sober yet, by these weak lines I write:
Onely I do't for this, to let you see
Whos'ere paid for the ale, I'm sure't paid me

I also managed to read a great deal of modern literature from America and France as well as Britain. Besides his novels, I read the letters and essays of D.H. Lawrence, which often gave me new insights into politics; like Heine, he thought hard about everything he saw and heard, and expressed himself with a poet's verve and precision. I loved Conrad and Hemingway, and developed a taste for the type of social satire which developed from Norman Douglas through Aldous Huxley to Evelyn Waugh and Anthony Powell; I still prefer the early works which the last two were producing in the thirties, such as Waugh's *Decline and Fall* and *Vile Bodies*, and Powell's *Afternoon Men* and *From a View to a Death*. Their more ambitious later novels seem somewhat infected by what Koestler called 'the French flu'.

I knew just enough French to read Voltaire, Huysmans and de Maupassant with pleasure, and to indulge in Verlaine and Rimbaud; but I had to read Thomas Mann in English. As the inevitable war drew closer, however, my reading was more influenced by my politics. I ploughed through every single volume of the Left Book Club, and John Lehmann's anthologies of 'New Writing'.

The intellectual intoxication of university life shines out of Thomas Traherne:

> Having been at the University, and received there the Taste and Tincture of another Education, I saw that there were Things in this World of which I never Dreamed; Glorious Secrets, and Glorious Persons past Imagination. There I saw that Logic, Ethicks, Physicks, Metaphysicks, Geometry, Astronomy, Poesie, Medicine, Grammar, Music, Rhetorick, all kinds of Arts, Trades and Mechanicismes that Adorned the World, pertained to Felicity.
>
> At least, there I saw those Things which afterwards I knew to pertain unto it; and was Delighted in it. There I saw into the Nature of the Sea, the Heavens, the Sun, the Moon and Stars, the Elements, Mineralls and Vegetables. All which appeared like the King's Daughter, all Glorious within; and those Things which my Nurses, and Parents, should have talked of were there taught unto Me.

At the time, I did not feel that the work I had to do for my degree was as important as my innumerable extra-curricular activities. I spent only about twenty hours a week on my academic studies, which included two or three hours in tutorials with one or two other undergraduates, and five hours at lectures. I could never understand why it was necessary to spend an hour at a lecture when you could have read the whole thing yourself in five minutes, and understood it better. Even the tutorials were a waste of time with some tutors – though I was lucky in having a few who have had a permanent influence on my thinking – notably Sandy Lindsay for philosophy.

Nevertheless, I now realize that my academic work had even more influence on my future thinking than the other activities which I have described at greater length in my memoirs.

GREEK AND LATIN

My first five terms were spent studying the literature of Greece and
Rome. That may seem to be a poor preparation for my later life. I
disagree. There is no better way of training your mind to think
clearly and to express itself clearly than translating Latin into
English and vice versa. Clear thinking and self-expression are far
more valuable to anyone in public life than the pseudosciences of
economic and political theory, in which lessons learned twenty or
thirty years ago are likely to be irrelevant or dangerously mislead-
ing today.

   Latin poetry has never seemed to me as impressive as Greek. It
offers nothing comparable with the Greek dramatists, or with
Homer. Even the greatest lyric poets of Rome, such as Horace and
Catullus, pale in comparison with their Greek predecessors, such as
Sappho, Alcman, and Alcaeus. And, like Yeats, I found something
uncomfortably comic in unmarried elderly dons construing love
poetry:

> Bald heads forgetful of their sins,
> Old learned, respectable bald heads
> Edit and annotate the lines
> That young men, tossing on their beds,
> Rhymed out in love's despair
> To flatter beauty's ignorant ear.
>
> All shuffle there; all cough in ink;
> All wear the carpet with their shoes;
> All think what other people think;
> All know the man their neighbour knows.
> Lord, what would they say
> Did their Catullus walk that way?

The Greek language is far more difficult to learn than Latin. It
uses a different script, and underwent substantial changes even in
classical times; the languages of Homer and Euripides were almost
as different from one another as those of Chaucer and Shakespeare.
Yet it is worth the effort of learning Greek for the poetry alone.
Poetry depends for its effect so much on sound and rhythm that it
is impossible to translate adequately from one language into
another. Lord Chesterfield claimed that everything suffers from
translation except a bishop. The Italians say: '*traduttore, traditore*' – a

translator is a traitor. To take an example, English poets throughout the ages have used the daffodil as a symbol of happiness and spring. The Italian word for daffodil is *tromboncino* – literally, little trombone, which would look and sound ridiculous as a translation in a poem. The nearest Italian equivalent in sound is *asfodelo*; but the asphodel is quite a different flower that is traditionally a symbol of death and the underworld.

I find that Greek poetry is at once the greatest and most untranslatable of all. On the other hand Greek prose translates well into English. You can enjoy Plato's *Dialogues* in Jowett's translation, or Thucydides' *History* in Crawley's translation almost as much as in the original Greek. Henry David Thoreau spoke for me in *Walden*:

> Men sometimes speak as if the study of the classics would at length make way for more modern and practical studies; but the adventurous student will always study classics, in whatever language they may be written and however ancient they may be. For what are the classics but the noblest recorded thoughts of man? They are the only oracles which are not decayed, and there are such answers to the most modern enquiry in them as Delphi and Dodona never gave. We might as well omit to study Nature because she is old.
>
> No wonder that Alexander carried the *Iliad* with him on his expeditions in a precious casket. A written word is the choicest of relics. It is something at once more intimate with us and more universal than any other work of art. It is the work of art nearest to life itself. It may be translated into every language, and not only read but actually breathed from all human lips; – not be represented on canvas or in marble only, but be carved out of the breath of life itself. The symbol of an ancient man's thought becomes a modern man's speech. Two thousand summers have imparted to the monuments of Grecian literature, as to her marbles, only a maturer golden and autumnal tint, for they have carried their own serene and celestial atmosphere into all lands to protect them against the corrosion of time.

Virginia Woolf, in her seminal essay 'On Not Knowing Greek' reminds us that the Greek dramatists wrote for a large audience out of doors in brilliant sunlight:

> These Queens and Princesses were out of doors, with the bees buzzing past them, shadows crossing them, and the wind taking

their draperies. They were speaking to an enormous audience rayed round them on one of those brilliant southern days when the sun is so hot and yet the air so exciting. The poet, therefore, had to bethink him, not of some theme which could be read for hours by people in privacy, but of something emphatic, familiar, brief, that would carry, instantly and directly, to an audience of seventeen thousand people perhaps, with ears and eyes eager and attentive, with bodies whose muscles would grow stiff if they sat too long without diversion. Music and dancing he would need, and naturally would choose one of those legends, like our Tristram and Iseult, which are known to every one in outline, so that a great fund of emotion is ready prepared, but can be stressed in a new place by each new poet.

Sophocles would take the old story of Electra, for instance, but would at once impose his stamp upon it. Of that, in spite of our weakness and distortion, what remains visible to us? That his genius was of the extreme kind in the first place; that he chose a design which, if it failed, would show its failure in gashes and ruin, not in the gentle blurring of some insignificant detail; which, if it succeeded, would cut each stroke to the bone, would stamp each fingerprint in marble. His Electra stands before us like a figure so tightly bound that she can only move an inch this way, an inch that. . . . In six pages of Proust we can find more complicated and varied emotions than in the whole of the *Electra*. But in the *Electra* or in the *Antigone* we are impressed by something different, by something perhaps more impressive – by heroism itself, by fidelity itself. In spite of the labour and the difficulty it is this that draws us back and back to the Greeks; the stable, the permanent, the original human being is to be found there. Violent emotions are needed to rouse him into action, but when thus stirred by death, by betrayal, by some other primitive calamity, Antigone and Ajax and Electra behave in the way in which we should behave thus struck down; the way in which everybody has always behaved; and thus we understand them more easily and more directly than we understand the characters in the *Canterbury Tales*. These are the originals, Chaucer's the varieties of the human species.

. . . Here we meet them before their emotions have been worn into uniformity. Here we listen to the nightingale whose song echoes through English literature singing in her own Greek tongue. For the first time Orpheus with his lute makes men and beasts follow him. Their voices ring out clear and sharp; we see the hairy, tawny bodies at play in the sunlight among the olive trees, not posed gracefully on granite plinths in the pale corridors of the British Museum. And then suddenly, in the midst of all this sharpness and compression, Electra, as if she swept her veil over her face and forbade us to think of her any more, speaks of that very nightingale: 'that bird distraught with grief, the messenger of Zeus. Ah, queen of sorrow, Niobe, thee I deem divine – thee; who evermore weepest in thy rocky tomb.'

Auden points out that the historical discontinuity between Greek culture and our own makes it all the easier for each nation, and even each person, to fashion a classical Greece in its own image:

> For instance, here are two English caricatures:
> Professor X. Reade Chair of Moral Philosophy. 59. Married. Three daughters. Religion: C of E (Broad). Politics: Conservative. Lives in a small suburban house stuffed with Victorian knick-knacks. Does not entertain. Smokes a pipe. Does not notice what he eats. Hobbies: gardening and long solitary walks. Dislikes: foreigners, Roman Catholicism, modern literature, noise. Current worry: his wife's health.
> Mr Y. Classical tutor. 41. Unmarried. Religion: none. Politics: none. Lives in college. Has private means and gives wonderful lunch parties for favorite undergraduates. Hobbies: travel and collecting old glass. Dislikes: Christianity, girls, the poor, English cooking. Current worry: his figure.
> To X, the word Greece suggests Reason, the Golden Mean, emotional control, freedom from superstition; to Y it suggests Gaiety and Beauty, the life of the senses, freedom from inhibitions.

Any student of Greek will be able to classify his tutor into one of these two types.

Perhaps the most important thing I learned from my academic studies at Oxford was that variety is not the spice of life. It is life itself. I was led to this conclusion above all by reading philosophy. Philosophy, from its beginnings in ancient Greece right up to the present day, is concerned with what it shows to be the unknowable – the meaning of words like reality, goodness, and beauty.

Most people tend to regard a philosopher as someone separated from life in an ivory tower. Some philosophers justify this description. But the real subject matter of philosophy is of fundamental importance to all of us. I recall G.K. Chesterton saying that a landlady should be more concerned with her tenant's philosophy than with his wallet; it is the former which decides at all times whether he will pay his bill, the latter decides only once – when it is empty.

Even as a boy I puzzled over the eternal questions such as – if every effect has a cause, how can we have free will? or, if the universe is limited in time and space, what is outside it and what came before it? or, what is the relationship between truth and reality? One purpose of Greats is to make you think such problems through with the help of men who have studied them in the past.

I am all too aware that the next few pages may be hard going, as hard as the passages in *The Time of My Life* which try to explain the mysteries of economics and of nuclear strategy. Like economics and strategy, philosophy uses a vocabulary of its own in order to make its concepts more precise and manageable. I hope, however, that you will find mastering philosophy much more worthwhile; it is relevant to almost everything we think or do.

There is no place in Greats for D.H. Lawrence's pseudo-intellectual:

> A young man said to me:
> I am interested in the problem of reality.
> I said: Really!
> Then I saw him turn to glance, surreptitiously, in the
> big glass mirror at his own fascinating shadow.

I found that reading philosophy at Oxford was intellectually the most testing time of my life, and in retrospect the most useful. It helped me to understand some of the most difficult problems I was later to deal with in politics and economics. I have often quoted Kierkegaard's words: 'People hardly ever make use of the freedom which they have – for example freedom of thought; instead they demand freedom of speech as a compensation.'

Freedom of thought in philosophy started for me with the parable of the cave in Book VII of Plato's *Republic*. Plato compares human beings with prisoners in a cave, whose heads are immobilized so that they can see only the surface of the cave in front of them. Behind them objects are being carried so that their shadows are cast on the surface of the cave by a fire. The prisoners are bound to imagine that the distorted two-dimensional shadows they see in front of them are the only reality.

Most of the philosophers who followed Plato accept that the perception of the senses, on which his prisoners had to rely, can give at best only an incomplete and distorted picture of reality. But their attempts to use human reason in order to produce a better picture all came to grief. The central problem was put by Pascal in the seventeenth century: 'All the principles of sceptics, stoics, and atheists, etc. are true. But their conclusions are false, because the opposite principles are also true.'

The argument between faith and reason, between religion and science, came to a head in 1781 when Immanuel Kant published the *Critique of Pure Reason*. Kant, the son of simple but rigorously pious parents of Scottish extraction, lived in Prussia under the rule of Frederick the Great at Königsberg (later Kaliningrad). There was much of the puritan Scot about him too. He tells us that it was the Scottish empiricist, David Hume, who 'first interrupted my dogmatic slumber and gave my investigations in the field of speculative philosophy quite a new direction'.

Hume summed up his approach to philosophy in *An Enquiry Concerning Human Understanding* as follows:

> If we take in our hand any volume; of divinity or school metaphysics, for instance; let us ask, 'Does it contain any abstract reasoning concerning quantity or number?' No. 'Does it contain any experimental reasoning concerning matter of fact and existence?' No. Commit it then to the flames: for it can contain nothing but sophistry and illusion.

Kant did for me what Hume did for Kant. He showed me that the insolubility of the problems which I found so puzzling arose from attempting to apply the wrong sort of reason to them. Scientific logic is relevant only to things we can experience with our senses and prove or disprove by experiment; it cannot deal with problems of value like beauty and goodness.

I found, and still find, Kant's *Critique* appallingly difficult to read. What Heine described as his 'colourless, dry, packing-paper style' did not encourage my efforts. I was wrestling with Kant's passage on the 'originally synthetic unity of apperception' – his definition of the consciousness of self – on the morning of 3 September 1939 when I heard my mother running upstairs to tell me that Chamberlain had just declared that Britain was at war with Germany. The announcement came as a blessed release from my labours. Here is the passage in all its crystalline obscurity:

> For example, this universal identity of the apperception of the manifold given in intuition, contains a synthesis of representations, and is possible only by means of the consciousness of this synthesis.

For the empirical consciousness which accompanies different representations is in itself fragmentary and disunited, and without relation to the identity of the subject. This relation, then, does not exist because I accompany every representation with consciousness, but because I join one representation to another, and am conscious of the synthesis of them. Consequently, only because I can connect a variety of given representations in one consciousness, is it possible that I can represent to myself the identity of consciousness in these representations; in other words, the analytical unity of apperception is possible only under the presupposition of a synthetical unity.[1] The thought, 'These representations given in intuition, belong all of them to me,' is accordingly just the same as, 'I unite them in one self-consciousness, or can at least so unite them;' and although this thought is not itself the consciousness of the synthesis of representations it presupposes the possibility of it; that is to say, for the reason alone, that I can comprehend the variety of my representations in one consciousness, do I call them my representations, for otherwise I must have as many-coloured and various a self as are the representations of which I am conscious. Synthetical unity of the manifold in intuitions, as given *a priori*, is therefore the foundation of the identity of apperception itself, which antecedes *a priori* all determinate thought.

[1] All general conceptions – as such – depend, for their existence, on the analytical unity of consciousness. For example, when I think of *red* in general, I thereby think to myself a property which (as a characteristic mark) can be discovered somewhere, or can be united with other representations; consequently, it is only by means of a forethought possible synthetical unity that I can think to myself the analytical. A representation which is cogitated as common to *different* representations, is regarded as belonging to such as, besides this common representation, contain something *different*; consequently it must be previously thought in synthetical unity with other although only possible representations, before I can think in it the analytical unity of consciousness which makes it a *conceptas communis*. And thus the synthetical unity of apperception is the highest point with which we must connect every operation of the understanding, even the whole of logic, and after it our transcendental philosophy.

You may find this difficult, but one of my German friends at Balliol found Kant easier to read in this English translation than in the original German.

The heart of the *Critique* lies in a passage where Kant echoes Pascal, by showing that reason can be used to prove contradictory propositions on some of the most important issues which challenge our minds. He presents these 'antinomies of pure reason' as a series of four theses and antitheses:

> Thesis I. The world has a beginning in time, and is also limited in regard to space.
> Antithesis I. The world has no beginning, and no limits in space, but is, in relation both to time and space, infinite.
> Thesis II. Every composite substance in the world consists of simple parts: and there exists nothing that is not either itself simple, or composed of simple parts.
> Antithesis II. No composite thing in the world consists of simple parts; and there does not exist in the world any simple substance.
> Thesis III. Causality according to the laws of nature, is not the only causality operating to originate the phenomena of the world. A causality of freedom is also necessary to account fully for these phenomena.
> Antithesis III. There is no such thing as freedom, but everything in the world happens solely according to the laws of nature.
> Thesis IV. There exists either in, or in connection with the world – either as a part of it, or as the cause of it – an absolutely necessary being.
> Antithesis IV. An absolutely necessary being does not exist, either in the world, or out of it – as its cause.

In trying to explain how it was possible for reason to prove such contradictory propositions, Kant concluded that our knowledge is shaped by our senses and our reason together. Our senses experience things in space and time; space and time are subjective modes of sense-perception which have no reality outside our mind. Our reason operates through structures of logic which also do not exist outside our mind.

This was a revolution in thinking as fundamental as the revolution wrought by Copernicus in astronomy, with which it was often compared. By putting the nature and limitations of the human mind at the centre of knowledge Kant made it impossible to prove the existence of God by argument. Metaphysics was no longer a rational activity.

After I had spent months wrestling with the *Critique*, my eyes were finally opened to its meaning and importance by the German poet, Heinrich Heine. Again and again in later life I found that Heine's prose could illuminate the most difficult of problems by applying a poet's intuition, and above all, a poet's style.

To Heine, Kant had destroyed deism in Germany, if not God himself: his achievement in philosophy was as mighty as that of Robespierre in politics:

It is said that night-wandering spirits are filled with terror at night of the headsman's axe. With what mighty fear, then, must they be stricken when there is held up to them Kant's *Critique of Pure Reason*! This is the sword that slew deism in Germany.

To speak frankly, you French have been tame and moderate compared with us Germans. At most, you could but kill a king, and he had already lost his head before you guillotined him. For accompaniment to such deed you must needs cause such a drumming and shrieking and stamping of feet that the whole universe trembled. To compare Maximilian Robespierre with Immanuel Kant is to confer too high an honour upon the former. Maximilian Robespierre, the great citizen of the Rue Saint Honoré, had, it is true, his sudden attacks of destructiveness when it was a question of the monarchy, and his frame was violently convulsed when the fit of regicidal epilepsy was on; but as soon as it came to be a question about the Supreme Being, he wiped the white froth from his lips, washed the blood from his hands, donned his blue Sunday coat with silver buttons, and stuck a nosegay in the bosom of his broad vest.

The history of Immanuel Kant's life is difficult to portray, for he had neither life nor history. He led a mechanical, regular almost abstract bachelor existence in a little retired street of Königsberg, an old town on the north eastern frontier of Germany. I do not believe that the great clock of the cathedral performed in a more passionless and methodical manner its daily routine than did its townsman, Immanuel Kant. Rising in the morning, coffee-drinking, writing, reading lectures, dining, walking, everything had its appointed time, and the neighbours knew that it was exactly half-past three o'clock when Immanuel Kant stepped forth from his house in his grey, tight-fitting coat, with his Spanish cane in his hand, and betook himself to the little linden avenue called after him to this day the 'Philosopher's Walk.' Summer and winter he walked up and down it eight times, and when the weather was dull or heavy clouds prognosticated rain, the townspeople beheld his servant, the old Lampe, trudging anxiously behind him with a big umbrella under his arm, like an image of Providence.

What a strange contrast did this man's outward life present to his destructive, world-annihilating thoughts! In sooth, had the citizens of Königsberg had the least presentiment of the full significance of his ideas, they would have felt a far more awful dread at the presence of this man than at the sight of an executioner, who can but kill the body. But the worthy folk saw in him nothing more than a Professor of Philosophy, and as he passed at his customary hour, they greeted him in a friendly manner and set their watches by him.

But though Immanuel Kant, the arch-destroyer in the realm of thought, far surpassed in terrorism Maximilian Robespierre, he had many similarities with the latter, which induce a comparison between the two men. In the first place, we find in both the same inexorable, keen, poesyless, sober integrity. We likewise find in both the same talent of suspicion, only that in the one it manifested itself in the direction of thought and was called criticism, whilst in the other it was directed against mankind and was styled republican virtue. But both presented in the highest degree the type of the narrow-minded citizen. Nature had destined them for weighing out coffee and sugar, but fate decided that they should weigh out other things, and into the scales of the one it laid a king, into the scales of the other a God ... And they both gave the correct weight!

Heine found it difficult to understand how, after showing that it was impossible to prove the existence of God, Kant should have remained a pious Christian; he claimed that Kant pretended to believe in God just to please his loyal servant, Lampe:

Up to this point Immanuel Kant has pursued the path of inexorable philosophy; he has stormed heaven and put the whole garrison to the edge of the sword; the ontological, cosmological, and physico theological bodyguards lie there lifeless; Deity itself, deprived of demonstration, has succumbed; there is now no All-mercifulness, no fatherly kindness, no other-world reward for renunciation in this world, the immortality of the soul lies in its last agony – you can hear its groans and death-rattle; and old Lampe is standing by with his umbrella under his arm, an afflicted spectator of the scene, tears and sweat-drops of terror dropping from his countenance. Then Immanuel Kant relents and shows that he is not merely a great philosopher but also a good man; he reflects, and half good naturedly, half ironically, he says: 'Old Lampe must have a God, otherwise the poor fellow can never be happy. Now, man ought to be happy in this world; practical reason says so; – well, I am quite willing that practical reason should also guarantee the existence of God.' As the result of this argument Kant distinguishes between the *theoretical reason* and the *practical reason*, and by means of the latter, as with a magician's wand, he revivifies deism, which theoretical reason had killed.

But is it not conceivable that Kant brought about this resurrection, not merely for the sake of old Lampe, but through fear of the police? Or did he act from sincere conviction? Was not his object in destroying all evidence for the existence of God to show us how embarrassing it might be to know nothing about God? In doing so, he acted almost as sagely as a Westphalian friend of mine, who smashed all the lanterns in the Grohnder Street in Göttingen, and then proceeded to deliver to us in the dark a long lecture on the practical necessity of lanterns, which he had theoretically broken in order to show how, without them, we could see nothing.

Heine had completely missed the point.

Kant made it crystal clear in his preface to the second edition of the *Critique* that, far from destroying the belief in God, his purpose was to make belief possible: 'I must, therefore, abolish knowledge to make room for belief. The dogmatism of metaphysics is the true source of unbelief (always dogmatic) which militates against morality.'

In other words, as Benjamin Jowett said to Margot Asquith when she was a little girl: 'My dearest child, you must believe in God, in spite of all the clergy tell you' – sentiments I have often applied to Socialism when depressed by some of its ideologues.

In fact Kant clearly indicates his personal belief in a mystical reality beyond experience, in an extraordinary little pamphlet which he wrote to ridicule Swedenborg's belief in visions, called *Dreams of a man who sees spirits*:

> I know that will and understanding move my body, but I can never reduce by analysis this phenomenon, as a simple experience to another experience, and can therefore, indeed recognize it, but not understand it. That my will moves my arm is not more intelligible to me than if somebody told me that he could stop the moon in its orbit. The difference is only that the one I experience, but that the latter has never occurred to me. I recognize in myself changes as of a living subject, namely thoughts, power to choose, etc. etc., and, as these terms indicate things different in kind from any of those which, taken together, make up my body, I have good reason to conceive of an incorporeal and constant being.

All these issues were being debated with renewed ferocity when I was at Oxford. British philosophy in the thirties was dominated by the new fashion for Logical Positivism. In 1936, the year I went up to Balliol, Freddie Ayer produced a lucid account of it in his *Language Truth and Logic*, stressing its affinity with the empiricism of David Hume. I found Ayer's approach profoundly unsatisfying; though he built a good deal on Kant's case against metaphysics, he threw out the baby along with the bath-water.

Oddly enough, Ayer thought he was popularizing the thought of Ludwig Wittgenstein, who wrote his great *Tractatus Logico-Philosophicus* during the First World War as a soldier in the Austrian army after studying as an engineer. Wittgenstein carried Kant's work further by demonstrating the inadequacy of language itself to express the most important truths. He showed that language makes reasoning impossible on the fundamental issues, because the structure of syntax and the imprecision of words cannot produce meaningful propositions about reality. His *Tractatus* is only ninety pages long, and his use of algebraic symbols makes it even more difficult to master than Kant's *Critique*. But he concludes like Kant that there is an inexpressible reality to which the statements of natural science are irrelevant:

> My propositions are elucidatory in this way: he who understands me finally recognizes them as senseless, when he has climbed out through them, on them, over them. (He must so to speak throw away the ladder, after he has climbed up on it.)
>
> He must surmount these propositions; then he sees the world rightly.
>
> Whereof one cannot speak, thereof one must be silent.

Wittgenstein himself was tormented by the problems whereof one cannot speak. He met Bertrand Russell before the First World War when he was doing aeronautical research in Manchester, and went to study with him at Cambridge. Russell told how:

> He used to come and see me every evening at midnight, and pace up and down my room like a wild beast for three hours in agitated silence. Once I said to him, 'Are you thinking about logic or about your sins?' 'Both', he replied, and continued his pacing. I did not like to suggest that it was time for bed, as it seemed probable both to him and me that on leaving me he would commit suicide.

In fact three of his brothers did take their own lives. Soon after writing the *Tractatus* Wittgenstein abandoned philosophy to spend six years as an elementary schoolmaster in the Austrian countryside, teaching peasants to read and write. The parallel with Hopkins is interesting, particularly since Wittgenstein too was tortured by homosexual guilt. On the other hand he shared something with me – two of his favourite hobbies were Hollywood films and hard-boiled American detective stories.

Well before he died in 1951 Wittgenstein had repudiated his *Tractatus* and begun to study the meanings that language takes on as a means of communication in everyday life, which is the natural province of the playwright, novelist and poet.

I was spared his type of intellectual agony by my interest in music and painting, where meaning has always escaped imprisonment in words. But I was also helped enormously by the advice of my philosophy tutor, Sandy Lindsay, Master of Balliol and Popular Front candidate in the anti-appeasement by-election in 1938. He told me to read writers who were regarded as totally heretical both by my examiners for Greats, and by my Communist friends, particularly Kierkegaard and Shestov, who were among the founders of Existentialism.

Shestov was a Russian writer on philosophy and literature who wrote his first book in 1898 and continued writing in Paris after the Bolshevik Revolution. He found Tolstoy and Dostoevsky as illuminating as any of the conventional philosophers in dealing with the problems which are inaccessible to logic. In an early essay on the theory of knowledge he made a point which needs constant repetition:

> There is not the least necessity to make from an idea all the deductions to which it may lead. A man is a free agent and he can deduce if he has a mind to; if he has not, he will not; and there is no necessity to judge the character of a philosophic theory by its general postulates. The interest of mankind is not to put an end to the variety of philosophic doctrines but to allow that perfectly natural phenomenon wide and deep development.

In 1929 Shestov published the most extensive description of his views, *In Job's Balances*, which Lindsay persuaded me to read about ten years later. This drew my attention to two ancient philosophers who were largely ignored by Greats – Heraclitus, who lived a century before Plato, and Aristotle, and Tertullian, who lived two centuries after the birth of Christ.

Only a few fragments of Heraclitus have survived, but they have provided invaluable insights to politicians who have to cope with a world of rapid change: 'Everything is in flux,' and 'Upon those who step into the same rivers different and ever different waters flow down,' usually rendered as 'You cannot step into the same river twice.' Willy Brandt and Mikhail Gorbachev have both quoted him as their guide; Gorbachev may have been introduced to his work by his wife, Raisa, who studied philosophy at university.

Heraclitus also anticipated Hegel and Marx – and in a sense Kant's antinomies as well – in insisting on the interdependence of opposites. His cosmology treated fire as the basic material principle of an orderly universe. This inspired one of Hopkins' last and greatest poems:

THAT NATURE IS A HERACLITEAN FIRE AND OF THE COMFORT OF THE RESURRECTION

Cloud-puffball, torn tufts, tossed pillows ' flaunt forth, then chevy
    on an air-
built thoroughfare: heaven-roysterers, in gay-gangs ' they throng;
    they glitter in marches.
Down roughcast, down dazzling whitewash, ' wherever an elm
    arches,
Shivelights and shadowtackle in long ' lashes lace, lance, and pair.
Delightfully the bright wind boisterous ' ropes, wrestles, beats earth
    bare
Of yestertempest's creases; ' in pool and rutpeel parches
Squandering ooze to squeezed ' dough, crust, dust; stanches,
    starches
Squadroned masks and manmarks ' treadmire toil there
Footfretted in it. Million-fuelèd, ' nature's bonfire burns on.
But quench her bonniest, dearest ' to her, her clearest-selvèd spark
Man, how fast his firedint, ' his mark on mind, is gone!
Both are in an unfathomable, all is in an enormous dark
Drowned. O pity and indig ' nation! Manshape, that shone
Sheer off, disseveral, a star, ' death blots black out; nor mark
             Is any of him at all so stark
But vastness blurs and time ' beats level. Enough! the Resurrection,
A heart's-clarion! Away grief's gasping, ' joyless days, dejection.

> Across my foundering deck shone
> A beacon, an eternal beam. ' Flesh fade, and mortal trash
> Fall to the residuary worm; ' world's wildfire, leave but ash:
> In a flash, at a trumpet crash,
> I am all at once what Christ is, ' since he was what I am, and
> This Jack, joke, poor potsherd, ' patch, matchwood, immortal
>   diamond,
>   Is immortal diamond.

Tertullian was an early Christian, born in Carthage. He strongly resisted attempts to reconcile Christian doctrine with Greek philosophy, on the grounds that Athens could never agree with Jerusalem. Instead he insisted on the paradox – 'I am not ashamed – because it is shameful. It is absolutely credible – because it is absurd. It is certain – because it is impossible.' This is a drastic formulation, but may sometimes be the only way of breaking through the prison walls of logic which so often lock you away from reality.

Science has of course achieved wonders in the last four hundred years by working within the boundaries of logic and reason which Kant so rigorously defined. In the twentieth century, when its advance has accelerated at dizzy speed, it has owed more than might appear to the philosophers. Einstein's general theory of relativity linked space and time, as dependent on the position of the observer, in a way which would not have surprised Kant. Unlike Kant, however, he believed that natural science could produce a comprehensive truth about the world; he spent the latter part of his life vainly trying to prove that the universe is exactly engineered, since he was convinced that 'God is subtle but he is not malicious'.

None the less, Einstein believed profoundly that science depends on preserving a sense of wonder in the face of the natural world. He wrote:

> The most beautiful and profound emotion we can experience is the sensation of the mystical. It is the dower of all true science. He to whom this emotion is a stranger, who can no longer wonder and stand wrapped in awe, is as good as dead. To know that what is impenetrable to us really exists, manifesting itself as the highest wisdom and the most radiant beauty, which our dull faculties can comprehend only in the most primitive forms, this knowledge, this feeling is the centre of true religion.

Today chaos theory is the flavour of the age. It is defined as 'the theory of complex systems in a far-from equilibrium condition'. And computer scientists have developed 'fuzzy logic' to deal with problems which defy accurate and specific answers. I am told that an education in Greats is one of the best qualifications for working on the most formidable challenge to computer science – the creation of artificial intelligence.

I find it depressing, however, to discover how little many modern scientists have learned about the limitations of their profession as demonstrated by Kant and Wittgenstein. The cosmologists appear to think they are making meaningful statements when they talk of Big Bangs or Black Holes as the origin of the universe. The biologist Richard Dawkins even argues that by showing how complex things might have evolved from simple things, Darwin made faith irrelevant to real life: we can eliminate God from our inquiries because He is statistically improbable. Yet Dawkins himself thinks it is possible and necessary to make use of words like good and bad, or beautiful and ugly, without any reference to scientific reason. Even a modest acquaintance with philosophy might temper the arrogance of such scientists, and also persuade their theological opponents to avoid using scientific reason to justify their beliefs.

This brief caricature of my own encounter with philosophy at Oxford may appal some academics. However, following Shestov's advice, I have been more concerned here to pick out of my reading things which planted live seeds in my mind, than to give a balanced summary of the views of the philosophers concerned – as if that were possible!

In my first term at Balliol I read T.S. Eliot's 'Burnt Norton' – the first of his Four Quartets, which had recently been published. It crystallizes some of my own conclusions from philosophy:

> Words move, music moves
> Only in time; but that which is only living
> Can only die. Words, after speech, reach
> Into the silence. Only by the form, the pattern,
> Can words or music reach
> The stillness, as a Chinese jar still
> Moves perpetually in its stillness.
> Not the stillness of the violin, while the note lasts,
> Not that only, but the co-existence,
> Or say that the end precedes the beginning,

And the end and the beginning were always there
Before the beginning and after the end.
And all is always now. Words strain,
Crack and sometimes break, under the burden,
Under the tension, slip, slide, perish,
Decay with impression, will not stay in place,
Will not stay still. Shrieking voices
Scolding, mocking, or merely chattering,
Always assail them. The Word in the desert
Is most attacked by voices of temptation,
The crying shadow in the funeral dance,
The loud lament of the disconsolate chimera.

Better still, perhaps, the words of Guizot, the nineteenth-century French conservative, in a very different context: 'We cannot see clearly to the other side of the river. But the darkness does not destroy what it conceals.'

ANCIENT HISTORY

Greats also requires you to study the history of ancient Greece and Rome. You might think that was less relevant for a politician these days than the history of nineteenth or twentieth-century Europe. You would be wrong. To a politician the main value of history is as a guide to how societies develop and how people react to events. The problem with the history of the last few centuries is that it is written in the main by men who want to prove that their personal view of current events is correct – to prove a point about their own contemporary politics. Thus the great nineteenth-century English historians like Macaulay promoted what Herbert Butterfield called 'The Whig View of History'; for example they described the English Civil War of the seventeenth century in a way calculated to show that Gladstone was right two hundred years later. Similarly Karl Marx saw the past in terms of the class struggle which he thought was raging in nineteenth-century France and Germany. The French Revolution has been re-interpreted by each succeeding generation in the light of its own particular pre-occupations.

Karl Popper, who had a great influence on me when I read his work after the war, has spent much of his life attacking what he calls 'historicism'. He defines historicism as the illusion that it is possible to predict the future by discovering the laws or trends that underlie the evolution of history. He has attacked with particular force social or economic theories like Marxism, which assume that history is a science with immutable laws, on which a system can be built to explain any problem of human behaviour. I have no doubt he would be equally severe with the astonishing view of Francis Fukuyama that the end of the Cold War is the end of history. For Popper, as for me, 'behavioural science' is a contradiction in terms.

The current reaction against historicism has gone so far that Simon Schama's *Citizens*, for example, sees the French Revolution in terms of millions of events on which the historian imposes a pattern for aesthetic reasons. And here is the rub. There are indeed millions of things going on at any given time which may be relevant to any single historical event. Only a small fraction of these relevant facts is known to the historian, and whether that fraction contains the most important facts can never be known. So the pattern which a historian constructs, whether for political or aesthetic reasons, out of the facts he happens to know, may bear little relation to any historical reality. I suppose that is why Henry Ford said 'history is bunk' and why the opinion polls failed to predict the result of the British General Election in 1992.

And yet history is the only guide we have for understanding what is happening today. We are only just discovering that much which is at first sight difficult to understand in Eastern Europe or the former Soviet Union becomes all too intelligible if we read something of the history of those regions over the last thousand years. And it remains terribly true that those who do not learn from history are condemned to repeat it.

Even as an intellectual exercise the study of ancient history has a unique value. The facts that are known, and the documents or artefacts which survive, are comparatively few. Archeology is often as relevant as a contemporary account to understanding ancient history. So if you are a journalist or modern historian, ancient history can teach you to make sure that your interpretation of an event is consistent at least with all the evidence which is available.

Moreover some of the ancient historians had an understanding of the society of their day more penetrating than any of their successors except perhaps de Toqueville. My favourite was, and remains, Thucydides, who wrote the *History of the Peloponnesian War*, which lasted twenty-seven years in the fifth century before

Christ. He himself served in it as an Athenian general against the
Spartans and wrote its history during his twenty years in exile after
being dismissed for a military blunder. Like another of my
favourites, Tacitus, a historian of the early Roman Empire, he was
a conservative democrat, opposed equally to personal or oligarchic
dictatorship and to demagogic populism; inevitably his work
betrays his political bias.

The lasting attraction of Thucydides, however, lies in his ability
to define the moral and political issues underlying the events he
describes, usually through imaginary speeches or debates between
the protagonists. These debates give a timeless insight into some of
the most fundamental dilemmas facing politicians – more compelling even than the works of Machiavelli and Clausewitz – because
they are linked with historical events which have their counterpart
in every age. A century ago Matthew Arnold remarked that 'the
portion of history dealt with by Thucydides is only ancient in the
sense that the events related happened a long while ago; in other
respects it is more modern than the history of our own countrymen
in the Middle Ages.' In 1991 BBC television produced a riveting
commentary on the issues raised by the Gulf War, which consisted
entirely of actors reading extracts from speeches in Thucydides.

The History of the Peloponnesian War traces the development of a
political tragedy. It demonstrates how a war can destroy not only
democracy but the state itself. At the beginning Athens is a liberal
democracy; it became a model to future generations largely because
Thucydides described it in the great funeral oration of its leader,
Pericles:

> Our constitution does not copy the laws of neighbouring states; we
> are rather a pattern to others than imitators ourselves. Its administra-
> tion favours the many instead of the few; this is why it is called a
> democracy. If we look to the laws, they afford equal justice to all in
> their private differences; if to social standing, advancement in
> public life falls to reputation for capacity, class considerations not
> being allowed to interfere with merit; nor again does poverty bar
> the way, if a man is able to serve the state, he is not hindered by the
> obscurity of his condition. The freedom which we enjoy in our
> government extends also to our ordinary life. There, far from
> exercising a jealous surveillance over each other, we do not feel
> called upon to be angry with our neighbour for doing what he
> likes, or even to indulge in those injurious looks which cannot fail
> to be offensive, although they inflict no positive penalty. But all

this ease in our private relations does not make us lawless as citizens. Against this fear is our chief safeguard, teaching us to obey the magistrates and the laws, particularly such as regard the protection of the injured, whether they are actually on the statute book, or belong to that code which, although unwritten, yet cannot be broken without acknowledged disgrace. . . .

We cultivate refinement without extravagance and knowledge without effeminacy; weakness we employ more for use than for show, and place the real disgrace of poverty not in owning to the fact but in declining the struggle against it. Our public men have besides politics, their private affairs to attend to, and our ordinary citizens, though occupied with the pursuits of industry, are still fair judges of public matters; for, unlike any other nation, regarding him who takes no part in these duties not as unambitious but as useless, we Athenians are able to judge at all events if we cannot originate and instead of looking on discussion as a stumbling-block in the way of action, we think it an indispensable preliminary to any wise action at all. Again, in our enterprises we present the singular spectacle of daring and deliberation, each carried to its highest point, and both united in the same persons; although usually decision is the fruit of ignorance, hesitation or reflexion. But the palm of courage will surely be adjudged most justly to those, who best know the difference between hardship and pleasure and yet are never tempted to shrink from danger. In generosity we are equally singular, acquiring our friends by conferring not by receiving favours. Yet, of course, the doer of the favour is the firmer friend of the two, in order by continued kindness to keep the recipient in his debt; while the debtor feels less keenly from the very consciousness that the return he makes will be a payment, not a free gift. And it is only the Athenians who, fearless of consequences, confer their benefits not from calculations of expediency, but in the confidence of liberality.

In short, I say that as a city we are the school of Hellas.

At the end of the History, which stops in the twenty-first year of the war – six years of agony were still to follow – Athens has been exhausted by its disastrous colonial expedition to Syracuse; its army has been annihilated, its people demoralized, and its society corrupted. Moreover the war has spread. It has divided the whole of the ancient world along ideological lines, between democracy and dictatorship; the democracies are often behaving even worse than the dictatorships.

In fact, the Greek city states continued to fight one another for more than another hundred years. Then they simply collapsed in the face of Philip of Macedon, a kingdom on the fringe of Greek civilization. Philip's son, Alexander, built an empire which ultimately stretched from Egypt through the whole of the Middle East to India.

In recent years the collapse and disintegration not just of the Soviet Empire but of the whole culture of Communism – a New Civilization, as the Webbs called it – could have come as a surprise only to those who know nothing of Greek history.

I now realize that the work I did at Oxford on philosophy and ancient history gave me invaluable tools for my later career in politics. In particular they endowed me with a cautious scepticism against trying to understand human behaviour through the application of theories which claimed the certainties of science. Meanwhile Latin and Greek poetry, combined with my love of all the arts, which developed mightily at Oxford, showed me that there were alternative tools of understanding which were not only more helpful in many cases, but vastly more enjoyable.

POLITICS

In my time at Oxford, however, the Soviet Union still seemed the hope of the world. The failure of capitalism had produced fascism in Italy and Germany, had plunged the world into the Great Slump, and seemed incapable of dealing with the military threat from the dictators it had created. So on both sides of the Atlantic young people turned to Stalin for salvation, because he seemed to represent the opposite of capitalism; similarly in recent years young people in what was once the Soviet Empire have turned from the collapse of Communism to Thatcherism as its opposite.

The atmosphere in which we lived was well caught in 1938 by Louis MacNeice in his 'Autumn Journal':

> Conferences, adjournments, ultimatums,
>   Flights in the air, castles in the air,
> The autopsy of treaties, dynamite under the bridges,
>   The end of *laissez faire*.
> After the warm days the rain comes pimpling
>   The paving stones with white
> And with the rain the national conscience, creeping,
>   Seeping through the night.

And in the sodden park on Sunday protest
   Meetings assemble not, as so often, now
Merely to advertise some patent panacea
   But simply to avow
The need to hold the ditch; a bare avowal
   That may perhaps imply
Death at the doors in a week but perhaps in the long run
   Exposure of the lie.
Think of a number, double it, treble it, square it,
   And sponge it out
And repeat *ad lib.* and mark the slate with crosses;
   There is no time to doubt
If the puzzle really has an answer. Hitler yells on the wireless,
   The night is damp and still
And I hear dull blows on wood outside my window;
   They are cutting down the trees on Primrose Hill.
The wood is white like the roast flesh of chicken,
   Each tree falling like a closing fan;
No more looking at the view from seats beneath the branches,
   Everything is going to plan;
They want the crest of this hill for anti-aircraft,
   The guns will take the view
And searchlights probe the heavens for bacilli
   With narrow wands of blue.

The Spanish Civil War had begun in 1936 while I was cycling through Nazi Germany in the summer holiday between school and Oxford. Its impact on young intellectuals was anything but abstract, as illustrated by Hemingway's account of his visit to a Spanish hospital in 1937:

'Where's Raven?' I asked.

'I'm here,' said Raven.

The voice came from a high mound covered by a shoddy grey blanket. There were two arms crossed on the top of the mound and at one end there was something that had been a face, but now was a yellow scabby area with a wide bandage across where the eyes had been.

'Who is it?' asked Raven. He didn't have lips but he talked pretty well without them and with a pleasant voice.

'Hemingway,' I said. 'I came up to see how you were doing.'

'My face *was* pretty bad,' he said. 'It got sort of burned from the grenade but it's peeled a couple of times and it's doing better.'

'It looks swell,' I said. 'It's doing fine.'

I wasn't looking at it when I spoke.

'How are things in America?' he asked. 'What do they think of us over here?'

'Sentiment's changed a lot,' I said. 'They're beginning to realize the Government is going to win this war.'

'Do you think so?'

'Sure,' I said.

'I'm awfully glad,' he said. 'You know I wouldn't mind any of this if I could just watch what was going on. I don't mind the pain you know. It never seemed important really. But I was always awfully interested in things and I really wouldn't mind the pain at all if I could just sort of follow things intelligently. I could even be some use. You know I didn't mind the war at all. I did all right in the war. I got hit once before and I was back and rejoined the battalion in two weeks. I couldn't stand to be away. Then I got this.'

He had put his hand in mine. It was not a worker's hand. There were no callouses and the nails on the long, spatulate fingers were smooth and rounded.

'How did you get it?' I asked.

'Well, there were some troops that were routed and we went over to sort of reform them and we did and then we had quite a fight with the Fascists and we beat them. It was quite a bad fight, you know, but we beat them and then someone threw this grenade at me.'

Holding his hand and hearing him tell it, I did not believe a word of it. What was left of him did not sound like the wreckage of a soldier somehow. I did not know how he had been wounded but the story did not sound right. It was the sort of way everyone would like to have been wounded. But I wanted him to think I believed it.

'Where did you come from?' I asked.

'From Pittsburg. I went to the University there.'

'What did you do before you joined up here?'

'I was a social worker,' he said. Then I knew it couldn't be true, and I wondered how he had really been so frightfully wounded and I didn't care. In the war that I had known, men often lied about the manner of their wounding. Not at first; but later. I'd lied a little myself in my time. Especially late in the evening. But I was glad he thought I believed it and we talked about books, he wanted to be a writer, and I told him about what had happened north of Guadalajara and promised to bring some things from Madrid next time we got out that way. I hoped maybe I could get a radio.

'They tell me Dos Passos and Sinclair Lewis are coming over, too,' he said.

'Yes,' I said. 'And when they come I'll bring them up to see you.'

'Gee, that will be great,' he said. 'You don't know what that will mean to me.'

I joined the Labour Club as soon as I reached Balliol, and the following summer was persuaded by a young poet at Christ Church to join the Communist Party. Before long I was accepted as 'culture boss' in the Party. My main cultural activity, however, was in the New Oxford Art Society, which I started in 1938 with a few friends. Marxist theories of art seemed nonsense to me, as I explained in reviewing art exhibitions for *Oxford Forward*. I was no more impressed by the theory of Dialectical Materialism when I began studying philosophy for Greats. But although I rejected the Marxist theory of history, I was immensely impressed by Karl Marx himself as a political journalist and contemporary historian. I could forgive a lot to a man who could write *The Eighteenth Brumaire of Louis Bonaparte*. It begins as follows:

Hegel says somewhere that, upon the stage of universal history, all great events and personalities reappear in one fashion or another. He forgot to add that, on the first occasion, they appear as tragedy; on the second, as farce. Caussidière replaces Danton; Louis Blanc, Robespierre; the Mountain of 1848–1851, the Mountain of 1793–1795; the nephew Louis Bonaparte replaces his uncle. In the circumstances amid which the reissue of the *Eighteenth Brumaire* occurs (1869), we see the same caricature.

Men make their own history, but not just as they please. They do not choose the circumstances for themselves, but have to work upon circumstances as they find them, have to fashion the material handed down by the past. The legacy of the dead generations weighs like an alp upon the brains of the living. At the very time when they seem to be engaged in revolutionizing themselves and things, when they seem to be creating something perfectly new – in such epochs of revolutionary crisis, they are eager to press the spirits of the past into their service, borrowing the names of the dead, reviving old war-cries, dressing up in traditional costumes, that they may make a braver pageant in the newly-staged scene of universal history. Thus did Luther masquerade as Paul of Tarsus; thus did the revolution of 1789–1814, drape itself successively as the Roman Republic and the Roman Empire; and thus was it that the revolution of 1848 could find nothing better to do than to parody by turns 1789 and the revolutionary traditions of 1793–1795. In like manner, the learner of a new language begins by translating every word and every phrase into his mother tongue. He does not acquire the freedom of the city in his new speech, he is not at home there, until he has become able to break away from the memories of the language he learned in the nursery, and until he can use the new instrument without thinking of the old.

Moreover even when I was being deafened by one of my friends beating the ideological tom-tom, I could comfort myself with what Engels wrote in 1890:

The materialist conception of history also has a lot of friends nowadays to whom it serves as an excuse for not studying history. Just as Marx used to say about the French 'Marxists' of the late seventies: all I know is that I am not a Marxist.

The University Communist Party in those days, however, was able to laugh at itself. We made up songs which made fun of our own doctrine:

The rich men keep their women
In beautiful golden palaces
But the steadily declining profit rate
Exposes their worn out fallacies.
    So left, right, left
    So left, right, left
    There's a place, comrade, for you.
    March with us in the workers' united front
    For you are a worker too.

Many of our songs were sung to familiar tunes – for example, the following to the tune of 'The man who broke the bank at Monte Carlo':

As I stroll about the Red Square with a non-committal air, you
    can hear the girls declare:
'He must be a commissaire',
But they never would believe
That I'm laughing up my sleeve –
I'm the man that does the dirty work for Hitler.

As I crouch beneath the table where the Politburo meets,
They would startle from their seats,
If they knew of half the feats
Of diversionism and espionage,
And civil and military sabotage
That I perform the whole year round for Hitler.

Our fellow-students from the United States taught us not only political songs, but also moral ditties like the Ballad of Lilian:

Her name was Lil and she was a Cutie
She lived in a house of ill-reputy:
From far and near men came to see
Lilian in her deshabille.

She was lovely, she was fair,
She had lots of yellow hair:
But she was addicted to the demon rum,
She smoked hashish and opium.

Every day our Lil got thinner,
Insufficient protein in her;
She had great hollows in her chest
And had to go about completely dressed.

Clothes can make a girl go far,
But what's the good of clothes to a *fille de joie*?
Lilian's downfall started when
She covered up her abdomen.

Lilian went to her physician,
To prescribe for her condition:
She suffered, as we doctors say,
From pernicious an-aem-i-ae.

She lay for hours in the sun,
She tried Scott's emulsion.
She took liver, she tried yeast,
But still her clientele decreased.

One day Lil took up religion,
She went in for mysticism,
And every night as she went to sleep,
She prayed the Lord her soul to keep

In a penthouse in Park Avenue. . . .

> This is the story of a girl called Lilian.
> She was one girl in a million.
> The moral is not that you pay for your sins,
> But whatever your profession
> FITNESS WINS!

Nevertheless, neither I nor the bulk of my comrades could swallow the doctrine of violent revolution, which was fundamental to Marxism-Leninism. Watching the tragedy in Spain I could not forget Thucydides' account of the revolution in Corcyra, which he saw as typical of the ideological conflicts then tearing Greece apart:

> In peace and prosperity states and individuals have better sentiments, because they do not find themselves suddenly confronted with imperious necessities; but war takes away the easy supply of daily wants, and so proves a rough master, that brings most men's characters to a level with their fortunes. Revolution thus ran its course from city to city, and the places which it arrived at last, from having heard what had been done before, carried to a still greater excess the refinement of their inventions, as manifested in the cunning of their enterprises and the atrocity of their reprisals. Words had to change their ordinary meaning and to take that which was now given them. Reckless audacity came to be considered the courage of a loyal ally; prudent hesitation, specious cowardice; moderation was held to be a cloak for unmanliness; ability to see all sides of a question inaptness to act on any. Frantic violence became the attribute of manliness; cautious plotting, a justifiable means of self-defence. The advocate of extreme measures was always trustworthy; his opponent a man to be suspected. To succeed in a plot was to have a shrewd head, to divine a plot a still shrewder; but to try to provide against having to do either was to break up your party and to be afraid of your adversaries. In fine, to forestall an intending criminal, or to suggest the idea of a crime where it was wanting, was equally commended, until even blood became a weaker tie than party, from the superior readiness of those united by the latter to dare everything without reserve; for such associations had not in view the blessings derivable from established institutions but were formed by ambition for their overthrow; and the confidence of their members in each other rested less on any religious sanction than upon complicity in crime. The fair proposals of an adversary were met with jealous precautions by the stronger of the two, and not with a generous confidence. Revenge also was held of more account than self-preservation.

Oaths of reconciliation, being only proffered on either side to meet an immediate difficulty, only held good so long as no other weapon was at hand; but when opportunity offered, he who first ventured to seize it and to take his enemy off his guard, thought this perfidious vengeance sweeter than an open one, since, considerations of safety apart, success by treachery won him the palm of superior intelligence. Indeed it is generally the case that men are readier to call rogues clever than simpletons honest, and are as ashamed of being the second as they are proud of being the first. The cause of all these evils was the lust for power arising from greed and ambition; and from these passions proceeded the violence of parties once engaged in contention. The leaders in the cities, each provided with the fairest professions, on the one side with the cry of political equality of the people, on the other of a moderate aristocracy, sought prizes for themselves in those public interests which they pretended to cherish, and, recoiling from no means in their struggles for ascendancy, engaged in the direct excesses; in their acts of vengeance they went to even greater lengths, not stopping at what justice or the good of the state demanded, but making the party caprice of the moment their only standard, and invoking with equal readiness the condemnation of an unjust verdict or the authority of the strong arm to glut the animosities of the hour. Thus religion was in honour with neither party; but the use of fair phrases to arrive at guilty ends was in high reputation. Meanwhile the moderate part of the citizens perished between the two, either for not joining in the quarrel, or because envy would not suffer them to escape.

Revolutionary Leninism received its final blow for me when I read Dostoevsky's *The Possessed*, in which the plot revolves round the murder of a young 'reformist' called Shatov by a group of revolutionaries, as a means of binding them together by complicity in a crime. The organizer of the crime, Pyotr Verhovensky, is modelled on the real Russian terrorist, Nechaev. Nechaev was the leader of a small revolutionary sect called *Narodnaya Volna* – the People's Will. It is significant that Lenin's beloved elder brother, Alexandr Ulyanov, was hanged as a student when Lenin was seventeen, for conspiring with Nechaev to assassinate the Tsar. Lenin modelled the Bolshevik Party structure very much on that of *Narodnaya Volna*. Much of what Dostoevsky put into Verhovensky's mouth was all too reminiscent of what I sometimes heard in our Communist Party cells:

'Shigalov suggests a system of spying. Every member of the society spies on the others, and it's his duty to inform against them. Everyone belongs to all and all to everyone. All are slaves and equal in their slavery. In extreme cases he advocates slander and murder, but the great thing about it is equality. To begin with, the level of education, science, and talents is lowered. A high level of education and science is only possible for great intellects, and they are not wanted. The great intellects have always seized the power and been despots. Great intellects cannot help being despots and they've always done more harm than good. They will be banished or put to death. Cicero will have his tongue cut out, Copernicus will have his eyes put out, Shakespeare will be stoned – that's Shigalovism. Slaves are bound to be equal. There has never been either freedom or equality without despotism, but in the herd there is bound to be equality, and that's Shigalovism! Ha ha ha! Do you think it strange? I am for Shigalovism.'

To level the mountains is a fine idea, not an absurd one. I am for Shigalov. Down with culture. We've had enough science! Without science we have material enough to go on for a thousand years, but one must have discipline. The one thing wanting in the world is discipline. The thirst for culture is an aristocratic thirst. The moment you have family ties or love you get the desire for property. We will destroy that desire; we'll make use of drunkenness, slander, spying; we'll make use of incredible corruption; we'll stifle every genius in its infancy. We'll reduce all to a common denominator! Complete equality! 'We've learned a trade, and we are honest men; we need nothing more.' that was an answer given by English working-men recently. Only the necessary is necessary, that's the motto of the whole world henceforward. But it needs a shock. That's for us, the directors, to look after. Slaves must have directors. Absolute submission, absolute loss of individuality, but once in thirty years Shigalov would let them have a shock and they would all suddenly begin eating one another up, to a certain point, simply as a precaution against boredom. Boredom is an aristocratic sensation. The Shigalovians will have no desires. Desire and suffering are our lot, but Shigalovism is for the slaves.

'Listen. First of all we'll make an upheaval,' Verhovensky went on in desperate haste, continually clutching at Stavrogin's left sleeve. 'I've already told you. We shall penetrate to the peasantry. Do you know that we are tremendously powerful already? Our party does not consist only of those who commit murder and arson, fire off pistols in the traditional fashion, or bite colonels. They are only a hindrance. I don't accept anything without discipline. I am a scoundrel, of course, and not a socialist. Ha ha! Listen.

I've reckoned them all up: a teacher who laughs with children at their God and at their cradle is on our side. The lawyer who defends an educated murderer because he is more cultured than his victims and could not help murdering them to get money is one of us. The schoolboys who murder a peasant for the sake of sensation are ours. The juries who acquit every criminal are ours. The prosecutor who trembles at a trial for fear he should not seem advanced enough is ours, ours. Among officials and literary men we have lots, lots, and they don't know it themselves. On the other hand, the docility of schoolboys and fools has reached an extreme pitch; the schoolmasters are bitter and bilious. On all sides we see vanity puffed up out of all proportion; brutal, monstrous appetites. . . . Do you know how many we shall catch by little, ready-made ideas? When I left Russia, Littré's dictum that crime is insanity was all the rage; I come back and I find that crime is no longer insanity, but simply common sense, almost a duty; anyway, a gallant protest. "How can we expect a cultured man not to commit a murder, if he is in need of money?" But these are only the firstfruits. The Russian God has already been vanquished by cheap vodka. The peasants are drunk, the mothers are drunk, the children are drunk, the churches are empty, and in the peasant courts one hears: "Two hundred lashes or stand us a bucket of vodka." Oh, this generation has only to grow up. It's only a pity we can't afford to wait or we might have let them get a bit more tipsy!

The conclusion I drew from my political life at Oxford is well expressed in a poem by Robert Frost which I read many years later:

> I advocate a semi-revolution.
> The trouble with a total revolution
> (Ask any reputable Rosicrucian)
> Is that it brings the same class up on top.
> Executives of skilful execution
> Will therefore plan to go half-way and stop.
> Yes, revolutions are the only salves,
> But they're one thing that should be done by halves.

3

THE WAR

No drums they wished, whose thoughts were tied
To girls and jobs and mother,
Who rose and drilled and killed and died
Because they saw no other,

Who died without the hero's throb,
And if they trembled, hid it,
Who did not fancy much their job
But thought it best, and did it
　　　　– '*Epitaph on a New Army*', Michael Thwaites

For me, as for millions of other young men and women, my years in the army at war were a course of further education; I left the groves of Academe for the university of life. And, as at Oxford, I got my wartime education primarily from my own experiences and from those who shared them with me in the services.

I also continued to read omnivorously whenever I had time to spare, which was more often than you might imagine. In England I would scour the second-hand bookshops wherever I was stationed – a habit which I maintain to this day. In North Africa I was confined to the few books I was able to take with me – mainly verse; I spent many happy hours trying in vain to translate Greek lyrics into something which could masquerade as English poetry.

Once I reached Italy, however, my reading exploded. In Bari I bought philosophy at the publishers Laterza e Figli, who specialized in philosophy and were Benedetto Croce's publishing house. So besides reading Croce, who did not greatly appeal to me except for a brilliant essay on translation, I read in Italian a good deal of Nietzsche and the German existentialists Jaspers and Heidegger, as well of some of my beloved Shestov which was new to me.

Once north of Rome I was able to find second-hand British books. In a little bookshop near the Arno in Florence I made a wonderful haul of first editions of Yeats, Lawrence, and Virginia Woolf from the library of a lady called Leolyn Louise Everett – God bless her, whoever she was! It was the last thing I could ever have expected when I first joined up.

During my short period of pacifism at school I imagined that if war came I would adopt the attitude of Claude in Arthur Hugh Clough's 'Amours de Voyage':

> *Dulce* it is, and *decorum*, no doubt, for the country to fall, – to
> Offer one's blood an oblation to Freedom, and die for the Cause; yet
> Still, individual culture is also something, and no man
> Finds quite distinct the assurance that he of all others is called on,
> Or would be justified, even, in taking away from the world that
> Precious creature, himself. Nature sent him here to abide here
> Else why send him at all? Nature wants him still, it is likely.
> On the whole, we are meant to look after ourselves; it is certain
> Each has to eat for himself, digest for himself, and in general
> Care for his own dear life, and see to his own preservation;
> Nature's intentions, in most things uncertain, in this are decisive;

A handful of the pre-war intellectuals took this line. Auden and Isherwood, for example, went to the United States. My Oxford friends and I, however, volunteered to a man the day that war was declared. The horrors of the concentration camps had persuaded us that Belloc's realism was inescapable:

> Pale Ebenezer thought it wrong to fight,
> But roaring Bill, who killed him, thought it right.

So we found ourselves in khaki uniforms and stiff leather boots, spending our days drilling on parade-grounds, and sleeping at night in Nissen huts. Henry Reed caught our mood perfectly in his three poems, 'Lessons of the War'. I quoted the best, 'The Naming of Parts', in my memoirs. 'Judging Distances' is almost as good:

Not only how far away, but the way that you say it
Is very important. Perhaps you may never get
The knack of judging a distance, but at least you know
How to report on a landscape: the central sector,
The right of arc and that, which we had last Tuesday,
And at least you know

That maps are of time, not place, so far as the army
Happens to be concerned – the reason being,
Is one which need not delay us. Again, you know
There are three kinds of tree, three only, the fir and the poplar,
And those which have bushy tops to; and lastly
That things only seem to be things.

A barn is not called a barn, to put it more plainly,
Or a field in the distance, where sheep may be safely grazing.
You must never be over-sure. You must say, when reporting:
At five o'clock in the central sector is a dozen
Of what appear to be animals; whatever you do,
Don't call the bleeders *sheep*.

I am sure that's quite clear; and suppose, for the sake of example,
The one at the end, asleep, endeavours to tell us
What he sees over there to the west, and how far away,
After first having come to attention. There to the west,
On the fields of summer the sun and the shadows bestow
Vestments of purple and gold.

The still white dwellings are like a mirage in the heat,
And under the swaying elms a man and a woman
Lie gently together. Which is, perhaps, only to say
That there is a row of houses to the left of arc,
And that under some poplars a pair of what appear to be humans
Appear to be loving.

Well that, for an answer, is what we might rightly call
Moderately satisfactory only, the reason being,
Is that two things have been omitted, and those are important.
The human beings, now: in what direction are they,
And how far away, would you say? And do not forget
There may be dead ground in between.

There may be dead ground in between; and I may not have got
The knack of judging a distance; I will only venture
A guess that perhaps between me and the apparent lovers,
(Who, incidentally, appear by now to have finished,)
At seven o'clock from the houses, is roughly a distance
Of about one year and a half.

Soon we were being taught the elements of soldiering, best sum-
marized in phrases like: 'If it moves, salute it. If it doesn't move,
paint it,' and 'Sweat saves blood. Brains save sweat and blood.'

After my basic training I spent many months at railway stations in
bleak industrial towns. The atmosphere of desolation was well
captured by this typewritten poem on 'Sheffield in the Blitz' by an
anonymous soldier:

> This bloody town's a bloody cuss
> No bloody trains no bloody bus
> And no one cares for bloody us
> Oh bloody bloody woe.
> The bloody roads are bloody bad
> The bloody folks are bloody mad
> They even say what bloody cads
> Oh bloody bloody woe.
> And every thing's so bloody dear
> A bob for just a bloody beer
> And is it good? No bloody fear
> Oh bloody bloody woe.
> All bloody cloud all bloody rain
> No bloody kerbs no bloody drains
> The council's got no bloody brains
> Oh bloody bloody woe.
> The bloody films are bloody old
> All the bloody seats are sold
> You can't get in for bloody gold
> Oh bloody bloody woe.
> The bloody dances make you smile
> The bloody band is bloody vile
> It only cramps your bloody style
> Oh bloody bloody woe.
> No bloody sport no bloody games
> No bloody fun with bloody dames
> Wont even give their bloody names
> Oh bloody bloody woe.
> Best bloody place is bloody bed
> With bloody ice upon your head
> And then you think you're bloody dead
> Oh bloody bloody woe.

Many writers have tried to capture the atmosphere of wartime
Britain. I find the war novels of Evelyn Waugh and Anthony

Powell, despite their other qualities, too circumscribed by the attitudes of their particular class to speak for people like myself. The period of the phoney war, in particular, with its uncertainty, dread, and disintegration of social structure, is better caught for me by Dan Billany in *The Trap*, and by Joan Wyndham's adolescent diaries of a Chelsea girl, *Love Lessons* and *Love is Blue*.

I think it was a relief for us all when we were finally sent off to where the fighting was actually taking place. Even then, most of us spent far more time waiting than fighting. 'Why are we waiting, always bloody well waiting? Why are we waiting, oh why, oh why?' I suspect that song was sung more often than all the other soldiers' songs put together.

In Italy, one of our favourite songs was a response to Lady Astor's description of us as 'D-Day Dodgers', sung to the tune of the German soldiers' favourite, 'Lili Marlene'. I reprint it here because so many people wrote to ask me for the text after I broke down singing the last verse on television:

> We are the D-Day Dodgers out in ITALY
> Always on the vino – always on the spree
> Eighth Army skivers and the Yanks
> We live in Rome and stuff the twanks
> For we're the D-Day Dodgers – Out in ITALY
>
> We landed at SALERNO, a holiday with pay
> Tedesoi brought a band out to cheer us on our way
> Showed us the sights and gave us tea
> We all sang songs, the beer was free
> For we're the D-Day Dodgers – Out in ITALY
>
> NAPLES and CASSINO were taken in our stride
> We didn't get to fight there, we just went for the ride
> ANZIO and SANGRO were a farce, we did fuck all, sat on our arse
> For we are the D-Day Dodgers – Out in Italy.
>
> On the way to Florence we had a lovely time
> We ran a bus to Rimini right through the Gothic Line;
> Soon to Bologna we will go, when Jerry's fucked off beyond the Po
> For we're the D-Day Dodgers – Out in Italy.
>
> Once we had a bright light that we were going home
> Back to dear old Blighty, never more to roam;
> Then someone whispered 'In France you'll fight'
> We said 'Fuck that, we'll just sit tight'
> For we're the D-Day Dodgers – Out in Italy.

We hope the boys in France will soon be getting leave
After six months' service it's a shame they're not relieved;
But we can still carry on out here
For another two or three more years
For we're the D–Day Dodgers – Out in Italy.

Old Lady Astor please listen dear to this
Don't stand upon the platform and talk a lot of piss;
You're the nation's sweetheart, the nation's pride
But your bloody big mouth is far too wide,
That's from the D–Day Dodgers – Out in Italy.

If you look around the mountains in the mud and rain
You'll find the scattered crosses, some which bear no name.
Heartbreak and toil and suffering gone
The lads beneath them slumber on
For they were the D–Day Dodgers – Who'll stay in Italy.

For a young man who was single, however, the Italian campaign had many compensations – an infinite variety of lovely landscapes, a people of warm humanity, and a language both attractive to speak and easy to learn. I still cherish an English-Italian phrase-book published by G. Alfano which I picked up in Naples; I quote the English translation of a conversation at the barber's:

– Be quick and put on my wrapper and a white napkin, and strap [*sic*] your razors when you have lathered me.

– Ah! you have put the brush into my mouth.

– It was because you spoke when I did not expect it. The young bride's hair was black, thick, coarse, her forehead broad and square. An ordinary hairdresser would not have been able to hide the sternness of her features; but I have given her head a gentle and languishing expression.

– Truly, I am struck with admiration. But, mister artist, with all your talent you have cut me; I am bleeding. You have been shaving against the grain.

– No, sir; I have only taken off a little pimple. With a bit of courtplaster, it will not be seen.

– Doesn't my hair need to be freshened up a little?

– I will cut a little off behind; but I would not touch the tuft on the forehead nor about the ears.

– Why not?

– Because, sir, you would then appear to have too low a forehead and ears too long. Do you wish me to give you a touch of the curling irons, sir?

– It is unnecessary; my hair curls naturally.
– Shall I put on a little oil or pomatum?
– Put on a little scented oil.
– Please look in the glass.
– It will do very well. I see you are an artist worthy to shave and trim your contemporaries.

There have been some good books about the last war in Italy – notably Raleigh Trevelyan's *Rome 1944*. For me, however, nothing brings it back so vividly as the opening paragraphs of Ernest Hemingway's *Farewell to Arms*, which is about Italy during the First World War:

In the late summer of that year we lived in a house in a village that looked across the river and the plain to the mountains. In the bed of the river there were pebbles and boulders, dry and white in the sun, and the water was clear and swiftly moving and blue in the channels. Troops went by the house and down the road and the dust they raised powdered the leaves of the trees. The trunks of the trees too were dusty and the leaves fell early that year and we saw the troops marching along the road and the dust rising and leaves, stirred by the breeze, falling and the soldiers marching and afterward the road bare and white except for the leaves.

The plain was rich with crops; there were many orchards of fruit trees and beyond the plain the mountains were brown and bare. There was fighting in the mountains and at night we could see the flashes from the artillery. In the dark it was like summer lightning, but the nights were cool and there was not the feeling of a storm coming.

Sometimes in the dark we heard the troops marching under the window and guns going past pulled by motor-tractors. There was much traffic at night and many mules on the roads with boxes of ammunition on each side of their pack-saddles and gray motor trucks that carried men, and other trucks with loads covered with canvas that moved slower in the traffic. There were big guns too that passed in the day drawn by tractors, the long barrels of the guns covered with green branches and green leafy branches and vines laid over the tractors. To the north we could look across a valley and see a forest of chestnut trees and behind it another mountain on this side of the river. There was fighting for that mountain too, but it was not successful, and in the fall when the rains came the leaves all fell from the chestnut trees and the branches were bare and the trunks black with rain. The vineyards were thin and bare-branched too and all the country was wet and brown and dead with autumn. There were mists over the river and clouds on the mountain and the trucks splashed mud on the road and the troops were muddy and wet in their capes; their rifles were wet and under their capes the two leather cartridge boxes on the front of the belts, gray leather boxes heavy with packs of clips of thin, long 6.5 mm. cartridges, bulged forward under the capes so that the men, passing on the road, marched as though they were six months gone with child.

If I want to live again through the feelings I had as a soldier in the war, I turn to poems written at the time by other men and women who shared my experience.

The last two world wars were unique in our history, not least for the cultural shock they inflicted on the whole of our society. Each of them took millions of young men and women away from their families and friends at the most sensitive stage in their lives. It put them into uniform to serve under strict discipline with total strangers in closed communities. It sent them abroad to kill other young men and women hundreds or thousands of miles away – in cities, fields, and mountains, in deserts and jungles.

Finally, it subjected them to long periods of paralysing boredom, punctuated by short bursts of extreme excitement in which the prospect of death was always present.

For most of these men and women the war was the most intense experience they were ever to know. Thousands, who found the pressure almost too much to bear, turned to writing poetry as the only way of releasing it – for the first and often the last time in their lives. So both wars produced a cataract of poetry.

However, the poetry of the Second World War was very different from that of the First. Most of the poets we know of in the First World War were writing in the hope of publication. They were nearly all men – and men with university degrees, largely from public schools: Isaac Rosenberg was one of the few exceptions. The patriotic exaltation which led them to volunteer stumbled when they came face to face with the horrors of trench warfare. For the first time they began to ask how the war had come about. It was the old champion of the ordinary soldier, Rudyard Kipling, who gave them the answer: 'If any question why we died, Tell them, because our fathers lied.'

When my generation had to face the Second World War we

believed that we had no alternative but to fight the incontestable evil of Nazism; but we had no illusions about the fate which a-waited us. Wilfred Owen and Siegfried Sassoon had told us what to expect, though the nature of our ordeal turned out rather different.

Except for the Anzio beachhead, and the last winter on the Gothic Line in Italy, there was little trench warfare. Millions served in the Middle and Far East and north west Europe. The air force was far larger. There were many more women in uniform. And the home front was subjected to widespread air raids.

So poetry of the Second World War was far more diverse than that of the first. More important, most of its poets came from ordinary homes. Most wrote their poems with no thought of publication. Some of the best were from the Dominions, such as the South African Uys Krige, J.E. Brookes of the Australian infantry, and the New Zealander Les Cleveland. A few of the Scots preferred to write in Gaelic, making them even less acceptable to a literary establishment based in London.

For all these reasons the poetry of the Second World War made less impact on the peacetime public than that of the First. It offered no equivalent to the intense concentration on the horrors of trench warfare. It had no clear message, of hope or despair. As Dennis McHarrie wrote:

> 'He died who loved to live,' they'll say.
> 'Unselfishly so we might have today!'
> Like hell! He fought because he had to fight;
> He died that's all. It was his unlucky night.'

Some of the poets, such as Henry Reed, Sidney Keyes, Keith Douglas and Gavin Ewart became well-known at the time: others were published later. But the great majority would have remained unknown for ever but for the work of three young men serving in Cairo in 1942 – the most senior then a corporal. Victor Selwyn, David Burk, and the South African poet, Denis Saunders, appealed to all serving men and women in the Middle East to submit poems for inclusion in an anthology. Within three months they had collected 3,000 poems, selected 121, and persuaded another group of enthusiasts in the Salamander Society to get them printed.

In 1985 Everyman's (Dent) library published an Oasis selection, *Poems of the Second World War*. By then Victor Selwyn and his fellow-editors, Erik de Mauny and the late Professor Ian Fletcher, had collected over 14,000 poems written on active service, from every phase and theatre of the war.

Some of the best poems are by ordinary men and women who were moved to write only by the intensity of their feelings in the war. Anyone who served in the forces at that time will find poems which speak directly to them. As a beachmaster at Anzio I was particularly moved by Sean Jennett's trance-like apparition from an assault landing, Mahoney:

> Then Mahoney, standing in the surf,
> the convoy hanging in the misty sea
> and landing forces moving up the beach
> dropped down his arms, and said
> I wait, O God, I wait,
> and these were his last words of common speech.
>
> Christ in the shallows of the water walked
> or in the sweaty hollow of his palm
> appeared and spoke to his reluctant bone
> or moved about the chambers of his skull,
> the scourger of the temple, with a whip;
> and in his heart also the lash had been.
>
> So Mahoney stood and let his rifle fall
> into the sea, where lug-worms claimed it, and
> the servant tide; and heard his captain shout
> but did not move; and felt the weight of wheels
> and tracks across the cortex of his brain;
> but did not certainly hear the single shot.
>
> Wife, children, parents, weep for him, who now
> dead with the grey crabs and the starfish rests
> where surges heap on him the slow and secret sand.
> Yet even in the valleys of the sea
> the dead can feel the libel, and Mahoney
> in his stripped skull is tortured by a lie.

For those who think war is worthwhile because it makes a man of you, Frederick Horn sounded a sombre warning in 'Conscript':

> 'Of course, it's done him worlds of good', they said,
> 'He's twice the man he was — a puny chap
> he used to be, if you remember — always at books and that,
> but since he joined
> he's broadened out. They've made a man of him;
> You wouldn't know him now'.

Deep-sunk in rain-soaked ditch, with weeds and filth
stopping his mouth, the soldier lies;
swollen and black, his face turns to the skies
in blank, unquestioning stare, his body, tight
and big as flood-drowned pig, lurches and sways,
to wind and water. Yes, he's broadened out –
he's twice the man he was; a pity, though,
his life should run, like bright oil down a gutter,
to implement some politician's brag.

His world went out
through that neat hole in temple, quickly and easily
as words from windy mouths. And loves unknown,
and skies unseen, and books unread,
forever lost, he's dead.

You wouldn't know him now.

Most moving of all are some of the poems by young women, who describe not only the heartbreak of losing their loved ones but also the initial panic they felt at being thrown into barracks with other girls from totally different backgrounds.

Joy Corfield writes of her first night in barracks:

Don't cry, young woman,
In your badly made bed;
Pull the grey blanket
Over your head.

Your mother cries, too,
On your first night from home,
Fearing your safety
Now you're on your own.

Take comfort, young woman.
If only you knew
Most of the others
Are crying, too.

Olivia Fitzroy wrote about a pilot in the Fleet Air Arm:

'Good show!' he said, leaned his head back and laughed.
'They're wizard types!' he said, and held his beer
Steadily, looked at it and gulped it down
Out of its jamjar, took a cigarette

And blew a neat smoke-ring into the air.
'After this morning's prang I've got the twitch;
'I thought I'd had it in that teased-out kite.'
His eyes were blue and older than his face,
His single stripe had known a lonely war,
But all his talk and movements showed his age,
His jargon was of aircraft and of beer.
'And what will you do afterwards?' I said.
Then saw his puzzled face and caught my breath.
There was no afterwards for him but death.

Lisbeth David brings back the mixed feeling which many girls from sheltered backgrounds must have felt when the war ended, in 'Solemn Occasion':

Gay blows the flamboyant, green flutter the palms,
The winds of Colombo stretch longing their arms,
But hey nonny nonny the lark and the wren
I trow we shall never be meeting agin.

Now Gavin can cling to his bottle and glass
(Assisted by Dai) as the centuries pass,
And Layton will join them (regardless of cost)
Lamenting the love that they think they have lost,
And hey nonny nonny the lark and the wren
I trow we shall never be meeting again.

Now Steuart and Ted and the Vicar and all
Can devote their attention to hearing the call
And plough through the Hymnal in pious collusion
Without a disturbing soprano intrusion,
And hey nonny nonny, hey nonny nonny!

Now Gwilym and Ifor and Hari and Glyn
May return to the days before wrens butted in,
And Alun may sit at his desk in the sun,
Immersed in the trains he is trying to run,
And hey nonny nonny the lark and the wren
I trow we shall never be meeting agin.

Now Bob can perform undisturbed by his neighbour
And Julian live with Debussy and Weber,
And Gervase may dream with the masters long dead
And nothing but music will enter his head;
And hey nonny nonny the lark and the wren
I trow we shall never be meeting again.

And whether I like it and whether I choose
Good friends I have made and good friends I must lose,
So hey nonny nonny the lark and the wren,
I know we shall never be meeting again.

Mary Benson, whom I knew as a FANY in Italy and next met
twenty years later when she was a friend of Nelson Mandela and
deeply engaged in the struggle against Apartheid, paints a moving
picture of her life in the army in her autobiography, *A Far Cry*.

There is less soldiers' poetry than one might expect about the
Italian civilians who suffered most from the war. Norman Morris
describes a Sicilian town in 1943:

What was your crime, you little mountain town?
Why is that mother picking through those stones?
The entrails of the church stare to the sky;
The Military Police say: 'Out of Bounds.'

'No halting on the Road': the people stare
Blank-eyed and vacant, hollow-eyed and numb.
You do not seem to hate us: we are they
Who blew your town to dust with shell and bomb.

'Water not drinkable': 'One Way Street';
The road machine runts rubble from the track.
Was this a house, home of two lovers' joys,
Reduced by chemists' blast to pristine rock?

The moody mountain frowns, aloof, detached.
What was your crime, you little mountain town?
Just that you lay upon the Armies' route;
Two tracks met here by whim in ancient time.

Much of the war poetry is not of great literary value, but all is
deeply felt. Benjamin Jowett once said: 'Nowhere probably is
there more true feeling, and nowhere worse taste, than in a
churchyard. Scarcely a word of true poetry anywhere.' That may
be true; but in the war sometimes true feeling ennobled the verse
of people who might never write another poem in the rest of their
lives. 'D-Day Dodgers' is one example. Another is a long
anonymous poem which someone typed out for me when I was at
our headquarters in Florence. It achieves its effect like a Victorian
painting by William Frith, or Thomas Hood's remarkable poem
'My Village', by the accumulation of detail:

PANORAMA OF ITALY

If I were an artist, with nothing to do,
I'd paint a picture, a composite view
Of historic Italy, in which I'd show
Visions of contrasts, the high and the low.

There'd be towering mountains, a deep blue sea;
Filthy brats yelling 'Caramella' at me;
High plumed horses and coloured carts;
Two toned tresses on hustling tarts.

I'd show Napoleonic cops, the carabinieri;
Dejected old women with too much to carry;
A dignified gentleman with a 'Balbo' beard;
Bare-breasted bambino, both ends smeared.

Castle and palace, opera house too;
Hotel on a mountain, glorious view;
Homes made of weeds, brickbats and mud;
Folk covered with scabs, scurvy and crud.

Fine old homes, pride of the nation,
Beautiful to see, but no sanitation;
Well equipped schools, without a scholar;
Temples of learning, surrounded by squalor.

Chapels and churches, great to behold,
Each a king's ransom, in glittering gold;
Poverty and want, men craving for food,
Picking thru garbage, practically nude.

A hilltop village, a walled-in land;
Grimy old hags with pain as a brand;
Beautiful image, most Blessed of Mothers;
Scalped monks and alms-eating brothers.

Stately cathedrals, with rich-toned bells;
Ricovero shelters, with horrible smells;
Mouldering catacombs, a place for the dead;
Noisy civilians, clamouring for bread.

Palatial villas, with palm trees tall;
A stinking hovel, mere hole in the wall;
Tree-fringed lawns, swept by the breeze,
Goats wading in filth up to their knees.

Revealing statues, all details complete;
A sensual lass, with sores on her feet;

Big-busted damsels, but never a Bra;
Bumping against you, there should be a law.

Sweeping boulevard, a spangled team;
Alleys that wind like a dope fiend's dream;
Flowers blooming on the side of a hill;
A sidewalk latrine, with privacy nil.

Girls with shoe soles, two inches thick;
Unwashed peddlers whose wares make you sick.
Grapes, lemons, post cards and nuts,
Dolce and vino, to torture your guts.

Two-by-four shops with shelving all bare;
Gesturing merchants, arms flailing the air;
Narrow gauge side-walks, more like a shelf;
Butt-puffing youngster, scratching himself.

Lumbering carts, hugging the road;
Nondescript trucks, frequently towed;
Diminutive donkeys, loaded for bear,
Horse drawn taxis, seeking a fare.

Determined pedestrians, courting disaster;
Walk in the streets, where movement is faster;
Italian drivers, all accident bound,
Weaving and twisting, to cover the ground.

Home-made brooms, weeds tied to a stick,
Used on the streets, to clean off the bricks;
Bicycles and pushcarts, blocking your path;
Street corner politicos, needing a bath.

A crowded train, with fares in the cab.
More on the cow-catcher, breeding a scab;
Miserable buses, which move with a grind,
Packed to the roof, more left behind.

Arrogant wretches, picking up snipes;
Miniature Fiats, various types;
Young Street singers; hand organ tune;
Shoe shine boys, a sidewalk saloon.

Garbage strewn gutters, reeking with stench,
Weather beaten beggar, a God-awful wench;
A boy on the corner, yelling 'Gior-nal-e';
A half dressed urchin, fly covered belly.

Barbers galore, with manners quite mild,
Prolific women, all heavy with child;

Duce's secret weapon, kids by the score,
Caused by his bonus, which isn't any more.

No birth control in this fair land,
One child in arms, two by the hand;
Page Margaret Sanger, just turn her loose,
Her gospel is needed here, put it to use.

A beauteous maiden, a smile on her face,
With breath of garlic, fouling the place.
Listless housewife, no shoes on her feet,
Washing and cooking, right out in the street.

The family wash, of tattle tale gray,
Hung from a balcony, blocking the way;
Native coffee, God what a mixture;
Tile bathrooms, with one extra fixture.

Families dining, from one common bowl,
Next to a fish store, a terrible hole;
Italian zoot-suiters, flashily dressed,
Bare-footed beggars, looking oppressed.

Mud-smeared children, clustered about,
Filling their jugs at a community spout;
Dutiful mother, with look of despair,
Picking lice from a small daughter's hair.

Capable craftsmen, skilled in their art;
Decrepit old shacks, falling apart;
Intricate needlework, out on display,
Surrounded by filth, rot and decay.

Elegant caskets, carved out by hand;
Odorous factories, where leather is tanned;
A shoemaker's shop, a black market store;
Crawling with vermin, no screen on the door.

No sense of shame has the soliciting boy;
Unfortunate children, with nary a toy;
Pathetic monstrosity, with hunch-back dwarf;
Oil strewn shore, craft rotting at wharf.

I've tried to describe the things I have seen,
A panorama of Italy, the brown and the green;
I've neglected the war scars, visible yet,
But these are things we want to forget.

I'm glad I come, but damn anxious to go;
Give it back to the natives, I'm ready to blow.

Any war is an atrocity, as every soldier knows, however much
civilians may glorify it. A situation in which human beings are
compelled to kill and maim one another, and in which most of the
victims are innocent women and children, is an abomination.
Thomas Hardy, like Leo Tolstoy, was fascinated by war as a
phenomenon of human history, though unlike Tolstoy he never
fought as a soldier himself. After writing his last novel, *Jude the
Obscure*, he spent five years on an enormous drama called *The
Dynasts*, which presented the Napoleonic wars as the product of an
amoral Fate which he called the Immanent Will. However, when
the First World War broke out a little later he put it more
persuasively in the perspective of eternity in a short poem he called
'In time of the Breaking of Nations':

> Only a man harrowing clods
>   In a slow silent walk
> With an old horse that stumbles and nods
>   Half asleep as they stalk.
>
> Only thin smoke without flame
>   From the heaps of couch-grass;
> Yet this will go onward the same
>   Though Dynasties pass.
>
> Yonder a maid and her wight
>   Come whispering by:
> War's annals will cloud into night
>   Ere their story die.

I could not find sufficient comfort is such reflections. I believed,
and still believe, that we were right to fight the last war, so as to
stop Hitler dominating Europe. However, I tended also to share
Benjamin Franklin's view: 'There never was a good war, nor a bad
peace.' This did not prevent Franklin from supporting the
American War of Independence, which he had tried so hard to
prevent, any more than it stopped me volunteering in 1939. But I
remain convinced that wiser diplomacy could have prevented the
Second World War, as it could have prevented the First – and the
wars in Korea, the Falklands and the Gulf. So when I was
demobilized I decided not to write my great work on aesthetics as
a don at Oxford, but to go into politics – since there seemed no
other way of helping directly to prevent a Third World War.

My experience as a soldier had confirmed my conclusion as a

student — that there was no place for dogmatic systems of theory in politics any more than in war. Karl von Clausewitz had made the point: 'In war everything is uncertain — a continuous interaction of opposites. In war the will is directed at an animate object that reacts.'

The same point was made more recently by General Norman Schwarzkopf:

The analysts write about war as if it's a ballet. Yes, it's choreographed, and what happens is, the orchestra starts playing and some son of a bitch climbs out of the orchestra pit with a bayonet and starts chasing you around the stage. And the choreography goes right out the window.

I felt that, providing we remembered that peace is just as unpredictable, it might be possible to continue politics without adopting those 'other means' which made up Clausewitz's definition of war.

4

POLITICS

No man is an *Iland*, intire of it selfe; every man is a peece of the *Continent*, a part of the *maine*; if a *Clod* bee washed away by the *Sea*, *Europe* is the lesse, as well as if a *Promontorie* were, as well as if a *Mannor* of thy *friends* or of *thine owne* were; any mans *death* diminishes *me*, because I am involved in *Mankinde*; And therefore never send to know for whom the *bell* tolls; It tolls for *thee*.

– *Devotions*, John Donne

I cannot praise a fugitive and cloister'd vertue, unexercis'd and unbreath'd, that never sallies out and sees her adversary, but slinks out of the race, where that immortal garland is to be run for, not without dust and heat.

Areopagitica, John Milton

I agreed with John Donne that no man is an island; therefore Mrs Thatcher was wrong when she said that there is no such thing as society. Indeed this is the fundamental lesson which I, like so many others, learned from my experience in the army.

I also believed that society can be made better or worse by political action. So I agreed with John Milton that I had a duty to take part in the political race. There was plenty of dust and heat; I soon discovered that Harry Truman was right: 'If you can't stand the heat, don't go into the kitchen.' On the other hand, in politics even if you win the race you would be unwise to expect an immortal garland, certainly not from the spectators.

Few writers have a good word to say about politicians; only a dead politician can become a statesman. Some novelists have written objectively about politics. Stendhal in *Lucien Leuwen* paints a fascinating picture of young politicians in Paris after the revolution of 1830, when he himself took office under Louis-Philippe as a consul, first in Trieste then in Civitavecchia. As a moderate republican he stood between the Legitimists and the Ultras; but he was by no means a parliamentary democrat. 'Nothing in the world', he wrote, 'would make the author wish to live in a democracy like that of America, for the simple reason that he would rather pay court to the Minister of the Interior than to the grocer at the bottom of the road.'

Flaubert produced, in my opinion, the greatest novel about politics and society. He wrote *The Sentimental Education* twenty years after the events it describes; it is in part a sympathetic account of Flaubert's own youth in the 1840s, when his generation of romantic intellectuals was in revolt against the philistine mediocrity into which Louis-Philippe's regime had degenerated. He describes the society of the time, in which industrialization and high finance were changing both the face and the soul of France, with extraordinary insight. Parliamentary democracy had real meaning for the first time for Frenchmen after the revolution of 1848, which produced the Second Republic; but the Republic collapsed within three years because the young intellectuals who ran it had no idea of administration. Many of its incidents startle with their contemporary relevance. Flaubert's description of a selection conference in the provinces to choose a candidate would serve quite well today, and he even includes an obvious member of the Militant Tendency in the character of the sinister extremist Sénéchal.

The leading British political novelist is Anthony Trollope, whose 'Palliser' stories present political life in the nineteenth century as a struggle for place and preferment rather than for programmes and principles. To those who see politics as little more than a disagreeable jungle war, I always quote Trollope, to show there is little difference in this respect between any of the professions. Trollope's politicians differ little from his clerics in *The Barchester Chronicles* – or from the academics in C.P. Snow's *The Masters*.

In modern times America has produced some good political novels, notably *All the King's Men* which Robert Penn Warren based on the career of the Louisiana demagogue Huey Long. In my view the best contemporary writer about American politics is George V.

Higgins, who learned his trade in stories about the Boston underworld, such as *The Friends of Eddie Coyle*, before adapting his use of demotic dialogue to the politics of Washington and Vermont in, for example, *A Year or Two with Edgar* and *Victories*. The last impressive British political novel was *The New Machiavelli*, written by H.G. Wells before the First World War. In Germany, however, Günter Grass has written a superb novel around Willy Brandt's election campaign in 1970, in which he himself played an active role – *The Diary of a Snail*.

I enjoy reading good novels about politics; they throw a useful light on some aspects of my own career. However, since very few are written by full-time politicians, the one dimension which is usually missing is the genuine idealism which leads otherwise rational men to stick to a profession which is so poorly rewarded in money and respect. Disraeli's *Sybil* is the exception which proves the rule; its theme of 'the two nations' made it the bible of progressive Tories.

Most of the poets are even less kind than the novelists. Hilaire Belloc detested politicians as a breed:

> Here richly, with ridiculous display,
> The Politician's corpse was laid away.
> While all of his acquaintances sneered and slanged
> I wept, for I had longed to see him hanged.

And:

> The Politician, dead, and turned to clay,
> Will make a clout to keep the wind away.
> I am not fond of draughts, and yet I doubt
> If I could get myself to touch that clout.

The Second World War made me decide to enter politics, because I was determined to do my best to prevent a Third; whatever may be thought about the ability of politicians to make a lasting impact on a nation's economy, only governments decide whether there is peace or war, and it is difficult to influence a government's foreign policy except through politics.

The First World War led Kipling at first to the opposite conclusion because he blamed the politicians for allowing it to happen. After his son was killed in Flanders, he wrote this epitaph on 'A Dead Statesman':

I could not dig: I dared not rob:
Therefore I lied to please the mob.
Now all my lies are proved untrue
And I must face the men I slew.
What tale shall serve me here among
Mine angry and defrauded young?

I had read a good deal of Kipling as a boy, and enjoyed particularly *Kim* and *The Jungle Books*. However, I did not much like the poetry which he interspersed with the prose, and positively disliked the sort of verse which my father liked best, such as 'Gunga Din' and 'Recessional'; it seemed to me far too jingoistic, too macho in its rhetoric. It was only after the war that I read Kipling's poetry carefully and discovered that its values were much closer to mine than I imagined. He was usually on the side of the ordinary man, like the private soldier or the engineer, respected races other than his own, and above all showed a penetrating intelligence on every subject he chose to discuss.

His personality was carefully disguised in his writing. A sensitive, short-sighted boy with an unhappy childhood, bullied mercilessly at school, he liked to present himself as a man among men. Like most of his generation, he believed strongly in the civilizing mission of the Empire as 'the white man's burden', but had more respect for the Indian or the 'fuzzy wuzzy' than for the American or Frenchman. So while accepting the ideology of the Empire, he rejected the ethos of his minor public school, joining a group of insubordinate boys led by his hero Dunsterville, later a general on the North-West frontier of India, whom he immortalized as Stalky in *Stalky & Co*.

In one of Kipling's most savage stories, Stalky describes a visiting MP as a 'jelly-bellied flag-flapper'. Later, as a young journalist in India, he wrote a poem about a visiting MP which I have remembered more than once when I was on a Parliamentary delegation abroad:

Pagett, MP was a liar, and a fluent liar therewith, –
He spoke of the heat of India as 'The Asian Solar Myth';
Came on a four months' visit to 'study the East in November',
And I got him to make an agreement vowing to stay till
    September.

July was a trifle unhealthy, – Pagett was ill with fear,
Called it the 'Cholera Morbus', hinted that life was dear.

He babbled of 'Eastern exile', and mentioned his home with tears;
But I hadn't seen *my* children for close upon seven years.

We reached a hundred and twenty once in the Court at noon,
(I've mentioned that Pagett was portly) Pagett went off in a
    swoon.
That was an end to the business. Pagett, the perjured, fled
With a practical working knowledge of 'Solar Myths' in his head.

And I laughed as I drove from the station, but the mirth died out
    on my lips
As I thought of the fools like Pagett who write of their 'Eastern
    trips',
And the sneers of the travelled idiots who duly misgovern the
    land,
And I prayed to the Lord to deliver another one into my hand.

In his introduction to that poem Kipling makes the point less fiercely:

> The toad beneath the harrow knows
> Exactly where each tooth-point goes;
> The butterfly upon the road
> Preaches contentment to that toad.

After covering the Boer War, and developing an even greater admiration for the ordinary soldiers he encountered in South Africa, Kipling attacked with equal vigour both the right-wing Tories in the British Government and their Liberal opponents. He spoke for the common man with an eloquence rarely equalled in Britain, yet remained to the end an unrepentant Imperialist.

Kipling taught me never to judge writers on politics by their popular reputation, and never to pigeon-hole them as Left or Right according to their role in the politics of their time.

DEMOCRACY IN BRITAIN

Britain, unlike its neighbours across the Channel and across the Atlantic, has not had to endure the tragedy of civil war or enemy occupation for more than three hundred years. Its democracy has evolved gradually since the execution of Charles I, without the convulsions which have disrupted politics in Continental Europe and America, although it has been profoundly influenced by events in both continents. Since my main political interest has always been in international affairs, I have tried to learn something not only from Britain's own political history, but also from that of the other Western powers. Nothing has helped me more to understand the politics of the past than the poetry and literature of the time.

In the century which followed the Civil War, British politics seemed concerned with personalities rather than programmes. Eighteenth-century verse is particularly rich in political satire; but in the earlier decades it concentrates on the character and appearance of politicians rather than on their views about the issues of the day.

Perhaps the most wounding of all attacks on a politician is Alexander Pope's on Lord Hervey, whom he calls Sporus:

> Let Sporus tremble – 'What? that thing of silk,
> Sporus, that mere white curd of ass's milk?
> Satire or sense alas! can Sporus feel?
> Who breaks a butterfly upon a wheel?'
> Yet let me flap this bug with gilded wings,
> This painted child of dirt that stinks and stings;
> Whose buzz the witty and the fair annoys,
> Yet wit ne'er tastes, and beauty ne'er enjoys,
> So well-bred spaniels civilly delight
> In mumbling of the game they dare not bite.
> Eternal smiles his emptiness betray,
> As shallow streams run dimpling all the way.
> Whether in florid impotence he speaks,
> And, as the prompter breathes, the puppet squeaks;
> Or at the ear of Eve, familiar toad,
> Half froth, half venom, spits himself abroad,
> In puns, or politics, or tales, or lies,
> Or spite, or smut, or rhymes, or blasphemies.
> His wit all see-saw between *that* and *this*,
> Now high, now low, now Master up, now Miss,
> And he himself one vile antithesis.
> Amphibious thing! that acting either part,
> The trifling head, or the corrupted heart!
> Fop at the toilet, flatt'rer at the board,
> Now trips a Lady, and now struts a Lord.

> Eve's tempter thus the rabbins have expressed,
> A cherub's face, a reptile all the rest;
> Beauty that shocks you, parts that none will trust,
> Wit that can creep, and pride that licks the dust.

Hervey was an MP before he was made a peer, but had no particular views on politics, and little influence outside the court of George II. His memoirs, however, published a century after his death, give a marvellous picture of eighteenth-century England, since they were written for those who prefer to see the Great 'dressing and undressing rather than when they are playing their part on the public stage'.

In the eighteenth century and much of the nineteenth the average man had little role in Britain's parliamentary democracy. Only a small proportion of the male population had the vote, depending on their property. Women had to wait until after the First World War. Anthony Henry, the MP for Southampton from 1727 to 1734, wrote the following letter to his constituents when they asked him to vote against the Budget:

> *Gentlemen,*
> I have received your letter about the excise and I am surprised at your insolence in writing to me at all.
>
> You know, as I know, that I bought this constituency. You know, and I know, that I am now determined to sell it, and you know, what you think I don't know, that you are looking out for another buyer, and I know, what you certainly don't know, that I have found another constituency to buy.
>
> About what you said about the excise: May God's curse light on you all, and may it make your homes as open and as free to the excise officers as your wives and daughters have always been to me while I have represented your rascally constituency . . .

What Pope called the People was simply the property-owning minority:

> Well, if a King's a lion, at the least
> The People are a many-headed beast:
> Can they direct what measures to pursue,
> Who know themselves so little what to do?
> Alike in nothing but one lust of gold,
> Just half the land would buy, and half be sold:
> Their country's wealth our mightier misers drain,

Or cross, to plunder provinces, the main:
The rest, some farm the poor-box, some the pews;
Some keep assemblies, and would keep the stews;
Some with fat bucks on childless dotards fawn;
Some win rich widows by their chine and brawn;
While with the silent growth of ten per cent,
In dirt and darkness hundreds stink content.

In his 'Essay on Man' Pope expresses what was then the general view of the governing class, that God had established a natural hierarchy:

Cease then, nor ORDER Imperfection name:
Our proper bliss depends on what we blame.
Know thy own point: This kind, this due degree
Of blindness, weakness, Heav'n bestows on thee.
Submit – In this, or any other sphere,
Secure to be as blest as thou canst bear:
Safe in the hand of one disposing Pow'r,
Or in the natal, or the mortal hour.
All Nature is but Art, unknown to thee;
All Chance, Direction, which thou canst not see;
All Discord, Harmony, not understood;
All partial Evil, universal Good:
And, spite of Pride, in erring Reason's spite,
One truth is clear, 'Whatever IS, is RIGHT.'

His conclusion was inevitable:

For forms of government let fools contest
What'er is best administered is best

In the latter half of the eighteenth century British politics was shaped above all by the struggle of the American colonies for self-government and by the French Revolution. Though Pitt and Fox are seen as the great antagonists in the ensuing arguments, a large part was played by Irishmen – the writers Swift and Goldsmith, and the politicians Burke and Sheridan, who deployed their arguments more passionately than anyone before or since. Burke, too often seen as a conservative, because he opposed the French Revolution, spent most of his political life fighting for justice towards the American colonies, towards his native Ireland, and towards India.

He opposed the French Revolution for the same reasons as Liberals and democratic Socialists opposed the Soviet Revolution more than a century later – because it had destroyed the possibility of democracy in France and would lead to an aggressive military dictatorship.

Oliver Goldsmith produced a brilliant assessment of Edmund Burke as the intellectual in politics:

> Here lies our good Edmund, whose genius was such,
> We scarcely can praise it or blame it too much;
> Who, born for the universe, narrowed his mind,
> And to party gave up what was meant for mankind;
> Though fraught with all learning, kept straining his throat
> To persuade Tommy Townshend to lend him a vote;
> Who, too deep for his hearers, still went on refining,
> And thought of convincing, while they thought of dining;
> Though equal to all things, for all things unfit;
> Too nice for a statesman, too proud for a wit;
> For a patriot, too cool; for a drudge, disobedient;
> And too fond of the *right* to pursue the *expedient*.
> In short, 'twas his fate, unemployed or in place, sir,
> To eat mutton cold and cut blocks with a razor.

Burke's failure to exert more influence on British politics was one of the tragedies of history. His was the most eloquent voice against the stupidity of the British Government and Parliament in driving the American colonies to declare independence. Like some other politicians, he was simply too clever for his colleagues. Hazlitt's words could serve as Burke's political epitaph:

> His stock of ideas did not consist of a few meagre facts, meagrely stated, of half a dozen commonplaces tortured in a thousand different ways; but his mine of wealth was a profound understanding, inexhaustible as the human heart and various as the sources of nature.

The French Revolution had a dizzying impact on the young intellectuals in Britain, starting with William Wordsworth, who spent some years in France at the time, and had an illegitimate daughter there:

> Bliss was it in that dawn to be alive,
> But to be young was very Heaven!

The Revolution had a more lasting impact, however, on those of the upper-class such as Shelley and Byron. Inspired by William Godwin, whose daughter Mary, the author of *Frankenstein*, he later married, Shelley rejected the views of his father, a Whig MP, and became a fierce radical, writing a savage attack on George IV and the Regency in *England in 1819*:

> An old, mad, blind, despised, and dying king, –
> Princes, the dregs of their dull race, who flow
> Through public scorn, – mud from a muddy spring, –
> Rulers who neither see, nor feel, nor know,
> But leech-like to their fainting country cling,
> Till they drop, blind in blood, without a blow, –
> A people starved and stabbed in the untilled field, –
> An army, which liberticide and prey
> Makes as a two-edged sword to all who wield, –
> Golden and sanguine laws which tempt and slay;
> Religion Christless, Godless – a book sealed;
> A Senate, – Time's worst statute unrepealed, –
> Are graves, from which a glorious Phantom may
> Burst, to illumine our tempestuous day.

ACROSS THE CHANNEL

The rest of Europe was far more profoundly affected by the French Revolution than Britain. Napoleon's *Grande Armée* swept away the existing rulers all over the Continent. Freedom seemed invincible. Napoleon was seen at first as the great liberator by even the most intelligent radicals, like Heinrich Heine. Beethoven dedicated his *Emperor* Concerto to him. But before long the Congress of Vienna re-established the old regime and it became all too clear that the most lasting legacy of the French Revolution, and of the philosophers of the Enlightenment who inspired it, was nationalism rather than democracy. As today in the former Soviet Empire, the generous-minded young intellectuals who plotted to overthrow existing regimes all over Europe in the middle years of the nineteenth century found themselves fighting for national independence as much as for representative government. Too often when they succeeded they proved unable to meet the basic economic needs of their peoples. The confusion and despair which followed produced the greatest political parable of all time, the fable of the Grand Inquisitor from Dostoevsky's masterpiece, *The Brothers Karamazov*.

The three brothers Karamazov represent broadly the body, the mind, and the soul – or perhaps what Freud would call the id, the ego, and the superego. Ivan, the tortured intellectual who speaks for the mind, tells his brother Alyosha, who represents the soul, of a dream in which Jesus Christ comes back to earth while heretics are being burnt in Spain. Christ is recognized and adored by the crowds at the *auto da fe*, but put in prison by the police. The aged Grand Inquisitor visits him in his cell, recognizes him, and tells him that the religion he brought to earth is incompatible with human happiness:

> ' "The terrible and wise spirit, the spirit of self-destruction and non-existence," the old man went on, "the great spirit talked with you in the wilderness and we are told in the books that he apparently 'tempted' you. Is that so? And could anything truer have been said than what he revealed to you in his three questions and what you rejected, and what in the books are called 'temptations'? And yet if ever there has been on earth a real, prodigious miracle, it was on that day, on the day of the three temptations. Indeed, it was in the emergence of those three questions that the miracle lay . . . For in those three questions the whole future history of mankind is, as it were, anticipated and combined in one whole and three images are presented in which all the insoluble historical contradictions of human nature all over the world will meet . . .
>
> "Call to your mind the first question; its meaning, though not in these words, was this: 'You want to go into the world and you are going empty-handed, with some promise of freedom, which men in their simplicity and their innate lawlessness cannot even comprehend, which they fear and dread – for nothing has ever been more unendurable to man and to human society than freedom! And do you see the stones in this parched and barren desert? Turn them into loaves, and mankind will run after you like a flock of sheep, grateful and obedient, though for ever trembling with fear that you might withdraw your hand and they would no longer have your loaves.' But you did not want to deprive man of freedom and rejected the offer, for, you thought, what sort of freedom is it if obedience is bought with loaves of bread? You replied that man does not live by bread alone, but do you know that for the sake of that earthly bread the spirit of the earth will rise up against you and will join battle with you and conquer you, . . . 'Feed them first and then demand virtue of them!' – that is what they will inscribe on their banner which they will raise against you and which will destroy your temple. A new building will rise where your temple

stood, the dreadful Tower of Babel will rise up again, . . . And then we shall finish building their tower, for he who feeds them will complete it, and we alone shall feed them in your name, and we shall lie to them that it is in your name. Oh, without us they will never, never feed themselves. No science will give them bread so long as they remain free. But in the end they will lay their freedom at our feet and say to us, 'We don't mind being your slaves so long as you feed us!' They will, at last, realize themselves that there cannot be enough freedom and bread for everybody, for they will never, never be able to let everyone have his fair share! They will also be convinced that they can never be free because they are weak, vicious, worthless, and rebellious. You promised them bread from heaven, but, I repeat again, can it compare with earthly bread in the eyes of the weak, always vicious and always ignoble race of man? And if for the sake of the bread from heaven thousands and tens of thousands will follow you, what is to become of the millions and scores of thousands of millions of creatures who will not have the strength to give up the earthly bread for the bread of heaven? Or are only the scores of thousands of the great and strong dear to you, and are the remaining millions, numerous as the sand of the sea, who are weak but who love you, to serve only as the material for the great and the strong? No, to us the weak, too, are dear. They are vicious and rebellious, but in the end they will become obedient too. They will marvel at us and they will regard us as gods because, having become their masters, we consented to endure freedom and rule over them – so dreadful will freedom become to them in the end! But we shall tell them that we do your bidding and rule in your name. We shall deceive them again, for we shall not let you come near us again. That deception will be our suffering, for we shall be forced to lie. That was the meaning of the first question in the wilderness, and that was what you rejected in the name of freedom, which you put above everything else. And yet in that question lay hidden the great secret of this world. By accepting 'the loaves', you would have satisfied man's universal and everlasting craving, both as an individual and as mankind as a whole, which can be summed up in the words 'whom shall I worship?' Man, so long as he remains free, has no more constant and agonizing anxiety than to find as quickly as possible someone to worship. But man seeks to worship only what is incontestable, so incontestable, indeed, that all men at once agree to worship it all together. For the chief concern of those miserable creatures is not only to find something that I or someone else can worship, but to find something that all believe in and worship, and the absolutely essential thing is that they should do so *all together*. It is this need for *universal* worship that is the chief torment of every man individually and of mankind as a whole from the beginning of time. For the sake of that universal worship they have put each other to the sword. They have set up gods and called upon each other, 'Give up your gods and come and worship ours, or else death to you and to your gods!' And so it will be to the end of the world, even when the gods have vanished from the earth: they will prostrate themselves before idols just the same . . . It was you yourself, therefore, who laid the foundation for the destruction of your kingdom and you ought not to blame anyone else for it. And yet, is that all that was offered to you? There are three forces, the only three forces that are able to conquer and hold captive for ever the conscience of these weak rebels for their own happiness – these forces are: miracle, mystery, and authority. You rejected all three and yourself set the example for doing so. When the wise and terrible spirit set you on a pinnacle of the temple and said to you: 'If thou be the Son of God, cast thyself down: for it is written, He shall give his angels charge concerning thee: and in their hands they shall bear thee up, lest at any time thou dash thy foot against a stone, and thou shalt prove then how great is thy faith in thy Father.' But, having heard him, you rejected his proposal and did not give way and did not cast yourself down . . . you hoped that, following you, man would remain with God and ask for no miracle. But you did not know that as soon as man rejected miracle he would at once reject God as well, for what man seeks is not so much God as miracles. And since man is unable to carry on without a miracle, he will create new miracles for himself, miracles of his own, and will worship the miracle of the witch-doctor and the sorcery of the wise woman, rebel, heretic and infidel though he is a hundred times over. You did not come down from the cross when they shouted to you, mocking and deriding you: 'If thou be the Son of God, come down from the cross.' You did not come down because, again, you did not want to enslave man by a miracle . . . I swear, man has been created a weaker and baser creature than you thought him to be! Can he, can he do what you did? In respecting him so greatly, you acted as though you ceased to feel any compassion for him, for you asked too much of him – you who have loved him more than yourself! Had you respected him less, you would have asked less of him, and that would have been more like love, for his burden would have been lighter . . . Why is the weak soul to blame for being unable to receive gifts so terrible? Surely, you did not come only to the chosen and for the chosen? But if so, there is a mystery here and we cannot understand it. And if it is a mystery, then we, too, were entitled to preach a mystery and to teach them that it is neither the free verdict of their hearts nor love that matters, but the mystery which they must obey blindly, even against their con- science. So we have done. We have corrected your great work and have based it on *miracle, mystery, and authority*. And men rejoiced that they were once more led like sheep and that the terrible gift which had brought them so much suffering had at last been lifted from their hearts . . . we took from him Rome and the sword of Caesar and proclaimed ourselves the rulers of the earth, the sole rulers, though to this day we have not succeeded in bringing our work to total completion. But whose fault is it? Oh, this work is only beginning, but it has begun. We shall have to wait a long time for its completion and the earth will have yet much to suffer, but we shall reach our goal and be Caesars and it is then that we shall think about the universal happiness of man. And yet even in those days you could have taken up the sword of Caesar. Why did you reject that last gift? By accepting that third counsel of the mighty spirit, you would have accomplished all that man seeks on earth, that is to say, whom to worship, to whom to entrust his conscience and how at last to unite all in a common, harmonious, and incontestable ant-hill, for the need of universal unity is the third and last torment of men. Mankind as a whole has always striven to organize itself into a world state. There have been many great nations with great histories, but the more highly developed they were, the more unhappy they were, for they were more acutely conscious of the need for the world-wide union of men. The great conquerors, the Timurs and Ghenghis-Khans, swept like a whirl- wind over the earth, striving to conquer the world, but, though unconsciously, they expressed the same great need of mankind for a universal and world-wide union. By accepting the world and Caesar's purple, you would have founded the world state and given universal peace. For who is to wield dominion over men if not those who have taken possession of their consciences and in whose hands is their bread? And so we have taken the sword of Caesar and, having taken it, we of course rejected you and followed *him* . . . In receiving loaves from us, they will, of course, see clearly that we are taking the loaves made by their own hands in order to distribute them among themselves, without any miracle. They will see that we have not made stones into loaves, but they will, in truth, be more pleased with receiving them from our hands than with the bread itself! For they will remember only too well that before, without us, the bread they made turned to stones in their hands, but that when they came back to us, the very stones turned to bread in their hands. They will appreciate only too well what it means to submit themselves to us for ever! . . . We shall prove to them that they are weak, that they are mere pitiable children, but that the happiness of a child is the sweetest of all. They will grow timid and begin looking up to us and cling to us in fear as chicks to the hen. They will marvel at us and be terrified of us and be proud that we are so mighty and so wise as to be able to tame such a turbulent flock of thousands of millions. They will be helpless and in constant fear of our wrath, their minds will grow timid, their eyes will always be shedding tears like women and children, but at the slightest sign from us they will be just as ready to pass to mirth and laughter, to bright-eyed gladness and happy childish song. Yes, we shall force them to work, but in their leisure hours we shall make their life like a children's game, with children's songs, in chorus, and with innocent dances. Oh, we shall permit them to sin, too, for they are weak and helpless, and they will love us like children for allowing them to sin ... The most tormenting secrets of their conscience – everything, everything they will bring to us, and we shall give them our decision for it all, and they will be glad to believe in our decision, because it will relieve them of their great anxiety and of their present terrible torments of coming to a free decision themselves. And they will all be happy, all the millions of creatures, except the hundred thousand who rule over them. For we alone, we who guard the mystery, we alone shall be unhappy ... But then I will rise and point out to you the thousands of millions of happy babes who have known no sin. And we who, for their happiness, have taken their sins upon ourselves, we shall stand before you and say, 'Judge us if you can and if you dare.' Know that I am not afraid of you. Know that I, too, was in the wilderness, that I, too, fed upon locusts and roots, that I, too, blessed freedom, with which you have blessed men, and that I, too, was preparing to stand among your chosen ones, among the strong and mighty, thirsting 'to make myself of the number'. But I woke up and refused to serve madness. I went back and joined the hosts of those who have *corrected your work*. I went away from the proud and returned to the meek for the happiness of the meek. What I say to you will come to pass and our kingdom will be established. I repeat, tomorrow you will behold the obedient flock which at a mere sign from me will rush to heap up the hot coals against the stake at which I shall burn you because you have come to meddle with us. For if anyone has ever deserved our fire, it is you. Tomorrow I shall burn you. *Dixi!*' '

The Communist poet Bertholt Brecht, who wrote the great *Threepenny Opera* in Weimar Germany, put the Grand Inquisitor's point more briefly: '*Erst kommt das Fressen, dann kommt die Moral*' (Grub comes first, Morality comes later).

The influence of Dostoevsky on thinking throughout the West remains powerful to this day. It is even stronger in the East, where the words of the octogenarian Chinese leader Deng Xiao Ping, in criticizing Gorbachev, echo those of the Grand Inquisitor.

Unlike his great contemporaries Tolstoy and Turgenev, Dostoevsky was not a member of the Russian gentry. He was, in his own words 'an intellectual proletarian', who identified himself with the most deprived in his society; two of his first novels were *Poor Folk*, and *The Insulted and Injured*. At the age of twenty-eight he was condemned to be shot as a member of a small revolutionary group. His sentence was commuted just as he was being made ready for execution, and he was sent to Siberia for four years' hard labour, followed by four years as a soldier in the ranks.

During this period, he became a passionate convert to Christianity. This led him to believe both in the messianic mission of the common people and in Russia's national destiny to save the world from the evils of European civilization. Thus he was an important spokesman for the pan-Slav movement which Marx attacked so bitterly. This element in his thinking still exerts a powerful attraction in Russia, and has recently drawn new strength from the disintegration of the Soviet Union.

Dostoevsky was also tortured by a sense of guilt, partly rooted in his sexual proclivities; he was often overwhelmed by spiritual agony. His writings on the conflict between reason and the soul – of which the fable of the Grand Inquisitor is an example – have made him a major figure in religious and philosophical thinking over the last hundred years.

Yet Dostoevsky is a far more complex writer than his great contemporaries. As Virginia Woolf said, the plots of his novels are simply 'the little bits of cork which mark a circle upon the top of the waves, while the net drags the floor of the sea and encloses stranger monsters than have ever been brought to the light of day before.'

THE AMERICAN MODEL

Two oceans separate Russia physically from the United States; in political culture they belong to different universes. Although I had many American friends at Oxford, I did not appreciate how much

it differs from Europe until I began going there after the war. The
United States is still changing, as new waves of immigration flood
its shores – these days much more from Asia and Latin America
than from Europe. Its politics no longer reflect the values or style
of its founding fathers.

Whatever the shortcomings of its current political and business
leaders, the United States is still the one country in which millions
from the rest of the world would like to live – the land of
opportunity. Its creators established a model for democracy far
more impressive than any which existed in Europe at the time.
Washington's America was then the school of the world, as
Pericles' Athens was the school of Hellas – even if both depended
at the time on an underclass of slaves who were excluded from
their democracy. Yet Washington and the extraordinary group of
individuals who led the Revolutionary War and wrote the
American Constitution were men whose families had come from
England. Eight of the fifty-six signatories of the Declaration of
Independence had been born in Britain.

Washington, Jefferson, Hamilton, Madison, and Franklin
combined all that was best in eighteenth-century Britain with the
puritan simplicity of the early settlers. They matched reason with
integrity, common sense with vision, and expressed themselves
with a grace and clarity which later generations have rarely
matched. The preamble to the Declaration of Independence is
typical; it was written by Thomas Jefferson, with two small
amendments by others:

> When in the Course of human Events, it becomes necessary for one
> People to dissolve the Political Bands which have connected them
> with another, and to assume among the Powers of the Earth, the
> separate and equal Station to which the Laws of Nature and of
> Nature's God entitle them, a decent Respect to the Opinions of
> Mankind requires that they should declare the causes which impel
> them to the Separation.
>
> We hold these Truths to be self-evident, that all Men are created
> equal, that they are endowed by their Creator with certain unalien-
> able Rights, that among these are Life, Liberty, and the Pursuit of
> Happiness – That to secure these Rights, Governments are instituted
> among Men, deriving their just Powers from the Consent of the
> Governed, that whenever any Form of Government becomes de-
> structive of these then, it is the Right of the People to alter or to
> abolish it, and to institute new Government, laying its Foundation

on such Principles, and organizing its Powers in such Form, as to them shall seem most likely to effect their Safety and Happiness. Prudence, indeed, will dictate that Governments long established should not be changed for light and transient Causes; and accordingly all Experience hath shewn, that Mankind are more disposed to suffer, while Evils are sufferable, than to right themselves by abolishing the Forms to which they are accustomed. But when a long Train of Abuses and Usurpations, pursuing invariably the same Object, evinces a Design to reduce them under absolute Despotism, it is their Right, it is their Duty, to throw off such Government, and to provide new Guards for their future Security. Such has been the patient Sufferance of these Colonies; and such is now the Necessity which constrains them to alter their former Systems of Government.

My own favourite is Benjamin Franklin, partly because he was less austere and single-minded than his colleagues. Well before he involved himself in politics he had made himself famous as a journalist and scientist. His worldly wisdom was published in his almanacs under the pseudonym 'Poor Richard', and his scientific experiments made an important contribution to our knowledge of electricity. He had an insatiable curiosity about how things worked, and an inexhaustible desire to make them work better. So he invented the lightning rod and designed a new type of stove, which is still being manufactured. He established a fire company, an insurance company, a library, an academy and a hospital.

At the age of forty-seven he took his first public office, as Deputy Postmaster General in all the northern colonies. Then he became deeply involved in trying to persuade the British to come to terms with the American desire for greater autonomy. When that failed, at the age of sixty-nine he helped to draft the Declaration of Independence. He then spent nine years in Paris working as a representative of the new state, returning at seventy-nine to help draft the new American Constitution. During this period he invented bifocal spectacles. He died at eighty-four, to be celebrated in Turgot's immortal words: 'He snatched the lightning from the skies and the sceptre from tyrants.'

Franklin was as different from Dostoevsky as colonial America from Tsarist Russia. The only agony he ever admitted was caused by gout, not guilt. The nearest he approached to spiritual speculation was in his questions:

If your riches are yours, why don't you take them with you to t'other world?

If men are so wicked as we now see them with religion, what would they be if without it?

Work as if you were to live 100 years. Pray as if you were to die tomorrow.

If rascals knew the advantages of virtue they would become honest men out of rascality.

The essence of Franklin both as a man and as a politician was common sense; he believed that 'the most exquisite folly is made of wisdom spun too fine'. He warned his readers:

Laws too gentle are seldom obeyed; too severe, seldom executed.
Everything appears to promise that the American Constitution will last; but in this world nothing is certain except death and taxes.

He immensely enjoyed the company of intelligent women. During his mission to Paris in his seventies he flirted with several of the more brilliant hostesses, telling Madame Helvetius when he had to put off a visit: 'Madame, I am waiting till the nights are longer.'

Above all, he had a sense of humour. He prepared the following Prize Question for an imaginary Royal Academy – 'To discover some Drug wholesome and not disagreeable, to be mix'd with our common Food, or Sauces, that shall render the natural Discharges of Wind from our Bodies, not only inoffensive, but agreeable as Perfumes.' After gravely arguing that 'this Invention, if compleated, would be, as Bacon expresses it, bringing Philosophy home to Men's Business and Bosoms,' he concluded by saying that in comparison, the sciences of the philosophers 'are, all together, scarcely worth a FART-HING.

Sometimes his humour was addressed to more serious matters, as in his instructions:

How to make a STRIKING SUNDIAL, by which not only a Man's own Family, but all his Neighbours for ten Miles round, may know what o'Clock it is, when the Sun shines, without seeing the Dial.

Chuse an open Place in your Yard or Garden, on which the Sun may shine all Day without any Impediment from Trees or Buildings. On the Ground mark out your Hour Lines, as for a horizontal Dial, according to Art, taking Room enough for the Guns. On the Line for One o'Clock, place one Gun; on the Two o'Clock Line two Guns, and so of the rest. The Guns must all be charged with

Powder, but Ball is unnecessary. Your Gnomon or Style must have twelve burning Glasses annex'd to it, and be so placed as that the Sun shining through the Glasses, one after the other, shall cause the Focus or burning Spot to fall on the Hour Line of One, for Example, at one a Clock, and there kindle a Train of Gunpowder that shall fire one Gun. At Two a Clock, a Focus shall fall on the Hour Line of Two, and kindle another Train that shall discharge two Guns successively; and so of the rest.

Note, There must be 78 Guns in all. Thirty-two Pounders will be best for this Use; but 18 Pounders may do, and will cost less, as well as use less Powder, for nine Pounds of Powder will do for one Charge of each eighteen Pounder, whereas the Thirty-two Pounders would require for each Gun 16 Pounds.

Note also, That the chief Expence will be the Powder, for the Cannon once bought, will, with Care, last 100 Years.

Note moreover, That there will be a great Saving of Powder in cloudy Days.

Kind Reader, Methinks I hear thee say, *That it is indeed a good Thing to know how the Time passes, but this Kind of Dial, notwithstanding the mentioned Savings, would be very expensive; and the Cost greater than the Advantage.* Thou art wise, my Friend, to be so considerate beforehand; some Fools would not have found out so much, till they had made the Dial and try'd it. – Let all such learn that many a private and many a publick Project, are like this *Striking Dial*, great Cost for little Profit.

How many governments would have been better off if they had heeded this advice, not least President Reagan with his Star Wars programme!

Of later American politicians, only Abraham Lincoln ranks with those of that first Golden Age. He had all Franklin's common sense, humour and skill with words. In his second campaign speech in 1858 he said: 'Nobody has ever expected me to be President. In my poor, lean, lank face nobody has ever seen that any cabbages were sprouting.'

Lincoln had thought hard about the problem of government before he became President, and reached much the same conclusions as Adam Smith. In 1854 he wrote:

The legitimate object of government is to do for a community of people whatever they need to have done, but cannot do at all, or cannot so well do, for themselves, in their separate and individual capacities. In all the people can individually do as well for them-

selves, government ought not to interfere. The desirable things
which the individuals of a people cannot do, or cannot well do, for
themselves, fall into two classes: those which have relations to
wrongs, and those which have not. Each of these branch off into an
infinite variety of subdivisions.

The first – that in relation to wrongs – embraces all crimes,
misdemeanours, and non-performance of contracts. The other embraces all which, in its nature, and without wrong, requires combined action, as public roads and highways, public schools, charities,
pauperism, orphanage, estates of the deceased, and the machinery
of government itself.

From this it appears that if all men were just, there still would be
some, though not so much, need of government.

In the jargon of the Common Market, this is called 'subsidiarity'.

When Lincoln finally entered the White House his predecessor,
James Buchanan, told him: 'If you are as happy, my dear sir, on
entering this house as I am in leaving it and returning home, you
are the happiest man in this country.'

In fact, Lincoln soon found himself plunged into a civil war to
maintain the Constitution. More Americans were killed in that
civil war than in all the wars that followed, including two world
wars, Vietnam, and the Gulf. Yet its population was then only one
seventh as large as it is today. I have always seen this as a sombre
warning against federation as a means of uniting states; in recent
years the lesson has been rammed home in the Soviet Union and
Yugoslavia. The American Civil War is also a warning against the
belief, so fashionable today, that democracies never start wars or
fight one another; both the northern and southern states were
democratic.

The Civil War did abolish slavery in the United States, though
that was not part of Lincoln's original war aims. But it inflicted
some deep and lasting divisions on the American people. By
rapidly accelerating the pace of industrialization, it changed the
nature of American society and stimulated massive immigration
from Continental Europe. The culture of the British settlers, so
well enshrined in the Constitution, was replaced by the materialistic
melting pot we know today. It is an open question whether the
United States will be able to resolve the problems created by its
growing underclass and its unholy trinity of drugs, crime, and
racial division within the constitutional framework set by its
founding fathers.

NINETEENTH-CENTURY BRITAIN

While continental Europe went through the Age of Revolution and America fought its Civil War, politics in Britain pursued its comparatively tranquil way, 'broadening from precedent to precedent'. Like so many foreigners, the poet Heinrich Heine found this difficult to understand. No one has helped me more to understand the Europe of his time than Heinrich Heine. Besides being Germany's greatest lyric poet he was an incomparably acute observer of all aspects of the society he knew, as shown, for example, in his comments on Kant which I have already quoted. A Jewish upbringing in the Rhineland under French occupation, and travels in Germany, Italy, France and England, made him a true European – indeed a citizen of the world. His romantic idealism brought him to a close friendship with Karl and Jenny Marx in his middle age, when Marx was drafting the Communist Manifesto.

Heine had started his career running a firm in Hamburg called 'Harry Heine and Co.', dealers in British manufactured goods. When he first visited London as a writer some years later he was appalled by its materialism, and by the misery and poverty he saw around him. Yet he realized that in some respects the British might have discovered the secret of social peace:

'The Englishman bears the sight of a privileged aristocracy with far greater patience than the Frenchman. He is consoled by the possession of rights which prevent the aristocracy from disturbing his domestic comforts or daily wants. Nor does the aristocracy flaunt its privileges, as on the Continent. In London's streets and public places of resort you will see gay ribbons only on women's bonnets and gold and silver badges only on the coats of lackeys. Even that beautiful many-colored livery, which in Germany proclaims a privileged military class, is anything but a sign of honor in England. Just as an actor wipes off the paint after a performance, so an English officer hastens home to doff his red coat the moment he is off duty so that he may become a gentleman again, and appear in the plain coat of a gentleman. Only on the stage of St James's are those decorations and costumes which have been preserved from the rubble of the Middle Ages still of consequence. There you see the court decorations fluttering, stars glittering; there the satin trains and silken breeches rustle, gold spurs and old French phrases rattle. There the knight struts and the lady simpers. But what does a free Englishman care for all this courtly comedy at St James's, so long as it doesn't bother him and no one keeps him from playing a similar comedy in his own house, where he can have his domestics kneel before him and where he can toy with the cook's garter? *Honni soit qui mal y pense.*

In 1840, having travelled widely in Europe and finally settled in Paris as a political exile, he described what he saw as another reason for Britain's success:

But are the English really such clever heads at politics? In what does their superiority in this field consist? I believe it lies in the fact that they are arch-prosaic creatures; they do not allow themselves to be led astray by poetic illusions; they are not deceived by glowing wild fancies; they see everything in the most sober light; they keep the bare facts constantly before their eyes; they calculate accurately the conditions of time and place, and while doing so are not disturbed by the beating of their hearts or the flutterings of their noblest thoughts. Yes, their superiority consists in the fact that they do not possess imagination. This shortcoming constitutes the whole *forte* of the English, and is the ultimate reason for their success in politics, as in all realistic undertakings – industry, building of machinery, etc. They have no imagination. That is the whole secret. Their poets are merely brilliant exceptions to this rule. That is why they come into conflict with the people – the snub-nosed, low-browed people, without occiput – that chosen people of prose, who behave in India and in Italy in that same prosaic and calculating way in which they behave in Threadneedle Street. They are intoxicated by the perfume of the lotus as little as they are warmed by the fires of Vesuvius. They drag their urns to the edge of the crater, and there drink tea, seasoned with cant!

When I read the comments on nineteenth-century Britain by travellers like Heine and Taine, I am irresistibly reminded of Mr Podsnap's encounter with foreigners as Dickens described it in *Our Mutual Friend*:

'How do you like London?' Mr Podsnap now inquired from his station of host, as if he were administering something in the nature of a powder or potion to the deaf child; 'London, Londres, London?'
 The foreign gentleman admired it.

'You find it Very Large?' said Mr Podsnap, spaciously.

The foreign gentleman found it very large.

'And Very Rich?'

The foreign gentleman found it, without doubt, enormément riche.

'Enormously Rich, We say,' returned Mr Podsnap, in a condescending manner. 'Our English adverbs do Not terminate in Mong, and We Pronounce the "ch" as if there were a "t" before it. We say Ritch.'

'Reetch,' remarked the foreign gentleman.

'And Do You Find, Sir,' pursued Mr Podsnap, with dignity, 'Many Evidences that Strike You, of our British Constitution in the Streets of The World's Metropolis, London, Londres, London?'

The foreign gentleman begged to be pardoned, but did not altogether understand.

'The Constitution Britannique,' Mr Podsnap explained, as if he were teaching in an infant school. 'We Say British, But You Say Britannique, You Know' (forgivingly, as if that were not his fault). 'The Constitution, Sir.'

The foreign gentleman said, 'Mais, yees; I know eem.'

A youngish sallowish gentleman in spectacles, with a lumpy forehead, seated in a supplementary chair at a corner of the table, here caused a profound sensation by saying, in a raised voice, 'ESKER,' and then stopping dead.

'Mais oui,' said the foreign gentleman, turning towards him. 'Est-ce que? Quoi donc?'

But the gentleman with the lumpy forehead having for the time delivered himself of all that he found behind his lumps, spake for the time no more.

'I Was Inquiring,' said Mr Podsnap, resuming the thread of his discourse, 'Whether You Have Observed in our Streets as We should say, Upon our Pavvy as You would say, any Tokens . . .'

The foreign gentleman with patient courtesy entreated pardon; 'But what was tokenz?'

'Marks,' said Mr Podsnap; 'Signs, you know, Appearances – Traces.'

'Ah! Of a Orse?' inquired the foreign gentleman.

'We call it Horse,' said Mr Podsnap, with forbearance. 'In England, Angleterre, England, We Aspirate the "H", and We Say "Horse." Only our Lower Classes Say "Orse!"'

'Pardon,' said the foreign gentleman; 'I am alwiz wrong!'

'Our Language,' said Mr Podsnap, with a gracious consciousness of being always right, 'is Difficult. Ours is a copious Language, and Trying to Strangers. I will not Pursue my Question.'

But the lumpy gentleman, unwilling to give it up, again madly said, 'ESKER,' and again spake no more.

'It merely referred,' Mr Podsnap explained, with a sense of meritorious proprietorship, 'to Our Constitution, Sir. We Englishmen are Very Proud of our Constitution, Sir. It Was Bestowed Upon Us By Providence. No Other Country is so Favoured as This Country.'

'And ozer countries?' – the foreign gentleman was beginning, when Mr Podsnap put him right again.

'We do not say Ozer; we say Other: the letters are "T" and "H"; you say Tay and Aish, You Know;' (still with clemency). 'The sound is "th" – "th"!'

'And *other* countries,' said the foreign gentleman. 'They do how?'

'They do, Sir,' returned Mr Podsnap, gravely shaking his head; 'they do – I am sorry to be obliged to say it – *as* they do.'

'It was a little particular of Providence,' said the foreign gentleman, laughing; 'for the frontier is not large.'

'Undoubtedly,' assented Mr Podsnap; 'But So it is. It was the Charter of the Land. This Island was Blest, Sir, to the Direct Exclusion of such Other Countries as – as there may happen to be. And if we were all Englishmen present, I would say,' added Mr Podsnap, looking round upon his compatriots, and sounding solemnly with his theme, 'that there is in the Englishman a combination of qualities, a modesty, an independence, a responsibility, a repose, combined with an absence of everything calculated to call a blush into the cheek of a young person, which one would seek in vain among the Nations of the Earth.'

In later years those elements in the British political character which Heine described and Dickens caricatured were to infuriate Marx and Engels, and Lenin and Trotsky after them. British politicians, unlike the American colonists, have always found it difficult to shake off the legacy of the past. They still see Britain as a world power, and have shown great reluctance to adapt the class system to social and economic change. Our class structure is nowadays regarded by our competitors as a root cause of Britain's industrial weakness. And our lack of imagination has become a serious obstacle to innovation. So the factors which Heine saw as the source of Britain's commercial greatness have become the engines of her decline.

Such differences in history and culture play a vital role in the politics of nations. It is dangerous to formulate a foreign policy without taking them into account. My studies at Oxford helped me to understand them in theory. My six years as International Secretary of the Labour Party gave me a unique opportunity for observing them in practice and my reading has helped to fix them in my mind.

THE HOUSE OF COMMONS

When I first entered the portals of the House of Commons in February 1952 as a Member of Parliament I felt I was entering a different world. It was an experience for which H.G. Wells had prepared me in *The New Machiavelli*; it is a pity he later abandoned his realism for the utopias of science fiction. Wells' description of his hero's maiden speech is faultless, although he was never an MP himself:

> I can still recall quite distinctly my two futile attempts to catch the Speaker's eye before I was able to begin, the nervous quiver of my rather too prepared opening, the effect of hearing my own voice and my subconscious wonder as to what I could possibly be talking about, the realisation that I was getting on fairly well, the immense satisfaction afterwards of having on the whole brought it off, and the absurd gratitude I felt for that encouraging cheer.
>
> Addressing the House of Commons is like no other public speaking in the world. Its semi-colloquial methods give it an air of being easy, but its shifting audience, the comings and goings and hesitations of members behind the chair – not mere audience units, but men who matter – the desolating emptiness that spreads itself round the man who fails to interest, the little compact, disciplined crowd in the strangers' gallery, the light, elusive, flickering movements high up behind the grille, the wigged, attentive, weary Speaker, the table and the mace and the chapel-like Gothic background with its sombre shadows, conspire together, produce a confused, uncertain feeling in me as though I was walking upon a pavement full of trap-doors and patches of uncovered morass. A misplaced, well-meant 'Hear, Hear!' is apt to be extraordinarily disconcerting, and under no other circumstances have I had to speak with quite the same sideways twist that the arrangement of the House imposes. One does not recognize one's own voice threading out into the stirring brown. Unless I was excited or speaking to the mind of some particular person in the House, I was apt to lose my feeling of an auditor.

Aneurin Bevan describes in *In Place of Fear* the same experience, as an ex-miner from the Welsh valleys:

'The past lies like an Alp upon the human mind.' The House of Commons is a whole range of mountains. If the new Member gets there too late in life he is already trailing a pretty considerable past of his own, making him heavy-footed and cautious. When to this is added the visible penumbra of six centuries of receding legislators, he feels weighed to the ground. Often he never gets to his feet again.

His first impression is that he is in church. The vaulted roofs and stained-glass windows, the rows of statues of great statesmen of the past, the echoing halls, the soft-footed attendants and the whispered conversation, contrast depressingly with the crowded meetings and the clang and clash of hot opinions he has just left behind in his election campaign. Here he is, a tribune of the people, coming to make his voice heard in the seats of power. Instead, it seems he is expected to worship; and the most conservative of all religions – ancestor worship.

The first thing he should bear in mind is that these were not his ancestors. His forebears had no part in the past, the accumulated dust of which now muffles his own footfalls. His forefathers were tending sheep or ploughing the land, or serving the statemen whose names he sees written on the walls around him, or whose portraits look down upon him in the long corridors. It is not the past of his people that extends in colourful pageantry before his eyes. They were shut out from all this; were forbidden to take part in the dramatic scenes depicted in these frescoes. In him his people are there for the first time, and the history he will make will not be merely an episode in the story he is now reading. It must be wholly different; as different as is the social status which he now brings with him.

To preserve the keen edge of his critical judgment he will find that he must adopt an attitude of scepticism amounting almost to cynicism, for Parliamentary procedure neglects nothing which might soften the acerbities of his class feelings. In one sense the House of Commons is the most unrepresentative of representative assemblies. It is an elaborate conspiracy to prevent the real clash of opinion which exists outside from finding an appropriate echo within its walls. It is a social shock-absorber placed between privilege and the pressure of popular discontent.

The new Member's first experience of this is when he learns that passionate feelings must never find expression in forthright speech. His first speech teaches him that. Having come straight from contact with his constituents, he is full of their grievances and his own resentment, and naturally, he does his best to shock his listeners into some realisation of it.

He delivers himself therefore with great force and, he hopes and fears, with considerable provocativeness. When his opponent arises to reply he expects to hear an equally strong and uncompromising answer. His opponent does nothing of the sort. In strict conformity with Parliamentary tradition, he congratulates the new Member upon a most successful maiden speech and expresses the urbane hope that the House will have frequent opportunities of hearing him in the future. The Members present endorse this quite insincere sentiment with murmurs of approval. With that, his opponent pays no more attention to him, but goes on to deliver the speech he had intended to make. After remaining in his seat a little longer, the new Member crawls out of the House with feelings of deep relief at having got it over, mingled with a paralysing sense of frustration. The stone he thought he had thrown turned out to be a sponge.

I shared much of Bevan's reaction, as I explained in my memoirs. My literary idol Virginia Woolf, a daughter of the upper-class intelligentsia, was both less impressed by and less unkind about Parliament:

Certainly our own House of Commons from inside is not in the least noble or majestic or even dignified. It is as shiny and as ugly as any other moderate-sized public hall. The oak, of course, is grained yellow. The windows, of course, are painted with ugly coats of arms. The floor, of course, is laid with strips of red matting. The benches, of course, are covered with serviceable leather. Wherever one looks one says, 'of course.' It is an untidy, informal-looking assembly. Sheets of white paper seem to be always fluttering to the floor. People are always coming in and out incessantly. Men are whispering and gossiping and cracking jokes over each other's shoulders. The swing doors are perpetually swinging. Even the central island of control and dignity where the Speaker sits under his canopy, is a perching ground for casual members who seem to be taking a peep at the proceedings at their ease. Legs rest on the edge of the table where the mace lies suspended; and the secrets which repose in the two brass-bound chests on either side of the table are not immune from the prod of an occasional toe. Dipping and rising, moving and settling, the Commons remind one of a flock of birds settling on a stretch of ploughed land. They never alight for more than a few minutes; some are always flying off, others are always settling again. And from the flock rises the gabbling, the cawing, the croaking of a flock of birds, disputing merrily and with occasional vivacity over some seed, worm, or buried grain.

As her husband, Leonard, wrote, Virginia Woolf 'was the least political animal that has lived since Aristotle invented the expression.' She was also an appalling snob. But she produced some brilliant portraits of the politicians she met, from her cousin, H.A.L. Fisher, a typical Edwardian who was Minister of Education, through Beatrice and Sidney Webb, who were quintessential Fabians, to a working-class Socialist, Willie Gillies, who was my predecessor as International Secretary of the Labour Party.

On Fisher:

'He is a strange mixture of ascetic and worldling. The lean, secluded man now finds himself dazzled by office, and with all his learning and culture swept away by men of vitality and affairs. Such a tribute as he paid to Winston might have been paid by some dazzled moth to a lamp. He seems to see nothing clearly, or else some notion of responsibility forbids him to say what he thinks. He hums and haws when asked a plain question. His whole aspect is that of a worn and half obliterated scholar made spruce by tailors and doing his best to adopt the quiet distinguished manner of those who govern.'

On the Webbs:

Mrs Webb's brilliant idea of municipal bricks for children, inscribed with the names of organizations so that in putting them together they would learn their civic duties was almost too much in character to be suitable. . . . Even Sidney had his mild joke at her.

And when they came for a weekend and Virginia fills four or five pages of her diary on this, the following dialogue appears:

'The work of Government,' declared Sidney Webb, 'will be enormously increased in the future.'

'Shall I ever have a finger in the pie?' asked Virginia.

'Oh yes; you will have some small office no doubt. My wife and I always say that a railway guard is the most enviable of men. He has authority, and he is responsible to a government. That should be the state of each one of us.'

And the wonderful image she used, which I feel is all too true of many people I know in all parties, of the Webbs:

> In their efficiency and glibness one traces perfectly adjusted machinery; but talk by machinery does not charm, or suggest: it cuts the grass of the mind close at the roots. . . .
>
> She [Mrs Webb] asked me about my novel and I supplied her with a carefully arranged plot. I wished, so at least I said, to discover what aims drive people on, and whether these are illusory or not. She promptly shot forth: 'Two aims have governed my life: one is the passion for investigation by scientific means; the other the passion for producing a certain good state of society by those investigations'. Somehow she proceeded to warn me against the dissipation of energy in emotional friendship. One should have only one great personal relationship in one's life, she said, or at most two – marriage and parenthood. Marriage was necessary as a waste pipe for emotion, as security in old age when personal attractiveness fails, and as a help to work. We were entangled at the gates of the level crossing when she remarked, 'Yet I daresay an old family servant would do as well'.

Years later she met Mrs Webb again, and produced some wonderful passages of description. She describes her 'like the veins of a leaf when the pulp has been eaten away'. And just before her death the old woman, wearing a white-spotted headdress, 'was as alive as a leaf on an autumn bonfire: burning, skeletonised'.

Finally, on an unexpected visit by Gillies:

> Oh I'm so furious! Just as we'd cleared off our weekend visits, the telephone rings, and there comes to lunch late, hungry yet eating with the deliberation and mastication of a toad, Mr Gillies of the Labour Party. It's 5.30. He's still there, masticating. Half a plum cake has gone down crumb by crumb. Mercifully he was seized with such a choking fit that I made off to my lodge to write this. You can't conceive what the mind of a Labour Party leader is like – George [Duckworth] is advanced, Saxon [Sidney Turner] rash and Barbara [Bagenal] wildly imaginative in comparison. And they scrape their knives on their plates. . . .
>
> Never let Angelica marry a Labour leader: on the other hand, don't tell Leonard this, for he lives in the delusion that they are good men.

The economist, Maynard Keynes, was a close friend of Virginia

Woolf and a member of the so-called Bloomsbury Set. Though never directly involved in politics, he worked at the Treasury during the First World War and attended the subsequent Peace Conference. He finally resigned in disgust; his withering attack on the Versailles Treaty in 'The Economic Consequences of the Peace', made him famous. He omitted a passage he wrote about the personalities involved, but published it ten years later in his *Essays in Biography*. It makes a fascinating contrast to Virginia Woolf's descriptions of her political acquaintances, since, although written with equal brilliance, it concentrates on the three protagonists in their political roles; they emerge as very recognizable types. Clemenceau is described in terms which could be applied word for word to de Gaulle. President Wilson emerges as indistinguishable from Jimmy Carter, while at least two recent British politicians could stand in for Keynes' description of Lloyd George:

> The President, the Tiger, and the Welsh witch were shut up in a room together for six months and the Treaty was what came out. Yes, the Welsh *witch* – for the British Prime Minister contributed the female element to this triangular intrigue. I have called Mr Wilson a nonconformist clergyman. Let the reader figure Mr Lloyd George as a *femme fatale*. An old man of the world, a *femme fatale*, and a nonconformist clergyman – these are the characters of our drama. Even though the lady was very religious at times, the Fourteen Commandments could hardly expect to emerge perfectly intact.
>
> I must try to silhouette the broomstick as it sped through the twilit air of Paris. . . .
>
> In such a test of character and method as Paris provided, the Prime Minister's naturally good instincts, his industry, his inexhaustible nervous vitality were not serviceable. In that furnace other qualities were called for – a policy deeply grounded in permanent principle, tenacity, fierce indignation, honesty, loyal leadership. If Mr Lloyd George had no good qualities, no charms, no fascinations, he would not be dangerous. If he were not a syren, we need not fear the whirlpools.
>
> But it is not appropriate to apply to him the ordinary standards. How can I convey to the reader, who does not know him, any just impression of this extraordinary figure of our time, this syren, this goat-footed bard, this half-human visitor to our age from the hagridden magic and enchanted woods of Celtic antiquity? One catches in his company that flavour of final purposelessness, inner irresponsi-

bility, existence outside or away from our Saxon good and evil, mixed with cunning, remorselessness, love of power, that lend fascination, enthralment, and terror to the fair-seeming magicians of North European folklore. . . .

Lloyd George is rooted in nothing; he is void and without content; he lives and feeds on his immediate surroundings; he is an instrument and a player at the same time which plays on the company and is played on by them too; he is a prism, as I have heard him described, which collects light and distorts it and is most brilliant if the light comes from many quarters at once; a vampire and a medium in one.

Virginia Woolf disliked politics partly because it seemed to her a typically male activity – she saw politicians as little boys competing for power and status. I suspect this feeling is one reason why fewer women attempt to overcome the obstacles created by males to their participation in national politics. Wendy Cope put the problem in 'Men and their boring arguments':

> One man on his own can be quite good fun
> But don't go drinking with two –
> They'll probably have an argument
> And take no notice of you.
>
> What makes men so tedious
> Is the need to show off and compete.
> They'll bore you to death for hours and hours
> Before they'll admit defeat.
>
> It often happens at dinner parties
> Where brother disputes with brother
> And we can't even talk among ourselves
> Because we're not next to each other.
>
> Some men like to argue with women –
> Don't give them a chance to begin.
> You won't be allowed to change the subject
> Until you have given in.
>
> A man with the bit between his teeth
> Will keep you up half the night
> And the only way to get some sleep
> Is to say, 'I expect you're right.'

I expect you're right, my dearest love.
I expect you're right, my friend.
These boring arguments make no difference
To anything in the end.

Unfortunately these boring arguments are an essential part of the political process at every level, and some of the arguments may be tortuous, since as Kant wrote: 'Out of the crooked timber of humanity nothing straight was ever made.'

There are two sides to the politician's profession – to persuade people to entrust him with the power to take decisions on their behalf, and to take decisions that will fulfil that trust, in a world which can never be more than partially understood and which is constantly changing.

None of the people he must persuade – his constituents, his party, his civil servants, his foreign colleagues – are wholly rational beings. They are as likely to answer an appeal to their emotions, their interests, or their prejudices, as to their reason. Democracy relies above all on debate between opposing views; but as Bagehot said: 'Of all the pursuits ever invented by man for separating the faculty of argument from the capacity of belief, the art of debating is the most effective.'

Moreover both the politicians and the people they must persuade are prone to believe in the sort of abstract theories that I learned to distrust as a student. At present, as at periods in the past, the prevailing fashion attributes magical powers to the market economy. Rudyard Kipling dealt with this fantasy – and more – two generations ago in his poem 'The Gods of the Copybook Headings':

As I pass through my incarnations in every age and race.
I make my proper prostrations to the Gods of the Market-Place.
Peering through reverent fingers I watch them flourish and fall,
And the Gods of the Copybook Headings, I notice, outlast them all

We were living in trees when they met us. They showed us each in
   turn
That Water would certainly wet us, as Fire would certainly burn:
But we found them lacking in Uplift, Vision and Breadth of Mind,
So we left them to teach the Gorillas while we followed the March of
   Mankind.
We moved as the Spirit listed. *They* never altered their pace,

Being neither cloud nor wind-borne like the Gods of the Market-
  Place;
But they always caught up with our progress, and presently word
  would come
That a tribe had been wiped off its icefield, or the lights had gone
  out in Rome.
With the Hopes that our World is built on they were utterly out
  of touch,
They denied that the Moon was Stilton; they denied she was even
  Dutch.
They denied that Wishes were Horses; they denied that a Pig had
  Wings.
So we worshipped the Gods of the Market Who promised these
  beautiful things.

When the Cambrian measures were forming, They promised
  perpetual peace.
They swore, if we gave them our weapons, that the wars of the
  tribes would cease.
But when we disarmed They sold us and delivered us bound to
  our foe,
And the Gods of the Copybook Headings said: '*Stick to the Devil
  you know.*'

On the first Feminian Sandstones we were promised the Fuller Life
(Which started by loving our neighbour and ended by loving his
  wife)
Till our women had no more children and the men lost reason and
  faith,
And the Gods of the Copybook Headings said: '*The Wages of Sin
  is Death.*'

In the Carboniferous Epoch we were promised abundance for all,
By robbing selected Peter to pay for collective Paul;
But, though we had plenty of money, there was nothing our
  money could buy,
And the Gods of the Copybook Headings said: '*If you don't work
  you die.*'

Then the Gods of the Market tumbled, and their smooth-tongued
  wizards withdrew,
And the hearts of the meanest were humbled and began to believe
  it was true
That All is not Gold that Glitters, and Two and Two make Four –
And the Gods of the Copybook Headings limped up to explain it
  once more.

As it will be in the future, it was at the birth of Man –
There are only four things certain since Social Progress began: –
That the Dog returns to his Vomit and the Sow returns to her
    Mire,
And the burnt Fool's bandaged finger goes wabbling back to the
    Fire;

And that after this is accomplished, and the brave new world
    begins
When all men are paid for existing and no man must pay for his
    sins,
As surely as Water will wet us, as surely as Fire will burn,
The Gods of the Copybook Headings with terror and slaughter
    return!

The last two thousand years have produced a vast treasure-house of Copybook Headings from Machiavelli's *The Prince* to Cornford's *Cosmographica Academica* which encapsulate the common sense of their time; the eighteenth century was particularly prolific in the sort of aphorisms which Franklin recorded as Poor Richard. Certainly the wisdom they distil is more useful than many volumes of political or economic theory. But they too rarely admit the need for change. Here the novelists may be more helpful. In *Phineas Finn* an older MP gives good advice to a newcomer:

> Many who regarded legislation on the subject as chimerical, will now fancy that it is only dangerous, or perhaps not more than difficult. And so in time it will come to be looked on as among the things probable – and so at last it will be ranged in the list of those few measures which the country requires as being absolutely needed. That is the way in which public opinion is made.

I find it interesting to see how consistently this sort of wisdom reasserts itself from generation to generation, through massive changes in the political environment. As the franchise was gradually extended through the nineteenth century, elections began to involve the whole of the population. In *Pickwick Papers* Dickens described the Eatanswill election in words which were still not very remote from reality a hundred years later, in the nineteen thirties. Indeed many of Dickens' extravagances are familiar even today in the United States. 'The beating of drums, the blowing of horns and trumpets, the shouting of men, and tramping of horses' which he saw in Eatanswill are still staple fare at the American political conventions, as well as the antiphonal exchanges between audience and platform.

In England nowadays, however, the bribery is no longer retail, and at the candidate's expense; it is wholesale, and paid for by the voter himself as a taxpayer or borrower. Moreover, since I first won my seat in 1952, the public meeting has practically disappeared. Elections are fought instead on television, which can be watched in the comfort of the voter's home. Argument is replaced by the photo-opportunity and the sound-bite. The sound-bites become steadily shorter; in the American Presidential election of 1988 the average length of a sound-bite was cut from thirty seconds to nine in the course of the campaign.

One thing, however, has remained constant in all countries for a century-and-a-half — what Dickens in *Little Dorrit* called the Circumlocution Office:

> The Circumlocution Office was (as everybody knows without being told) the most important Department under Government. No public business of any kind could possibly be done at any time, without the acquiescence of the Circumlocution Office. Its finger was in the largest public pie, and in the smallest public tart. It was equally impossible to do the plainest right and to undo the plainest wrong, without the express authority of the Circumlocution Office. If another Gunpowder Plot had been discovered half an hour before the lighting of the match, nobody would have been justified in saving the parliament until there had been half a score of boards, half a bushel of minutes, several sacks of official memoranda, and a family-vault full of ungrammatical correspondence, on the part of the Circumlocution Office.
>
> This glorious establishment had been early in the field, when the one sublime principle involving the difficult art of governing a country, was first distinctly revealed to statesmen. It had been foremost to study that bright revelation, and to carry its shining influence through the whole of the official proceedings. Whatever was required to be done, the Circumlocution Office was beforehand with all the public departments in the art of perceiving — HOW NOT TO DO IT.

It is not surprising that frustration often breeds cynicism about the whole political process. William Butler Yeats in an extraordinary poem called '*Ego Dominus Tuus*' imagines a dialogue between his two selves, *Hic* and *Ille*, which like much of his work makes no distinction between art and politics as public activities:

> *Hic*: 'Yet surely, there are men who have made their art
> Out of no tragic war, Lovers of life,
> Impulsive men that look for happiness,
> And sing when they have found it.'
> *Ille*: 'No, not sing.
> For those that love the world serve it in action,
> Grow rich and popular and full of influence
> And, should they paint or write, still it is action,
> The struggle of the fly in marmalade.'

Yeats' disillusionment with political action was much increased when the 'terrible beauty' he saw born in Easter 1916 turned into a self-destructive civil war:

> Now days are dragon-ridden, the nightmare
> Rides upon sleep: a drunken soldiery
> Can leave the mother, murdered at her door,
> To crawl in her own blood, and go scot-free;
> The night can sweat with terror as before
> We pieced our thoughts into philosophy,
> And planned to bring the world under a rule,
> Who are but weasels fighting in a hole.

Leonard Woolf, whose love sustained the tragic genius of his wife for so many years, unlike her was a dedicated politician. He spent most of his life helping the Labour Movement and working for collective security. Even after 1945, when Virginia was dead and he was sixty-five years old, he was as active as ever. He went on working in London as Secretary of the Labour Party's Advisory Committee on International Relations and Secretary of the Labour Party's Advisory Committee on Imperial Questions. He was also at that time on the Executive Committee of the Fabian Society, he was Chairman of its International Bureau, on which I also sat, he was Chairman of its Imperial Bureau, he was on the Committee of the Anglo-Soviet Society, he was a Director of the *New Statesman* and *Nation*, Editor of the *Political Quarterly*, and even sat on the Civil Service Arbitration Tribunal. And on top of all that, when he got down to Sussex, he was Clerk to the Rodmell Parish Council for seventeen years, and Manager of Rodmell Primary

School, and, glory be, President of the Rodmell Horticultural Society which he founded.

At the end of his life he wondered if it had all been worthwhile:

> It is extremely difficult to answer honestly the question why I spent so many thousands of hours in these drab occupations. I do not really like sitting on committees, and I am not a good rank-and-file committee man, though I can be a very good secretary and even, when I take the trouble, a good chairman. There is, of course, a kind of childish or ignoble pleasure in the feeling of male importance which everyone feels when he takes his seat at a committee meeting. If you are chairman or secretary, you can feel at least a faint additional pleasure in the exercise of power, however feeble. Then too, as I have said, I find it extremely interesting to watch the psychological antics of five, ten, or fifteen men sitting round a table, each with his own selfish or unselfish axe to grind. I have always found the battle of brains and wills, boxing, wrestling or jujitsu, with no blows or holds barred, which goes on round the table fascinating. Indeed, one of the reasons why I am ordinarily not a good rank-and-file committee man is that I tend to forget everything in the silent amusement of observing highly intelligent men fighting for Will-o'-the-wisps or even windmills as if for their own dear lives, converting their own pet molehills into God's Mount Sinais. Looking back upon the aeons of slowly passing minutes that I have spent in the House of Commons and other less distinguished committee rooms, I must admit that I have enjoyed the spectacle of many great men or little men of great political expertise performing as if for my personal benefit; the wily, treacherous Ramsay MacDonald in the old ILP; the mouselike Clem Attlee who, when you least expected it, would suddenly show himself to be a masterful or even savage mouse, in the New Fabian Research Bureau; Bernard Shaw's gala performances of irrelevant wit and dialectic in the Fabian Society; the ruthless virtuosity of Sidney Webb . . ., the new school of hard-headed, no-nonsense common sense of Harold Laski, G.D.H Cole, Hugh Gaitskell, Hugh Dalton, Harold Wilson in the Fabian Society and Labour Party; the strange succession of Maynard Keynes, Kingsley Martin, John Freeman and Jock Campbell on the *New Statesman* board.

Peter Calvocoressi, who knew Leonard well, sent me a letter in which he said 'Leonard also told me how he was in some body concerned with Labour Party foreign policy which contained also Harold Wilson. He observed Harold Wilson making his way up the ladder as from time to time some misfortune occurred to the person immediately ahead of him. "When he got next to me", said Leonard, "I resigned!"'.

But Leonard Woolf never felt he had achieved very much through this enormous investment of time and effort. He wrote in the last volume of his autobiography, at the end of his life:

> Looking back at the age of eighty-eight over the fifty-seven years of my political work in England, knowing what I aimed at and the results, meditating on Britain and the history of the world since 1914, I see clearly that I achieved practically nothing. The world today and the history of the human anthill during the last fifty-seven years would be exactly the same as it is if I had played ping-pong instead of sitting on committees and writing books and memoranda. I have therefore to make the rather ignominious confession to myself and to anyone who may read this book that I must have in a long life ground through between 150,000 and 200,000 hours of perfectly useless work.

Perhaps. Yet for anyone who cares about the state of the world and thinks he might be able to improve it, there can be no escape from politics.

The Polish ex-Communist philosopher Lesjek Kolakowski sets modest objectives. He defined Socialism as 'an obstinate will to erode by inches the conditions which produce avoidable suffering'. I agree. And those who show this obstinate will must not expect credit for it. Archbishop Helder Camara of Brazil recently made a telling point: 'When I give food to the poor they call me a saint. When I ask why the poor have no food they call me a Communist.'

It is difficult to endure such criticism without believing in values which transcend everyday life. For Archbishop Helder, and so many other Christian Socialists, it is religion. For Heine, as a young man who did not believe in God, it was freedom:

> Yes, it will be a beautiful day, my heart repeated in soft prayer, and trembled with anguish and joy. It *will* be a beautiful day! The sun of freedom will warm the earth more gladly than the entire aristocracy of nocturnal stars. A new race will rise, engendered in free embrace; and not in the forced nuptials or under the eye of clerical tax-collectors. Together with free birth, freer thoughts and feelings will come into the world – of which we, who were born in

servitude, have no conception. Ah! they will not understand how horrible was the night in whose darkness we were compelled to live; how bitterly we had to fight with frightful ghosts, stupid owls, and sanctimonious sinners! Alas, we poor warriors who have had to squander our lives in such combat, and are weary and spent, now that victory is at hand! The sunrise glow can no longer flush our cheeks and warm our hearts. We perish like the waning moon. All too brief is man's allotted course, and his end is the implacable grave!

Truly, I do not know whether I deserve that a laurel wreath be placed on my bier: Poetry, much as I loved it, has always been to me only a sacred plaything, or, at best, a consecrated means to a heavenly end. I have never laid great store by poetic glory, and whether my songs are praised or blamed matters little to me. But lay a sword on my bier, for I have been a good soldier in the wars of human liberation.

Shelley often expressed his dedication to freedom in similar words.

One of Leonard Woolf's friends and fellow-Socialists was the economic historian Richard Tawney, whose life was also an endless series of committees and campaigns. He was more successful than Woolf because he was mainly concerned to change society in Britain rather than to reorganize the world as a whole; he was responsible for raising the school-leaving age, for extending workers' education, and for fixing minimum wages. His robust faith in Socialism was rooted in his Christianity. In 1929, at the beginning of the great slump, he produced a book on *Equality*, which later had a great influence on my friend Tony Crosland, and through him on a generation of young Socialists in Britain. He starts by describing the problem:

When the gods are unpropitious, the first instinct of the tribe is not to question their power, but to redouble its appeals. It is natural that a nation which has been imbued by its history with the conviction that the secret of success is the elaboration of machinery should suppose that it can extricate itself from its embarrassments by invoking with a heightened devotion the tradition of the elders. Englishmen, it is perhaps true to say, are more noted for business acumen than for intellectual flexibility, and, if tactically bold, are strategically timid. So they approach the closed doors of economic well-being with a flourish of the old key, and are not troubled by doubts whether it will fit the new lock. Accustomed for three generations to the spectacle of prosperity, pouring, as from an

enchanted spring, from technical accomplishment, they are disposed
to take it for granted that the problem which confronts them is the
improvement of technique, without pausing to consider whether
deficiencies of technique may not themselves be a symptom of
more fundamental failings. Nurtured in a belief in the omnipotence
of externals, they are apt to assume that their economic organization
can be adjusted to the needs of an unforeseen situation, without
being disturbed by the question whether the condition of readjust-
ment may not be an alteration in their intellectual outlook, and the
abandonment of certain of the cherished proprieties of their social relations.

His conclusion lays the foundation for the sort of democratic
Socialism for which, with all its imperfections, the Labour Party
stands.

He listens 'to the dialectical battle':

In a world where revolutions, carried out with varying degrees of
violence, treachery, and heroism, are the source whence the most
respectable of states derive their title, to greet with cries of scandal-
ized propriety a diagnosis which refers to them is obviously, he will
say, either naif or insincere. It is like ignoring war, because war is
atrocious, while condoning its causes and hugging its spoils. The
reality of a class struggle in modern society, whatever may be
thought of the theory, is, unhappily, too insistent, and the indignation aroused by the phrase is itself evidence of the fact. But to
suppose that such phenomena are preordained and unavoidable – to
find their source in inexorable historical tendencies, and the laws of
social evolution, and the force of things, instead of in the obvious,
commonplace operations of folly and greed, which can either be
indulged till they bring their nemesis, or chastened and repressed –
is not science, but superstition. It is a piece of solemn, spectacled
mystification, which is analogous to the confidence of the eighteenth
century in the invisible hand of economic self-interest, or to the
belief of the nineteenth in the saving virtues of the struggle for
existence, or to any other of the fetishes that from time to time
have masqueraded as oracles.

Democracy is neither white magic nor black, neither a formula
of easy salvation nor a sanctimonious fraud. It is a tool which, like
any other tool, is to be judged by its results, which, like any other
tool, can be blunted or mishandled till it is flung aside in disgust,
but which can be used to correct inequalities, if there is a will to
correct them, since, in fact, on a humble scale, it has been already so

used. Differences of individual endowment are a biological phenomenon. Contrasts of environment, and inherited wealth, and educational opportunity, and economic security, with the whole sad business of snobbery and servility which such contrasts produce, are the creation, not of nature, but of social convention. They are the work of the lovable, but exasperating animal, man, whose follies are redeemed by his capacity for criticizing them. *Il est plus honteux de se défier de ses amis que d'en être trompé:* it is more contemptible to be intimidated by distrust of human nature than to be duped by believing in it. Men have given one stamp to their institutions; they can give another. They have idealized money and power; they can 'choose' equality.

I do not believe it is possible to sustain the will to change the world, on however small a scale, without some faith which goes beyond the world as seen by science alone. As Yeats wrote in his searing attack on conventional politics, *On the Boiler*: 'Man has made mathematics, but God reality'. That faith found its finest expression this century after the trial of Sacco and Vanzetti.

In 1921 two young Italian immigrants in Massachusetts were arrested and found guilty for a crime they did not commit. Both were anarchists. For six years attempts were made by supporters of civil liberty to prove them innocent. They failed, and the men were finally executed by the electric chair in 1927. After receiving sentence Bartolomeo Vanzetti made the following statement, at once more true and more poetic than Heine's:

If it had not been for these thing, I might have live out my life talking at street corners to scorning men. I might have die, unmarked, unknown, a failure. Now we are not a failure. This is our career and our triumph. Never in our full life could we hope to do such work for tolerance, for joostice, for man's onderstanding of man as now we do by accident. Our words – our lives – our pains – nothing! The taking of our lives – lives of a good shoe-maker and a poor fish-peddler – all! That last moment belongs to us – that agony is our triumph.

5

THE ARTS

For, don't you mark, we're made so that we love
First when we see them painted, things we have passed
Perhaps a hundred times nor cared to see;
And so they are better painted – better to us,
Which is the same thing. Art was given for that;
God uses us to help each other so,
Lending our minds out.
                    – *'Fra Lippo Lippi'*, Robert Browning

Oxford, the war, and politics all taught me the limitations of scientific reason as a guide to human beings. Fortunately I have always found the arts an inexhaustible source, not only of pleasure, but also of knowledge and understanding.

As a little boy of four or five I loved to sit in the tiny garden outside our wooden bungalow near Woolwich, drawing with coloured chalks, and finding inspiration from the saucer in front of me, which was full of glistening white segments of an apple which my mother had 'peeled, cut and cored'.

It was through nursery rhymes that I learned to read at my infant school in Keighley; my love for poetry increased throughout my schooldays.

Music came only a little later, when I took piano lessons in Riddlesden. But my musical education took off when I was at school in Bradford. I heard Eva Turner sing Turandot at the Alhambra theatre with the Carl Rosa Opera; I also heard them give one of the first performances of *Koanga* by the Bradford-born composer Delius. I went to the subscription concerts given by the Hallé Orchestra under Hamilton Harty. I remember vividly how he put the trumpet player in a corridor behind the stage, so that his call in the 'Leonora' overture would sound suitably far away. Many of the greatest musicians of the time – Schnabel, Cortot, Fischer, Szigeti and Huberman – introduced me to concertos from Mozart to Sibelius.

On Fridays I used to race across the road from school to the Church Bookshop to spend my pocket money on colour postcards of paintings by Van Gogh, Monet, Manet and Cézanne. I continued the habit until well after the war; so I have albums full of postcards from galleries all over Europe, from Albi to Amsterdam, from Berlin to Budapest.

The war brought a new stimulus to my love of the arts. In North Africa it was the hot dry Mediterranean air which led me to try translating the Greek poets. Italy inevitably encouraged my love of opera. Butterfly was any Italian girl with a lover in the allied forces, and Tosca was the story of the resistance in Rome. My colonel, Jack Donaldson, who later became a Labour Minister for the Arts, joined me in organizing concerts of chamber music with members of the San Carlo orchestra in Naples. And I was able to enjoy the great paintings of the Renaissance, often in their original settings. Piero della Francesca captivated me when I saw the grave purity of his *Madonna and Child with Angels* at the Palazzo Borghese in Rome, so when we moved north I contrived a special visit to Arezzo to admire his astonishing murals of the Battle of Constantinople. In Tuscany I saw the great Sienese painters for the first time. Most magical of all, on a visit to the Sitwell villa at Montegufoni, I walked into the drawing room and saw Botticelli's *Birth of Venus* illuminated in a shaft of sunlight; it had been moved there for safety from the Uffizi Gallery.

When the war was over, my political duties gave me the chance of hearing operas rarely performed in England, for example Dvořák's *Rusalka* in Prague and Moniusko's *Halka* in Warsaw. Visits to the United States revealed great paintings where I would least have expected them, like the collection of Degas, another life-long passion of mine, at the Norton Simon museum in Pasadena. One of the few compensations for innumerable boring committees on the Common Market in Brussels was a chance to visit the Brueghels at the Musée des Beaux Arts; my role as the Labour

Party's International Secretary had already allowed me to see the stupendous collection of Brueghels in Vienna, where I later made acquaintance with Schiele and Klimt, painters hitherto unknown to me.

As Chancellor of the Exchequer I was able to visit Glyndebourne regularly, and to do my own bit for music by persuading the Italian Finance Minister to help in financing exchange visits between Covent Garden and Milan's La Scala.

All this experience of art not only lightened the burdens I carried as a politician, but also deepened my general understanding and knowledge of the world.

The arts, like politics, change in both style and content with the society around them. You will find it easier to enjoy the arts – and politics – if you understand the nature and causes of these changes. The best teachers are the artists themselves, when they write about their own work or that of other artists. Fortunately many great artists and musicians have been able to express themselves in words as well as in paint or sounds.

Though there are comparatively few periods in which artists and politicians have been intimately associated with one another, painters, architects, poets and composers have often worked closely together, from the Italian Renaissance to the Bloomsbury set, from Inigo Jones to David Hockney.

There is no adequate substitute for looking at pictures and listening to music. That is why I so much enjoy presenting my favourite music in recordings on radio. But since this book is neither an art gallery nor a concert hall, I shall try to communicate my enthusiasm for those arts in words – wherever possible the words of artists.

John Ruskin was deeply concerned with politics and became one of the founders of British socialism. He was also a good draughtsman and watercolour painter. Above all, he was probably the greatest British writer on art; he championed both Turner and the Pre-Raphaelites before they were generally accepted. At the end of his life he wrote his autobiography, *Praeterita*. He admits that he might never have written the second volume of his masterpiece, *Modern Painters*, if he had read the lectures on moral philosophy given twenty years earlier by Sydney Smith, who is generally remembered simply as a clerical wit. Ruskin quotes the following passage as an example of 'the most wise, because most noble thought, and most impressive, because steel-true language to be found'; it is concerned as much with knowledge of the arts as with any other form of knowledge:

> But while I am descanting so minutely upon the conduct of the understanding, and the best modes of acquiring knowledge, some men may be disposed to ask, 'Why conduct my understanding with such endless care? and what is the use of so much knowledge?' What is the use of so much knowledge? – what is the use of so much life! What are we to do with the seventy years of existence allotted to us? and how are we to live them out to the last? I solemnly declare that, but for the love of knowledge, I should consider the life of the meanest hedger and ditcher as preferable to that of the greatest and richest man here present: for the fire of our minds is like the fire which the Persians burn in the mountains, – it flames night and day, and is immortal, and not to be quenched! Upon something it *must* act and feed, – upon the pure spirit of knowledge, or upon the foul dregs of polluting passions. Therefore, when I say, in conducting your understanding, love knowledge with a great love, with a vehement love, with a love coeval with life, what do I say, but love innocence, love virtue, love purity of conduct, love that which, if you are rich and great, will sanctify the blind fortune which has made you so, and make men call it justice; love that which, if you are poor, will render your poverty respectable, and make the proudest feel it unjust to laugh at the meanness of your fortunes; love that which will comfort you, adorn you, and never quit you, – which will open to you the kingdom of thought, and all the boundless regions of conception, as an asylum against the cruelty, the injustice, and the pain that may be your lot in the outer world.

A surprising number of the people I have met in public life have also been invigorated by the arts. Ted Heath and Helmut Schmidt both play the organ and the piano. Enoch Powell, Grey Gowrie and Norman Willis write poetry. Sir Patrick Nairne, who was my private secretary at the Ministry of Defence, is an accomplished painter in watercolours. Even the dismal science of economics is sometimes illuminated by music: the banker Jim Wolfensohn is a good cellist, and that most uncomfortable thorn in every recent Chancellor's flesh, Wynne Godley, plays the oboe. Maynard Keynes and Arthur Cockfield both married ballet dancers.

However, it is unusual nowadays to find a creative artist actively engaged in public life. It was not always so. Dante was exiled from Florence for his political activities. His contemporary, Giotto, the

father of Renaissance painting, was so active in business that he
had to employ a horde of lawyers; his frescoes in the Scrovegni
chapel at Padua are among the greatest works of Christian art –
but they were painted to commemorate a notorious money-lender.
Chaucer, the father of English poetry, served King Edward III
both as a diplomat and comptroller of the customs. Rubens acted
as a diplomat for the Spanish Hapsburgs in the Low Countries.
Andrew Marvell was MP for Hull, where three centuries later
another poet, Philip Larkin, was librarian. Sheridan was MP for
Stafford, Undersecretary for Foreign Affairs, and later Treasurer of
the Navy.

Although many artists took part in the revolutions of 1830 and
1848, this type of connection between the arts and public life had
greatly diminished by the end of the nineteenth century. Van
Gogh spoke for many of his fellows when he complained:

> Giotto and Cimabue, as well as Holbein and Van Dyck, lived in an
> obeliscal solidly-framed society, architecturally constructed, in
> which each individual was a stone and all the stones clung together,
> forming a monumental society. . . . But, you know, we are in the
> midst of downright *laisser-aller* and anarchy. We artists who love
> order and symmetry isolate ourselves and are working to define
> *only one thing*. . . . We *can* paint an atom of the chaos, a horse, a
> portrait, your grandmother, apples, a landscape. . . .
>
>   We do not feel that we are dying, but we do feel the truth that
> we are of small account, and that we are paying a hard price to be a
> link in the chain of artists, in health, in youth, in liberty, none of
> which we enjoy, any more than the cab-horse that hauls a coachful
> of people out to enjoy the spring.

The comparatively recent gulf between the arts and politics is due
in part to the greater complexity of modern life and the explosion
of knowledge, both of which tend to compel people to narrow
their field of interest. It is also due in part to the heavy burdens
which fall on a politician in a modern democracy. Nowadays it
seems possible for an artist to be a politician only during and after
a revolution. The pianist Paderewski became President of Poland
when it became independent after the First World War. The
writer Vaclav Havel became President of Czechoslovakia in 1989,
and a little later the musicologist Landsbergis became President of
Lithuania.

Indeed the pattern was set by William Butler Yeats in a small way, when he became a Senator in the newly formed Republic of Ireland, and even served as Chairman of the Committee of the Coinage – a link of which I was inordinately proud when, as Chancellor of the Exchequer, I was Master of the Mint in Britain. To Yeats, however, even poetry required an excessive involvement in public life once it was published and began to make money. I imagine he was thinking of himself when he wrote:

> Toil and grow rich
> What's that but to lie
> With a foul witch
> And after, drained dry
> To be brought
> To the chamber where
> Lies one long sought
> With despair.

Wystan Auden, who was deeply political in his early years as a poet, later turned against politics because he claimed that politics denied the importance of the individual. But he remained acutely sensitive to the politician in every poet. He wrote in *The Dyer's Hand*:

Every British or American poet will agree that Winston Churchill is a greater figure than Charles II, but he will also know that he could not write a good poem on Churchill, while Dryden had no difficulty in writing a good poem on Charles. To write a good poem on Churchill, a poet would have to know Winston Churchill intimately, and his poem would be about the man, not about the Prime Minister. All attempts to write about persons or events, however important, to which the poet is not intimately related in a personal way are now doomed to failure. Yeats could write great poetry about the Troubles in Ireland, because most of the protagonists were known to him personally and the places where the events occurred had been familiar to him since childhood.

Every age is one-sided in its political and social preoccupation and in seeking to realize the particular value it esteems most highly, it neglects and even sacrifices other values. The relation of a poet, or any artist, to society and politics is, except in Africa or still backward semifeudal countries, more difficult than it has ever been because, while he cannot but approve of the importance of *everybody* getting enough food to eat and enough leisure, this problem has nothing whatever to do with art, which is concerned with *singular persons*, as they are alone and as they are in their personal relations. Since these interests are not the predominant ones in his society; indeed, in so far as it thinks about them at all, it is with suspicion and latent hostility – it secretly or openly thinks that the claim that one is a singular person, or a demand for privacy, is putting on airs, a claim to be superior to other folk – every artist feels himself at odds with modern civilization.

In our age, the mere making of a work of art is itself a political act. So long as artists exist, making what they please and think they ought to make, even if it is not terribly good, even if it appeals to only a handful of people, they remind the Management of something managers need to be reminded of, namely, that the managed are people with faces, not anonymous members, that *Homo Laborans* is also *Homo Ludens*.

Poets are, by the nature of their interests and the nature of artistic fabrication, singularly ill-equipped to understand politics or economics. Their natural interest is in singular individuals and personal relations, while politics and economics are concerned with large numbers of people, hence with the human average (the poet is bored to death by the idea of the Common Man) and with impersonal, to a great extent involuntary, relations. The poet cannot understand the function of money in modern society because for him there is no relation between subjective value and market value; he may be paid ten pounds for a poem which he believes is very good and took him months to write, and a hundred pounds for a piece of journalism which costs him but a day's work. If he is a successful poet – though few poets make enough money to be called successful in the way that a novelist or playwright can – he is a member of the Manchester school and believes in absolute *laisser-faire*; if he is unsuccessful and embittered, he is liable to combine aggressive fantasies about the annihilation of the present order with impractical daydreams of Utopia. Society has always to beware of the utopias being planned by artists *manqués* over cafeteria tables late at night.

All poets adore explosions, thunderstorms, tornadoes, conflagrations, ruins, scenes of spectacular carnage. The poetic imagination is not at all a desirable quality in a statesman.

The true men of action in our time, those who transform the world, are not the politicians and statesmen, but the scientists. Unfortunately poetry cannot celebrate them because their deeds are concerned with things, not persons, and are, therefore, speechless.

When I find myself in the company of scientists, I feel like a shabby curate who has strayed by mistake into a drawing room full of dukes.

I would not wish more artists to turn politician, or even to attempt to convey a political message, unless they feel deeply that they must. Politics should be a vocation, like art itself. But I would encourage every politician to cherish a love for art, if only as an escape from the element of drudgery in politics, and as a protection against the temptation to see society solely in terms of statistics. The individual must lie at the heart of all political action. That is why I believe it is so important for a politician to represent a constituency in which he is responsible for helping individuals – perhaps the most rewarding of all his roles. For the same reason I am reluctant to embrace any form of proportional representation which depends on national lists of candidates, and breaks the link with constituencies as we know it in Britain.

In earlier times the distinction between the various arts and branches of knowledge was also less rigid. Michelangelo was not only a sculptor, painter, and architect, but also a major poet; his sonnets have a clarity of meaning and density of texture comparable with those of Donne and Hopkins. Leonardo da Vinci was not only a master of all the visual arts, but also a leading scientist and engineer. When he offered his services to Ludovico Sforza, the ruler of Milan, he put his skills as an artist last, almost as a footnote to his inventions in military technology:

> My Most Illustrious Lord, having now sufficiently seen and considered the achievements of all those who count themselves masters and artificers of instruments of war, and having noted that the invention and performance of the said instruments is in no way different from that in common usage, I shall endeavour, while intending no discredit to anyone else to bring myself to the attention of Your Excellency for the purpose of unfolding to you my secrets, and thereafter offering them at your complete disposal, and when the time is right bringing into effective operation all those things which are in part briefly listed below:

> 1. I have plans for very light, strong and easily portable bridges with which to pursue and, on some occasions, flee the enemy, and others, sturdy and indestructible either by fire or in battle, easy and convenient to lift and place in position. Also means of burning and destroying those of the enemy.

After running through another eight fields of military technology he concludes his letter:

10. In time of peace I believe I can give as complete satisfaction as any other in the field of architecture, and the construction of both public and private buildings, and in conducting water from one place to another.

Also I can execute sculpture in marble, bronze and clay. Likewise in painting I can do everything possible as well as any other, whosoever he may be.

Moreover, work could be undertaken on the bronze horse which will be to the immortal glory and eternal honour of the auspicious memory of His Lordship your father, and of the illustrious house of Sforza.

And if any of the above-mentioned things seems impossible or impracticable to anyone, I am most readily disposed to demonstrate them in your park or in whatever place shall please Your Excellency, to whom I commend myself with all possible humility.

Leonardo did not distinguish between art and science. His motto was *saper vedere* – one of those untranslatable phrases which implies both 'knowing how to see' and 'getting knowledge from seeing'. Much art is easier to appreciate if you know something about the artist as a human being. Very little about the personalities of the artists of ancient times has come down to us. In the case of most of the great sculpture and painting of Egypt and Asia we do not know even the artists' names. Whether Homer was a man, a woman, or a group of people is still the subject of academic argument. Practically the only story about Aeschylus which has survived is that he was killed when an eagle dropped a tortoise on his bald head – and that was probably made up!

Even William Shakespeare is almost unknown to us except through his works. So the Germans can call him 'Unser Shakespeare', the French can imagine that his real name was 'Jacques Père', and in modern times Colonel Gaddafi has claimed him as an Arab called 'Sheikh Spear'! Even in his native England there have been arguments about the identity of Shakespeare. At one time it was fashionable to claim that his works were written by Francis Bacon. As I was revising this book I came across two more theories about Shakespeare. The technology correspondent of *The Times* reported that an American consultant had carried out a computerized analysis of the Shakespeare portrait in the First Folio of his works, and discovered a striking resemblance to a painting of Queen Elizabeth I; it was a small step to speculating that the Queen may have helped to write his plays!

Scarcely less bizarre was a book by the Poet Laureate, Ted Hughes, called *Shakespeare and the Goddess of Complete Being*. Hughes presents Shakespeare as a shaman of Old Catholicism who turned into 'a prophetic shaman of the Puritan revolution', as illustrated by the contrast between *The Rape of Lucrece* and *Venus and Adonis*. Hughes' fellow-poet Tom Paulin, who is also a brilliant literary critic, explains his 'batty syncretism' as 'an epic prose poem born out of the experience of Thatcherism', and admires 'the stink of its Protestant guilt'. Great fun! The Argentinian writer Jorge Luís Borges has perhaps the last word on Shakespeare. He tells a parable in which Shakespeare at the end of his life found himself in the presence of God and told him:

'I who have been so many men in vain want to be one and myself.' The voice of God answered from a whirlwind: 'Neither am I anyone: I have dreamt the world as you dreamt your work, my Shakespeare, and among the forms in my dreams are you, who like myself are many and no one.'

Vasari wrote the lives of the great artists of the Italian Renaissance and Cellini, of course, wrote a brilliant account of his own career. The personality of the artist, however, did not become the subject of major interest until, towards the end of the eighteenth century, artists began to cultivate personalities which would set them apart from the common herd. They began to write their memoirs, and to arrange for their letters and diaries to be published. Moreover they began to write about one another, with an insight denied to those who have not shared the same experience of creation.

Indeed, even the baroque extravagance of Ted Hughes on Shakespeare reminds us that poets inhabit a world in which the creative stimulus of one poet's phrase can explode centuries later in a completely different type of poet. Sometimes I wish that politicians could communicate as productively.

Milton described Shakespeare's 'native wood-notes wild' and Wordsworth wrote a sonnet to Milton which is all too relevant today:

Milton! thou shouldst be living at this hour:
England hath need of thee: she is a fen
Of stagnant waters: altar, sword, and pen,
Fireside, the heroic wealth of hall and bower,
Have forfeited their ancient English dower

Of inward happiness. We are selfish men;
Oh! raise us up, return to us again;
And give us manners, virtue, freedom, power.
Thy soul was like a Star, and dwelt apart;
Thou hadst a voice whose sound was like the sea:
Pure as the naked heavens, majestic, free,
So didst thou travel on life's common way,
In cheerful godliness; and yet thy heart
The lowliest duties on herself did lay.

Blake also wrote a long poem about Milton, but he was more concerned with Milton's philosophy than with his poetry; he regarded him as being 'of the Devil's party without knowing it'. In my opinion, the greatest of all attempts by one poet to describe another's poetry is Heinrich Heine's coruscating description of the old German epic, the *Nibelungenlied*, on which Wagner based *The Ring*; he also comments on the anonymity of much great art:

This *Nibelungenlied* is a great and mighty poem. A Frenchman can hardly form an idea of it, or even of the language in which it is written. Its language is as of stone, and its verses are metrical granite blocks. Here and there, in the clefts, red flowers break forth, like drops of blood, or long ivy trails like green trickles of tears. You dainty little people can scarcely conceive the massive passions which inspire this poem. Imagine a clear summer night. The stars are silver-bright, but huge as the sun, they come forth in the blue heavens. Imagine all the Gothic cathedrals of Europe meeting at a rendezvous on a large plain. Imagine the Cathedral of Strassburg advancing calmly; then the Cathedral of Cologne, the Campanile of Florence, of Rouen, etc. And they are gallantly courting beautiful Notre Dame de Paris. It is true that their gait is somewhat unsteady; some of them are ungainly. Their amorous awkwardness is amusing. But our laughter dies when we see them falling into a passion, and proceeding to strangle each other. Notre Dame, in despair, stretches her two arms of stone toward heaven, and then suddenly taking hold of a sword, beheads the grandest of all the cathedrals. No. Even you can have no idea of the principal characters of the *Nibelungenlied*. No tower is so high, and no stone so hard as grim Hagen and vindictive Kriemhilde.

But who wrote the poem? We know that as little as we know the names of the authors of our folksongs. It is strange that we so seldom know the originators of the most admirable books, poems, buildings, and other monuments of art. What builder devised the

Cathedral of Cologne? Who painted the altar piece there, on which the lovely Mother of God is so engagingly depicted with the Three Holy Kings? Who composed the Book of Job, which has comforted so many generations of suffering humanity? Man all too soon forgets the names of his benefactors. The good and noble who have toiled for the weal of their fellow-men are seldom on the lips of the people, whose weak memory retains only the names of their oppressors and cruel warrior-heroes. The tree of humanity is forgetful of the silent gardener who protected it against the cold, watered it when it was dry, and defended it against harmful creatures. But it faithfully retains the names which have mercilessly been engraved in its bark with sharp steel, and transmits them – ever greater – to succeeding generations.

A few years after Charlotte Brontë died Emily Dickinson, her spiritual sister, wrote her an epitaph from three thousand miles away:

> All overgrown by cunning moss,
> All interspersed with weed,
> The little cage of 'Curser Bell'
> In quiet 'Haworth' laid.
>
> Gathered from many wanderings –
> Gethsemane can tell
> Thro' what transporting anguish
> She reached the Asphodel!
>
> Soft fall the sounds of Eden
> Upon her puzzled ear –
> Oh what an afternoon for Heaven
> When 'Bronte' entered there.

Tennyson described some of his contemporaries as 'lice on the locks of poetry'. Poets of our own age have been kinder to their colleagues. In February 1939, a month after Yeats died, and on the eve of the Second World War, Auden paid him this tribute:

> I
> He disappeared in the dead of winter:
> The brooks were frozen, the airports almost deserted.
> And snow disfigured the public statues;
> The mercury sank in the mouth of the dying day.
> What instruments we have agree.
> The day of his death was a dark cold day.

Far from his illness
The wolves ran on through the evergreen forests,
The peasant river was untempted by the fashionable quays;
By mourning tongues
The death of the poet was kept from his poems.

But for him it was his last afternoon as himself,
An afternoon of nurses and rumours;
The provinces of his body revolted.
The squares of his mind were empty,
Silence invaded the suburbs,
The current of his feeling failed; he became his admirers.

Now he is scattered among a hundred cities
And wholly given over to unfamiliar affections.
To find his happiness in another kind of wood
And be punished under a foreign code of conscience.
The words of a dead man
Are modified in the guts of the living.

But in the importance of noise of to-morrow
When the brokers are roaring like beasts on the floor of the Bourse.
And the poor have the sufferings to which they are fairly
    accustomed.
And each in the cell of himself is almost convinced of his freedom.
A few thousand will think of this day
As one thinks of a day when one did something slightly unusual.
What instruments we have agree
The day of his death was a dark cold day.

II

You were silly like us; your gift survived it all:
The parish of rich women, physical decay,
Yourself. Mad Ireland hurt you into poetry.
Now Ireland has her madness and her weather still,
For poetry makes nothing happen: it survives
In the valley of its making where executives
Would never want to tamper, flows on south
From ranches of isolation and the busy griefs,
Raw towns that we believe and die in: it survives,
A way of happening, a mouth.

III

Earth, receive an honoured guest:
William Yeats is laid to rest
Let the Irish vessel lie
Emptied of its poetry.

In the nightmare of the dark
All the dogs of Europe bark,
And the living nations wait,
Each sequestered in its hate;

Intellectual disgrace
Stares from every human face,
And the seas of pity lie
Locked and frozen in each eye.

Follow, poet, follow right
To the bottom of the night,
With your unconstraining voice
Still persuade us to rejoice;

With the farming of a verse
Make a vineyard of the curse,
Sing of human unsuccess
In a rapture of distress;

In the deserts of the heart
Let the healing fountain start,
In the prison of his days
Teach the free man how to praise.

Sidney Keyes died as a prisoner of war before he reached the age of twenty-one. Before he joined the army, at the age of nineteen, he wrote this poem about Wordsworth:

No room for mourning: he's gone out
Into the noisy glen, or stands between the stones
Of the gaunt ridge, or you'll hear his shout
Rolling among the screes, he being a boy again.
He'll never fail nor die
And if they laid his bones
In the wet vaults or iron sarcophagi
Of fame, he'd rise at the first summer rain
And stride across the hills to seek
His rest among the broken lands and clouds.
He was a stormy day, a granite peak
Spearing the sky; and look, about its base
Words flower like crocuses in the hanging woods,
Blank though the dalehead and the bony face.

Very recently Seamus Heaney gave us this posthumous comment on Philip Larkin:

Larkin's shade surprised me. He quoted Dante:

Daylight was going and the umber air
Soothing every creature on the earth,
Freeing them from their labours everywhere.

I alone was girding myself to face
The ordeal of my journey and my duty
And not a thing had changed, as rush-hour buses

Bore the drained and laden through the city.
I might have been a wise king setting out
Under the Christmas lights – except that

It felt more like the forewarned journey back
Into the heartland of the ordinary.
Still my old self. Ready to knock one back.

A nine-to-five man who had seen poetry.

A.E. Housman wrote *The Shropshire Lad*, a nostalgic cycle of pastoral elegies which commemorates his early love for another young man. In his later role as Professor of Latin he could be savage and cantankerous. Although he gave it towards the end of his life, his lecture on 'The Name and Nature of Poetry' recalls his earlier sensitivity; nevertheless some of his generalizations are preposterous, particularly on William Blake. By distinguishing between verse and poetry he is able to exclude most of the eighteenth century from his canon. He quotes Coleridge with approval: 'Poetry gives most pleasure when only generally and not perfectly understood.' Housman himself asserts roundly: 'Meaning is of the intellect, poetry is not . . . Even Shakespeare, who had so much to say, would sometimes pour out his loveliest poetry in saying nothing.

Take O take those lips away
　That so sweetly were forsworn,
And those eyes, the break of day,
　Lights that do mislead the morn;
But my kisses bring again,
　　　　　　　bring again,
Seals of love, but seal'd in vain,
　　　　　　　seal'd in vain.

That is nonsense, but it is ravishing poetry.'

Housman quotes the six simple words of Milton – 'Nymphs and shepherds, dance no more' – and asks 'what is it that can draw tears, as I know it can?' adding

Poetry indeed seems to me more physical than intellectual ...
Experience has taught me, when I am shaving of a morning, to
keep watch over my thoughts, because, if a line of poetry strays
into my memory, my skin bristles so that the razor ceases to act.
This particular symptom is accompanied by a shiver down the
spine; there is another which consists in a constriction of the throat
and a precipitation of water to the eyes.

Emily Dickinson told her friend Colonel Higginson: 'If I read a book and it makes my whole body so cold no fire can ever warm me, I know that is poetry. If I feel physically as if the top of my head were taken off, I know that is poetry.' For me, tears are an infallible proof.

I was over seventy when I first read Emily Dickinson's poems in full, though I had been immensely impressed by the handful of poems which appeared in anthologies, particularly:

Safe in their Alabaster Chambers –
Untouched by Morning –
And untouched by Noon –
Lie the meek members of the Resurrection –
Rafter of Satin – and Roof of Stone!

Grand go the Years – in the Crescent – above them –
Worlds scoop their Arcs –
And Firmaments – row –
Diadems – drop – and Doges – surrender –
Soundless as dots – on a Disc of Snow –

She is now recognized as one of the major poets of the English language, yet she was known in her lifetime only to a small circle of her friends. Her complete poems were first published in 1955, nearly seventy years after she died at the age of fifty-five. In her last twenty years she dressed only in white and scarcely ever moved outside the confines of her house and garden in the country town of Amherst, Massachusetts; even then she would usually hide in her bedroom when visitors called.

She explained her reluctance to have her poems published many
times:

>Publication – is the Auction
>Of the Mind of Man –
>Poverty – be justifying
>For so foul a thing
>
>Possibly – but We – would rather
>From Our Garret go
>White – Unto the White Creator –
>Than invest – Our Snow –
>
>Thought belong to Him who gave it –
>Then – to Him Who bear
>
>Its Corporeal illustration – Sell
>The Royal Air –
>
>In the Parcel – Be the Merchant
>Of the Heavenly Grace –
>But reduce no Human Spirit
>To Disgrace of Price –

*

>To see the Summer Sky
>Is Poetry, though never in a Book it lie –
>True Poems flee –

*

>Fame is a fickle food
>Upon a shifting plate
>Whose table once a
>Guest but not
>The second time is set.
>
>Whose crumbs the crows inspect
>And with ironic caw
>Flap past it to the
>Farmer's Corn –
>Men eat of it and die.

*

>Fame is a bee.
>   It has a song –
>It has a sting –
>   Ah, too, it has a wing.

Yet she craved for approval from those whose judgment she could respect, like Colonel Thomas Wentworth Higginson, who had written an article of advice to young poets in the *Atlantic Monthly*, and her fellow poet Helen Hunt Jackson. What little we know of her appearance we owe to these friends. Apologizing that she had no photograph to send him, she told Higginson: 'I am small like the Wren, and my hair is bold, like the Chestnut Burr, and my eyes, like the Sherry in the Glass, that the Guest leaves.'

When he was finally able to meet her in Amherst, Higginson describes

> a step like a pattering child's in entry and in glided a little plain woman with two smooth bands of reddish hair . . . in a very plain and exquisitely clean white piqué and a blue net worsted shawl. She came to me with two day lilies, which she put in a sort of childlike way into my hand and said 'These are my introduction' in a soft frightened breathless childlike voice.

Helen Jackson wrote to her:

> Truly you seemed so white and mothlike (and) your hand felt like such a wisp in mine – I felt like a great ox, talking to a white moth and begging it to come and eat grass with me to see if it could turn itself into beef!

Yet this frail husk concealed one of the most powerful and active intellects in poetry, with an extraordinary range of understanding. Emily Dickinson's verse always has meaning – contrary to Housman's preference – but it is also sublime poetry. Often her letters are poetry too, since she was incapable of avoiding the rhythm and imagery of poetry in anything she wrote:

> They shut me up in Prose –
> As when a little Girl
> They put me in the Closet –
> Because they liked me 'still' –
>
> Still! Could themself have peeped –
> And seen my Brain – go round –
> They might as wise have lodged a Bird
> For Treason – in the Pound –

> Himself has but to will
> And easy as a Star
> Abolish his Captivity —
> And laugh — No more have I —

She avoided excessive clarity:

> Tell all the Truth but tell it slant —
> Success in Circuit lies
> Too bright for our infirm Delight
> The Truth's superb surprise
>
> As Lightning to the Children eased
> With explanation kind
> The Truth must dazzle gradually
> Or every man be blind —

She felt that too much eagerness for truth can not only blind, but also breed disaster or despair:

> A Word dropped careless on a Page
> May stimulate an eye
> When folded in perpetual seam
> The Wrinkled Maker lie
>
> Infection in the sentence breeds
> We may inhale Despair
> At distances of Centuries
> From the Malaria —
>
> *
>
> I stepped from Plank to Plank
> A slow and cautious way
> The Stars about my Head I felt
> About my Feet the Sea.
>
> I knew not but the next
> Would be my final inch —
>
> This gave me that precarious Gait
> Some call Experience.

Like Virginia Woolf, whom she so much resembles, she found politics boring and even meaningless. In October 1870, when the Germans were besieging Paris, she wrote to a friend:

Life is the finest secret . . . How lonesome to be an article! I mean –
to have no soul. An Apple fell in the night and a Wagon stopped. I
suppose the Wagon ate the Apple and resumed its way. How fine
it is to talk. What Miracles the news is! Not Bismarck but ourselves.

Yet, again like Virginia Woolf, she could show a malicious wit
when writing about her own circle:

Mrs – re-decided to come with her son Elizabeth. Aunt Lucretia
shouldered arms. I think they lie in my memory, a muffin and a
bomb. Now they are gone and the crickets are pleased. Their
bombazine reproof still falls upon the twilight, and checks the
softer uproars of the departing day.

She wrote about some other acquaintances:

> What Soft – Cherubic Creatures –
> These Gentlewomen are –
> One would as soon assault a Plush –
> Or violate a Star –
>
> Such Dimity Convictions –
> A Horror so refined
> Of freckled Human Nature –
> Of Deity – ashamed –
>
> It's such a common – Glory –
> A Fisherman's – Degree –
> Redemption – Brittle Lady –
> Be so – ashamed of Thee –

The intensity of her imagination owes much to her self-imposed
exile from society. She did not spend her spiritual energy on
meeting any but her closest friends, and then it was normally by
letter rather than physical contact. Yet she read widely, particularly
other woman poets such as Charlotte Brontë and Christina Rossetti, and could press anything she read in the newspapers or
magazines into the service of her poetry.

Reading Emily Dickinson's life, I am often reminded of the
little old lady in Buckden, where Edna and I spent our honeymoon,
who used to disturb us by appearing with a candle through the
trapdoor into the loft where we slept, to read us her poems. The
arts produce many eccentrics, and not a few who escape from the

pressure into madness. As Shakespeare wrote: 'the lunatic, the lover, and the poet are of imagination all compact.' The intensity of feeling required for great art too easily overstrains the mind. John Clare and Virginia Woolf had periods of madness. William Blake saw three-dimensional visions in front of him. Van Gogh spent his last years painting some of his greatest pictures in an asylum.

It is possible to show how a poem achieves its effects, through the choice of words, sound and rhythm. Edith Sitwell, herself a good poet, did this well. William Empson, another poet, showed in *The Seven Types of Ambiguity* how poetry is enriched by the use of words which have multiple meanings or associations. But it is not possible to learn the art of poetry. As Gerard Manley Hopkins wrote while still an undergraduate:

> It is a happy thing that there is no royal road to poetry. The world should know by this time that one cannot reach Parnassus except by flying thither. Yet from time to time more men go up and either perish in its gullies fluttering 'excelsior' flags or else come down again with full folios and blank countenances. Yet the old fallacy keeps its ground.

Dylan Thomas gave the following advice to a young woman who asked him about the art of poetry:

> Read the poems you like reading. Don't bother whether they're important, or if they'll live. What does it matter what poetry *is*, after all? If you want a definition of poetry, say: 'Poetry is what makes me laugh or cry or yawn, what makes my toenails twinkle, what makes me want to do this or that or nothing,' and let it go at that. All that matters about poetry is the enjoyment of it, however tragic it may be. All that matters is the eternal movement behind it, the vast under-current of human grief, folly, pretension, exaltation, or ignorance, however unlofty the intention of the poem.'
>
> You can tear a poem apart to see what makes it technically tick, and say to yourself, when the works are laid out before you, the vowels, the consonants, the rhymes and rhythms, 'Yes, this is *it*. This is why the poem moves me so. It is because of the craftsmanship.' But you're back again where you began. You're back with the mystery of having been moved by words. The best craftsmanship always leaves holes and gaps in the works of the poem so that something that is *not* in the poem can creep, crawl, flash, or thunder in.

The joy and function of poetry is, and was, the celebration of man, which is also the celebration of God.

Let me conclude this passage on poetry as an art with a poem by William Blake, whom Housman believed to be superior even to Shakespeare for giving us poetry 'neat, or adulterated with so little meaning that nothing except poetic emotion is perceived and matters' – a compliment which Blake himself would have rejected with outrage since most of his poems are explicitly didactic:

> O Rose, thou art sick!
> The invisible worm,
> That flies in the night,
> In the howling storm,
>
> Has found out thy bed
> Of crimson joy;
> And his dark secret love
> Does thy life destroy.

Poetry exists outside space and time, although it draws its images from both. Thomas Lovell Beddoes, for example, who started writing at the end of Blake's life, was fascinated by time:

> Why what's the world and time? a fleeting thought
> In the great meditating universe,
> A brief parenthesis in chaos.

He brings me to my next theme:

> I begin to hear
> Strange but sweet sounds, and the loud rocky dashing
> Of waves, where time into Eternity
> Falls over ruined worlds

Music, as Auden wrote, is 'the best means we have of digesting time'. It exists in time alone, and has nothing to do with either space or knowledge in the scientific sense; though many scientists, like Einstein, see it as a bridge between the world of the senses and a pure science, like mathematics.

Yet no other art has the same power to excite our emotions. Thus, while Samuel Johnson said that 'music is the only sensual pleasure without vice', Bernard Shaw could describe it as 'the brandy of the damned'. I find it more deeply charged with spiritual meaning than any of the other arts.

One of the prices I paid for being a busy politician is that I had no time to practise on my piano. My capacity for reading piano music seems to improve with age, even after long periods without playing. But the piano does depend on continual practice. At my best, I could stagger through Bach, Haydn, Mozart and Beethoven, as well as the easier romantic compositions of Chopin and Brahms. Nowadays my fingers stubbornly refuse to obey my eyes, and too often I cannot even enjoy my own playing – I long ago gave up the idea of pleasing others!

However, I listen to music more than ever. I bought a Sony Walkman in Minneapolis when they were first produced, and have never since been without a miniature cassette player. So I regularly listen to music in the train, and to the cassette player in my car. It is difficult to imagine that recorded music was practically unknown before I was born; nowadays almost everything which was ever composed is available in the best performances recorded since the First World War, at the price of a round of drinks. I look back with longing on the days when I could sneak out of the Ministry of Defence at lunch-time to buy Saga or Supraphon records for seven and sixpence at Waterloo station across the Thames. But the drinks were cheaper then as well.

Thanks to modern technology, classical music is still growing in popularity. Two thirds of the 225,000 sales of Nigel Kennedy's interpretation of Vivaldi's *Four Seasons* went to people who had no other classical recordings at all. It is difficult to justify complaints about Nigel Kennedy's punk hairstyle and demotic speech if they contribute to the diffusion of good music. I first met Kennedy myself on the television programme *Face the Music* and found him deeply serious, with an attractive innocence. Although no doubt his promoters have encouraged his recent change of image, I cannot help feeling that it must have started, at least, as an attempt to recover the years of a normal adolescence, which he had lost in practising his violin.

The arts are a taskmaster at least as hard as politics. Musicians of all types have as little spare time as members of Parliament, and, as they rise in their profession, they tend to travel as much as ministers. The consequent toll levied on their families is equally heavy.

One of my greatest delights is to watch young musicians playing in their annual competitions or learning from more experienced musicians in a television master class. They gave me some hours of blessed relief from the rigours of the 1992 Election. Even an amateur like myself can learn more from such programmes than from a lifetime of reading about music. I also enormously enjoy putting together my own collections of music for radio programmes, and make time to accept such invitations, however busy I am with politics. Indeed this book would serve its purpose far better if it included good performances of music as well. Technology may well make that possible within my lifetime. Meanwhile, I have to be content with exploring music through the writing, not only of musicians, but of other artists, since, like painting and poetry, music is essentially a means of self–expression. Mozart told his father:

> I do not know how to write poetically, I am no poet. I do not know how to distribute my phrases so that they cast shadows and light, I am no painter. Nor do I know how to express my feelings, my thoughts with gestures and mime, I am no dancer. But I can do all this with notes, because I am a musician.

The great art critic, Max J. Friedlander, recognized that all the arts are kin:

> The arts have a common root, are interconnected in the depths: poetry, music, and the arts of the eye. Whoever is bound to convey by word the impression of a picture or a piece of sculpture, finds himself impelled towards poetical expression, while his intelligence cautions him to avoid poetry. Not wholly unjustifiably it has been said by somebody that one ought to be musical in order fully to understand formative art. There is some truth in this sweeping maxim inasmuch as music, in preference to all other arts, is absolute art.

Most poets have loved music, and have succeeded in expressing their feeling well. John Milton describes one sort of music in 'L'Allegro':

> Lap me in soft Lydian airs
> Married to immortal verse
> Such as the meeting soul may pierce
> In notes, with many a winding bout

> Of linkèd sweetness long drawn out,
> With wanton heed and giddy cunning,
> The melting voice through mazes running;
> Untwisting all the chains that ty
> The hidden soul of harmony.

In 'Il Penseroso' Milton evokes another sort of music:

> There let the pealing Organ blow,
> To the full voic'd Quire below,
> In Service high, and Anthems cleer
> As may with sweetness, through mine ear
> Dissolve me into extasies,

Shakespeare has Olivia remind us of the cloying power of music:

> If music be the food of love, play on:
> Give me excess of it, that, surfeiting,
> The appetite may sicken, and so die.
> That strain again! It hath a dying fall:
> O! It came o'er my ear like the sweet sound
> That breathes upon a bank of violets,
> Stealing and giving odour! Enough! no more:
> 'Tis not so sweet now as it was before.

Yet Shelley made a more important point:

> Music when soft voices die
> Vibrates in the memory.

Whenever I am not thinking about anything, I have some piece of music going through my head – sometimes quite irrelevant to my situation at the time, sometimes inspired by circumstance or memory. Noël Coward speaks for all of us when he has Amanda say in *Private Lives*: 'Extraordinary how potent cheap music is.'

Music has a unique power of conjuring up past experience. I find the folk music of foreign countries an infallible means of recreating their cultural atmosphere. So when I go abroad I try to bring back one or two records of the local music, to play when I watch my colour slides.

The mixture of music with poetry in song or opera is an art in itself. In the songs of Schubert and Richard Strauss the poetry is sometimes as good as the music – 'Who is Sylvia', for example. Opera libretti, however, are notoriously inferior to the music they serve; it is the plot and situation rather than the poetry which matters – except in a few cases like Hugo von Hofmannstahl's libretti for *Rosenkavalier* and *Arabella*. Even Boito had to mangle Shakespeare's poetry a little in translation to fit the supreme music of Verdi in *Otello* and *Falstaff*.

A marriage of equals is, however, achieved more easily in less ambitious works like Weill's settings of Brecht, and the cabaret songs written by Jacques Prevert and put to music by Kosma – especially when sung by the young Yves Montand; *Barbara* still brings tears to my eyes with its evocation of wartime France. Indeed cabaret songs are new art forms, like the musical comedies of Gershwin, Bernstein and Werner and Lowe.

The Elizabethan poets wrote wonderful songs, which have challenged composers of many ages besides their own. Ben Jonson, like Campion, wrote at least one song which almost creates its own music:

> Slow, slow, fresh fount, keep time with my salt tears;
>   Yet slower yet, oh faintly, gentle springs;
> List to the heavy part the music bears,
>   Woe weeps out her division when she sings.
>   Droop herbs and flowers,
>   Fall grief in showers;
>   Our beauties are not ours;
>   Oh, I could still
> (Like melting snow upon some craggy hill)
>   Drop, drop, drop, drop,
> Since nature's pride is, now, a withered daffodil.

In the nineteenth century contact between the arts was as close as at any time in history. Heine wrote with his infallible verve about Berlioz, Liszt, and above all, Chopin:

Chopin was born in Poland of French parents, and was partly educated in Germany. The influences of three nations have shaped a most remarkable personality; for in this way he has absorbed what is best in all three. Poland gave him a chivalrous spirit and her historic sorrow. France endowed him with gentle amiability and grace. Germany bestowed upon him a romantic depth of feeling. And Nature gave him an elegant, slender, somewhat spare frame, and the noblest heart and genius. Yes, we must admit that Chopin possesses genius in the fullest meaning of the word. He is not only a virtuoso; he is also a poet. He reveals the poetry which dwells in his soul. He is a tone-poet; and nothing can compare with the pleasure we experience when he improvises at the piano. Then he is neither Pole, nor Frenchman, nor German. He manifests a far nobler descent. We see that he comes from the land of Mozart, Raphael, and Goethe – that his true fatherland is the dream-world of poesy. When he improvises, it seems to me as if I were being visited by a compatriot from my beloved homeland, and were listening to all the singular things that had taken place in my absence . . . Sometimes I am tempted to interrupt him and ask, 'Tell me how is the lovely water-nixie who used to bind her silver veil so coquettishly around her green locks? Does the white-bearded sea-god still pursue her with his foolish, faded old love? And are our roses still as fiery-proud as ever? And do the trees sing as sweetly in the moonlight as they used to?

Berlioz wrote memoirs which are among the most lively and attractive I know. He describes a banquet in Prague at which Liszt gave the after-dinner speech:

When the first toast was called, he rose and in the name of the whole company addressed me for a full quarter of an hour with a warmth of feeling, a wealth of ideas and a turn of phrase which many orators would envy. I was deeply touched. Unhappily if he spoke well, he drank likewise. That fatal cup set such tides of champagne flowing that all Liszt's eloquence was shipwrecked in it. Belloni and I were still reasoning with him in the street at two in the morning, and urging on him the advisability of waiting until daylight before engaging in single combat with pistols at two yards' range with a Bohemian who had drunk even better than he.

Nietzsche was a close friend of Wagner, but later turned against him as too Romantic and too German:

The 'good old' time is past, it sang itself out in Mozart – how happy are *we* that his *rococo* still speaks to us, that his 'good company,' his tender enthusiasm, his childish delight in the Chinese and its flourishes, his courtesy of heart, his longing for the elegant, the amorous, the tripping, the tearful, and his belief in the South, can still appeal to *something left* in us! Ah, some time or other it will be over with it! – but who can doubt that it will be over still sooner with the intelligence and taste for Beethoven! For he was only the last echo of a break and transition in style, and *not*, like Mozart, the last echo of a great European taste which had existed for centuries. Beethoven is the intermediate event between an old mellow soul that is constantly breaking down, and a future over-young soul that is always *coming*; there is spread over his music the twilight of eternal loss and eternal extravagant hope, – the same light in which Europe was bathed when it dreamed with Rousseau, when it danced round the Tree of Liberty of the Revolution, and finally almost fell down in adoration before Napoleon. But how rapidly does *this* very sentiment now pale, how difficult nowadays is even the *apprehension* of this sentiment, how strangely does the language of Rousseau, Schiller, Shelley, and Byron sound to our ear, in whom *collectively* the same fate of Europe was able to *speak*, which knew how to *sing* in Beethoven! – Whatever German music came afterwards, belongs to Romanticism, that is to say, to a movement which, historically considered, was still shorter, more fleeting, and more superficial than that great interlude, the transition of Europe from Rousseau to Napoleon, and to the rise of demo-cracy.

As this extract shows, Nietszche was fiercely opposed to all forms of nationalism and anti-Semitism. His popular reputation as a proto-Nazi was a fiction deliberately spread by his sister after his death; she was both an anti-Semite and a racist German nationalist.

The French painter Delacroix was a close friend of Chopin. His *Journal* shows an astonishing breadth of interest, in politics and philosophy as well as the arts. Indeed he was thought by some to be the illegitimate son of the great diplomatist Talleyrand. This is the entry for 7 April 1849:

Went with Chopin for his drive at about half-past three. I was glad to be of service to him although I was feeling tired. The Champs-Élysées, l'Arc de l'Étoile, the bottle of quinquina wine, being stopped at the city gate, etc.

We talked of music and it seemed to cheer him. I asked him to explain what it is that gives the impression of logic in music. He made me understand the meaning of harmony and counterpoint; how in music, the fugue corresponds to pure logic, and that to be well versed in the fugue is to understand the elements of all reason and development in music. I thought how happy I should have been to study these things, the despair of commonplace musicians. It gave me some idea of the pleasure which true philosophers find in science. The fact of the matter is, that true science is not what we usually mean by that word – not, that is to say, a part of knowledge quite separate from art. No, science, as regarded and demonstrated by a man like Chopin, is art itself, but on the other hand, art is not what the vulgar believe it to be, a vague inspiration coming from nowhere, moving at random, and portraying merely the pictur-esque, external side of things. It is pure reason, embellished by genius, but following a set course and bound by higher laws. And here I come back to the difference between Mozart and Beethoven. As Chopin said to me, 'Where Beethoven is obscure and appears to be lacking in unity, it is not, as people allege, from a rather wild originality – the quality which they admire in him – it is because he turns his back on eternal principles'. Mozart never does this. Each part has its own movement which, although it harmonizes with the rest, makes its own song and follows it perfectly. This is what is meant by counterpoint, '*punto contrapunto*'. He added that it was usual to learn harmony before counterpoint, that is to say, to learn the succession of notes that leads to the harmonies. In Berlioz's music, the harmonies are set down and he fills in the intervals as best he can.

Those men, who are so taken up with style that they put it before everything else, prefer to be stupid rather than not to *appear serious*. Apply this to Ingres and his school.

Delacroix reminds us that 'the craft of the painter is the most difficult of all and it takes the longest to learn. Like composing, painting requires erudition, but it also requires execution, like playing the violin.' He thought very hard about his work concentrating particularly on the role of colour:

A picture should be laid-in as if one were looking at the subject on a grey day, with no sunlight or clear-cut shadows. Fundamentally, lights and shadows do not exist. Every object presents a colour mass, having different reflections on all sides. Suppose a ray of sunshine should suddenly light up the objects in this open-air scene under grey light, you will then have what are called lights and shadows but they will be pure accidents. This, strange as it may appear, is a profound truth and contains the whole meaning of colour in painting. How extraordinary that it should have been understood by so few of the great painters, even among those who are generally regarded as colourists!

I quite realize that to call a man a colourist is considered more of a disadvantage than a recommendation by modern schools which regard the study of drawing as a virtue in itself and are willing to sacrifice everything to it. It would appear that colourists are solely concerned with the inferior, the more mundane aspects of painting, that fine drawing is infinitely finer when combined with a depressing colour-scheme, and that colour merely serves to distract attention from more sublime qualities that can very easily stand without the support of its prestige. This might be called the *abstract* side of painting in which the contour is the prime object. Apart from colour, such a conception subordinates other essential factors of painting, for example the right distribution of effect, and even composition itself.

He had no doubt of the superiority of painting to poetry:

> What I have been saying about the power of *painting* now becomes clear. If it has to record but a single moment it is capable of concentrating the *effect* of that moment. The painter is far more master of what he wants to express than the poet or musician who are in the hands of interpreters; even though his memory may have a smaller range to work on, he produces an effect that is a perfect unity and one which is capable of giving complete satisfaction. Moreover, the painter's work does not suffer so much from variations in the manner in which it is understood in different periods. Fashions change, and the bias of the moment may cause a different value to be set upon his work, but ultimately it is always the same, it remains what the artist intended it to be, whereas this cannot be said of the art of the theatre, which has to pass through the hands of interpreters. When the artist's mind is not there to guide the actors or singers the performance no longer corresponds to his original intention; the accent disappears, and with it, the most subtle part of the work is lost. Happy indeed is the author whose work is not mutilated, an insult to which he is exposed even during his lifetime. Even the change of an actor alters the whole character of a work.

Yet he was, like his contemporary Berlioz, a great admirer of Shakespeare:

> Shakespeare is intensely sophisticated. When with his deep perception he portrayed emotions which the early writers ignored or did not even realize the existence of, he revealed a little world of sentiments which, albeit confusedly, have been common to men of every age but seemed doomed never to reach the light or to be analysed until some specially gifted genius carried his torch into the

dark corners of the soul. It seems that a writer ought to be tremendously learned, but we know how easy it is to be deceived and how much reality lies beneath a show of universal knowledge.

The poet Baudelaire wrote an impassioned obituary of Delacroix, who had been his friend, and in whom he saw much of the novelist Stendhal:

'Nature is but a dictionary, he [Delacroix] kept repeating. Properly to understand the extent of meaning implied in this sentence, you should consider the numerous ordinary uses of a dictionary. In it you look for the meaning of words, their genealogy and their etymology – in brief, you extract from it all the elements that compose a sentence or a narrative; but no one has ever thought of his dictionary as a *composition*, in the poetic sense of the word. Painters who are obedient to the imagination seek in their dictionary the elements which suit with their conception; in adjusting those elements, however, with more or less of art, they confer upon them a totally new physiognomy. But those who have no imagination just copy the dictionary. The result is a great vice, the vice of banality, to which those painters are particularly prone whose speciality brings them closer to what is called inanimate nature – landscape-painters, for example, who generally consider it a triumph if they can contrive not to show their personalities. By dint of contemplating and copying, they forget to feel and think.

Like the Impressionists, whom he inspired, Delacroix was much influenced by the landscapes of John Constable, who certainly did not copy out the dictionary of nature. Constable's paintings appear to spring spontaneously from nature and fresh air. In fact they are the product of deep thought. His friend and fellow-painter C.R. Leslie wrote memoirs of his life which included some fascinating insights from Constable's letters and notes:

When young, I was extremely fond of reading poetry, and also fond of music, and I played myself a little; but as I advanced in life and in art, I soon gave up the latter; and now after thirty years, I must say that the sister arts have less hold on my mind in its occasional ramblings from my one pursuit than the sciences, especially the study of geology, which, more than any other, seems to satisfy my mind. . . .
    In such an age as this, painting should be *understood*, not looked

on with blind wonder, nor considered only as a poetic aspiration, but as a pursuit, *legitimate, scientific,* and *mechanical.* . . .

I have seen him [Constable] admire a fine tree with an ecstasy of delight like that with which he would catch up a beautiful child in his arms. The ash was his favourite, and all who are acquainted with his pictures cannot fail to have observed how frequently it is introduced as a near object, and how beautifully its distinguishing peculiarities are marked. I remember his pointing out to me, in an avenue of Spanish chestnuts, the great elegance given to their trunks by the spiral direction of the lines of the bark. . . .

The world is wide; no two days are alike, nor even two hours; neither were there ever two leaves of a tree alike since the creation of the world; and the genuine productions of art, like those of nature, are all distinct from each other. . . .

There is nothing ugly; *I never saw an ugly thing in my life*: for let the form of an object be what it may, – light, shade, and perspective will always make it beautiful. It is perspective which improves the form of this. . . .

He [Constable] would never admit of a distinction which is sometimes made between poetry and truth. He felt that the *supernatural* need not be the *unnatural.* Neither did he admit that the *conventional* in art, though it may be found in the works of the greatest masters, was to be considered in any other light than as an evidence of human imperfection. He looked upon the imitation by modern painters of that which is conventional in the works of their predecessors, as one great cause of the deterioration of art. 'Raphael and Michael Angelo,' he said, 'would be greatly astonished could they rise from their graves, at the theories on which it has been supposed their works were formed; as, for instance, that the charms of colour, or chiaroscuro, would detract from the intellectual dignity of their inventions.'

Yet Constable admired landscape painters with whom at first sight he had little in common, telling his wife: 'I do not wonder at you being jealous of Claude [Lorrain]. If anything could come between our love it is him.'

Van Gogh was another painter who thought deeply about the meaning of his work. He studied other painters and read widely in French and English as well as his native Dutch:

Alone or almost alone amongst painters Rembrandt has . . . that heartbroken tenderness, that glimpse into a superhuman infinitude that seems so natural there; you come upon it in many places in Shakespeare.

There are many things which one must believe and love. There is something of Rembrandt in Shakespeare, and of Correggio in Michelet, and of Delacroix in Victor Hugo ... And in Bunyan there is something of Maris or of Millet, and in Beecher Stowe there is something of Ary Scheffer ... I am very fond of the portrait of a man by Fabritius. Yes, but I am as fond of Sydney Carton, in the *A Tale of Two Cities* by Dickens ... My God, how beautiful Shakespeare is! Who is mysterious like him? His language and style can indeed be compared to an artist's brush, quivering with fever and emotion. But one must *learn* to read, as one must *learn* to see, and *learn* to live.

I always feel greatly drawn to the figures either of the English graphic artists or of the English authors, because of their Monday-morning-like sobriety and studied simplicity and gravity and analytical candour, as something solid and robust which can give us strength in our times of weakness. The same holds good, among French authors, for Balzac and Zola too ... I have been re-reading Dickens' Christmas Books these days. There are things in them so profound that one must read them over and over; there are tremendously close connections with Carlyle.

In fact Van Gogh could use words almost as well as he used pencil and paint. As a young man he spent some time with a branch of the family firm in London, and later worked as a teacher without pay at a school in Ramsgate, where he describes a storm:

The sea was yellowish especially near the shore; at the horizon a streak of light and above it the immense dark grey clouds from which the rain poured down in slanting streaks. The wind blew the dust from the little white path on the rocks into the sea and swayed the blooming hawthorn bushes and wallflowers that grow on the rocks. To the right were fields of young green corn and in the distance the town that looked like the town that Albrecht Dürer used to etch. A town with its turrets, mills, slate roofs and houses built in Gothic style, and below, the harbour between two dykes, projecting far into the sea. I also saw the sea last Sunday night, everything was dark and grey, but at the horizon the day began to dawn.

It was still very early but a lark was singing already. So were the nightingales in the gardens near the sea. In the distance shone the light from the lighthouse, the guardship, etc.

That same night I looked from the window of my room on the roofs of the houses that can be seen from there and on the tops of the elm trees, dark against the night sky. Over those roofs, one single star, but a beautiful, large, friendly one. And I thought of you all and of my own past years and of our home, and in me arose the words and the feeling: 'Keep me from being a son who makes ashamed, give me Thy blessing, not because I deserve it but for my mother's sake. Thou art love, cover all things. Without Thy continued blessings we succeed in nothing.'

Enclosed is a little drawing of the view from the window of the school, through which the boys wave good-bye to their parents after a visit when they are going back to the station. None of us will ever forget the view from the window. You ought to have seen it this week when we had rain, especially in the twilight when the lamps were on and their light reflected in the wet street.

Days like that could put Mr Stokes into a bad temper, and when the boys made more noise than he liked, it sometimes happened that they had to go without their supper.

Even when he had become totally committed to painting, he could recreate a painting in words:

Here is a description of a canvas which is in front of me at the moment. A view of the park of the asylum where I am staying; on the right a grey terrace and a side wall of a house. Some deflowered rose bushes, on the left a stretch of the park – red ochre – the soil scorched by the sun, covered with fallen pine needles. This edge of the park is planted with large pine trees, whose trunks and branches are red-ochre, the foliage green gloomed over by an admixture of black. These high trees stand out against the evening sky with violet stripes on a yellow ground, which higher up turns into pink, into green. A wall – also red-ochre – shuts off the view, and is topped only by a violet and yellow-ochre hill. Now the nearest tree is an enormous trunk, struck by lightning and sawed off. But one side branch shoots up very high and lets fall an avalanche of dark green pine needles. This sombre giant – like a defeated proud man – contrasts, when considered in the nature of a living creature, with the pale smile of a last rose on the fading bush in front of him. Underneath the trees, empty stone benches, sullen box trees; the sky is mirrored – yellow – in a puddle left by the rain. A sunbeam, the last ray of daylight, raises the sombre ochre almost to orange. Here and there small black figures wander among the tree trunks.

You will realize that this combination of red-ochre, of green gloomed over by grey, the black streaks surrounding the contours, produces something of the sensation of anguish, called 'rouge-noir,' from which certain of my companions in misfortune frequently suffer. Moreover, the motif of the great tree struck by lightning, the sickly green-pink smile of the last flower of autumn serve to confirm this impression.

I am telling you (about this canvas) to remind you that one can try to give an impression of anguish without aiming straight at the historic Garden of Gethsemane.

To Van Gogh the appearance was the symbol of reality. To the Impressionists the appearance was the reality itself. Monet wrote:

When you go out to paint, try to forget what objects you have in front of you, a tree, a field . . . merely think, here is a little square of blue, here an oblong of pink, here a streak of yellow, and paint it just as it looks to you, the exact colour and shape, until it gives your own naïve expression of the scene.

Auden quotes a passage from Virginia Woolf's *The Waves* as 'the best description of the creative process that I know', yet it describes a very different approach to art from that of Monet:

There is a square: there is an oblong. The players take the square and place it upon the oblong. They place it very accurately; they make a perfect dwelling-place. The structure is now visible; what is inchoate is here stated; we are not so various or so mean; we have made oblongs and stood them upon squares. This is our triumph; this is our consolation.

Paul Klee, in his essay 'On Modern Art', puts yet another view:

In the womb of nature, at the source of creation, where the secret key to all lies guarded.

But not all can enter. Each should follow where the pulse of his own heart leads.

So, in their time, the Impressionists – our opposites of yesterday – had every right to dwell within the matted undergrowth of every-day vision.

But our pounding heart drives us down, deep down to the source of all.

What springs from this source, whatever it may be called, dream or idea or fantasy – must be taken seriously only if it unites with the proper creative means to form a work of art.

The most obvious distinction between approaches to painting is between the linear and the painterly. At the opposite extreme from Monet, William Blake stands for the linear approach in *The Golden Rule*:

> The great and golden rule of art, as well as of life, is this: that the more distinct, sharp, and wiry the bounding line, the more perfect the work of art; and the less keen and sharp, the great is the evidence of weak imagination, plagiarism, and bungling. Great inventors in all ages knew this: Protogenes and Apelles knew each other by this line. Raphael and Michael Angelo and Albert Dürer are known by this and this alone ... Leave out this line, and you leave out life itself; all is chaos again, and the line of the almighty must be drawn out upon it before man and beast can exist.

Blake detested the 'slobberings' of Sir Joshua Reynolds partly because he did not observe this golden rule; he wrote:

> When Sir Joshua Reynolds died
> All Nature was degraded
> The King dropped a tear into the Queen's Ear,
> And all his Pictures Faded.

The most ambitious and successful attempt to classify painting into categories was made by Heinrich Woelfflin, in his *Principles of Art History*. He distinguishes between 'Classical' and 'Romantic' by using the antinomies Linear and Painterly, Plane and Recession, Closed and Open Form, Multiplicity and Unity, Clearness and Unclearness. I first read Woelfflin at school, and still find his antinomies exceptionally useful. They can be applied to people as well as to all the arts. But like all generalizations, Woelfflin's break down when confronted with a unique genius like Brueghel or Shakespeare or Bach or Mozart.

In fact it is as difficult to discuss painting with words alone as to discuss music. Even with reproductions of the paintings in front of us, analyses of style cannot encompass what is most important in them. Nevertheless, if I understand how the painter saw his subject and what he was trying to do with it, I will enjoy it more. No one would judge Debussy by the same criteria as Bach. It is just as absurd to judge Picasso by the same criteria as Piero. What is most mysterious is why artists tend to see the same things in different ways at different periods in history, and why changes of style often affect all the arts in the same way at a given time. Delacroix, Victor Hugo, and Berlioz all represent the same phase of romantic art. Debussy, Monet and Verlaine are all in the same sense, Impressionists. The art of Vienna before the First World War, or of Berlin in the twenties, obviously reflect the decadence of the societies from which they sprang. Yet the Marxist art historians have made fools of themselves by trying to trace all such shifts in style to changes in the class structure or modes of production. There is obviously some link between art and society at a given time, although its nature is obscure and irregular; often we cannot tell whether society is influencing the art or art the society.

I love almost all schools of painting and of music, and refuse to be drawn into putting one school above another. On the other hand I do find it possible, up to a point, to rank artists inside a particular school. To me Beethoven is as obviously superior to Spohr as Rembrandt is to Fabritius, or Shakespeare to Marlowe, although I enjoy Spohr, Fabritius and Marlowe greatly. On the other hand I do see certain artists as uniquely great in the depth of their penetration and range of their sympathies. And despite my inability to explain my judgement, I see Beethoven's last quartets along with much of Bach's choral music and some of Mozart's operas standing on pinnacles higher than even Haydn, Brahms and Verdi can attain. Among the writers, I put Shakespeare and the Greek tragic dramatists on equally lonely pinnacles. I have more difficulty in singling out a few supremely great painters. How can you rank Dürer against Rembrandt, Goya against Velasquez, Michelangelo against Mantegna, Vermeer against Piero della Francesca, or even Van Eyck against Van Gogh?

Moreover nothing can prevent individuals of different types and periods from seeing pictures differently. Take a painting of Christ on the cross. Quentin Bell tells us that Roger Fry at one time was 'deeply and almost exclusively concerned with plastic values; I have heard him describe the agonized body of Christ upon the cross as "this important mass".'

In describing Grünewald's *Crucifixion* the Belgian decadent J.K. Huysmans could see nothing but the horror of a rotting corpse:

The hour of putrefaction had arrived; the watery wound in the side streamed more thickly, soaking the hip with blood dark like the juice of mulberries; pinkish liquid, a sort of diluted whey resembling the Moselle *vins gris*, oozed from the chest and soaked the belly below which undulated a puffed-out patch of loin-cloth; then the knees, drawn together convulsively, brought the knee-caps into collision, and the twisted legs arched out all the way to the feet which, one crossed over the other, stretched and sprouted in full decay, turning green amid the torrents of blood. Those feet, spongy and distended, were horrible; their flesh swelled over the nail-head and their shrivelled toes conflicted with the imploring gesture of the hands, threatening, almost scratching at the iron-filled, ochre soil, like the purple earth of Thuringia, with the blue horn of their toe-nails.

This corpse in eruption was topped by a head huge and tormented; encircled by a shaggy crown of thorns, it hung, exhausted, with one sunken, barely-opened eye where still quivered a look of pain and fear; the face was distorted, the forehead creased, the cheeks drained, every battered feature dissolved, while the slack mouth grimaced, its jaw contracted in appalling, tetanus like shock.

Friedlander, however, sees the same picture quite differently, asking:

Why does it not release a torrent of horror, which sweeps away all pleasurable contemplation? Because, in spite of the utmost closeness to nature, not the tortured body but the picture of it rises before us; because the master communicates to us his vision and, thereby, his religious fervour in such purity and so decisively, that our imagination, removed far away from disturbing, unrelenting actuality, experiences the distant, sublime myth; and the fearsomeness becomes deeply affecting drama. In the picture Christ dies not once, not here; on the contrary, everywhere and always; hence never and nowhere.

There is a story about a man passing a building site which makes the same point. He asks each of three labourers what he is doing. The first replies: 'I'm breaking stones.' The second says: 'I'm earning a living.' The third says: 'I'm helping to build a cathedral.' Politicians fall into the same three types.

The value of good writing about art, however perverse it may sometimes appear, is that it directs your mind to something important which you might otherwise have missed. Fashions in art have a similar value in concentrating your attention on one type of painting or one aspect of a particular painting at a time. Great paintings can bear many interpretations, and carry different messages for different ages.

Two of the greatest pieces of writing about painting are by Walter Pater and Wystan Auden.

Pater's famous description of Leonardo's *Mona Lisa* could only have been written by an academic in nineteenth-century England:

La Gioconda is, in the truest sense, Lionardo's masterpiece, the revealing instance of his mode of thought and work. In suggestiveness, only the Melancholia of Dürer is comparable to it; and no crude symbolism disturbs the effect of its subdued and graceful mystery. We all know the face and hands of the figure, set in its marble chair, in that cirque of fantastic rocks, as in some faint light under sea. Perhaps of all ancient pictures time has chilled it least. As often happens with works in which invention seems to reach its limit, there is an element in it given to, not invented by, the master. In that inestimable folio of drawings, once in the possession of Vasari, were certain designs by Verrocchio, faces of such impressive beauty that Lionardo in his boyhood copied them many times. It is hard not to connect with these designs of the elder by-past master, as with its germinal principle, the unfathomable smile, always with a touch of something sinister in it, which plays over all Lionardo's work. Besides, the picture is a portrait. From childhood we see this image defining itself on the fabric of his dreams; and but for express historical testimony, we might fancy that this was but his ideal lady, embodied and beheld at last. What was the relationship of a living Florentine to this creature of his thought? By what strange affinities had she and the dream grown thus apart, yet so closely together? Present from the first, incorporeal in Lionardo's thought, dimly traced in the designs of Verrocchio, she is found present at last in Il Giocondo's house. That there is much of mere portraiture in the picture is attested by the legend that by artificial means, the presence of mimes and flute-players, that subtle expression was protracted on the face. Again, was it in four years and by renewed labour never really completed, or in four months and as by stroke of magic, that the image was projected?

The presence that thus so strangely rose beside the waters is expressive of what in the ways of a thousand years man had come to desire. Hers is the head upon which all 'the ends of the world are come', and the eyelids are a little weary. It is a beauty wrought out from within upon the flesh, the deposit, little cell by cell, of strange thoughts and fantastic reveries and exquisite passions. Set it for a moment beside one of those white Greek goddesses or beautiful women of antiquity, and how they would be troubled by this beauty, into which the soul with all its maladies has passed? All the thoughts and experience of the world have etched and moulded there in that which they have of power to refine and make expressive the outward form, the animalism of Greece, the lust of Rome, the reverie of the middle age with its spiritual ambition and imaginative loves, the return of the Pagan world, the sins of the Borgias. She is older than the rocks among which she sits; like the vampire, she has been dead many times, and learned the secrets of the grave; and has been a diver in deep seas, and keeps their fallen day about her; and trafficked for strange webs with Eastern merchants; and, as Leda, was the mother of Helen of Troy, and, as Saint Anne, the mother of Mary; and all this has been to her but as the sound of lyres and flutes, and lives only in the delicacy with which it has moulded the changing lineaments and tinged the eyelids and the hands. The fancy of a perpetual life, sweeping together ten thousand experiences, is an old one; and modern thought has conceived the idea of humanity as wrought upon by, and summing up in itself, all modes of thought and life. Certainly Lady Lisa might stand as the embodiment of the old fancy, the symbol of the modern idea.

Similarly Auden's poem on Brueghel's *Fall of Icarus* can only be the product of twentieth-century alienation:

About suffering they were never wrong,
The Old Masters: how well they understood
Its human position; how it takes place
While someone else is eating or opening a window or just walking
    dully along;
How, when the aged are reverently, passionately waiting
For the miraculous birth, there always must be
Children who did not specially want it to happen, skating
On a pond at the edge of the wood:
They never forgot
That even the dreadful martyrdom must run its course
Anyhow in a corner, some untidy spot
Where the dogs go on with their doggy life and the torturer's horse
Scratches its innocent behind on a tree,
In Brueghel's *Icarus*, for instance: how everything turns away
Quite leisurely from the disaster; the ploughman may
Have heard the splash, the forsaken cry,
But for him it was not an important failure; the sun shone

As it had to on the white legs disappearing into the green
Water; and the expensive delicate ship that must have seen
Something amazing, a boy falling out of the sky,
Had somewhere to get to and sailed calmly on.

In recent years, however, schools of criticism, of literature as well as of the visual arts, have sprung up which 'murder to dissect'. They make me ask, like William Blake:

Why would thou examine every little fibre of my soul,
Spreading them out before the sun like stalks of flax to dry?
The infant joy is beautiful, but its anatomy
Horrible, ghast and deadly: Nought shalt thou find in it
But death, despair and everlasting brooding melancholy.

Critics have never been popular with artists, as Kipling showed:

When the flush of a new-born sun fell first on Eden's green and
    gold,
Our father Adam sat under the Tree and scratched with a stick in
    the mould:
And the first rude sketch that the world had seen was joy to his
    mighty heart,
Till the Devil whispered behind the leaves. 'It's pretty, but is it
    Art?'

For a long time it was the rule of the Academies which creative artists found most difficult to bear. The Academies have little influence these days. On the contrary, as Quentin Bell admits in his stimulating book, *Bad Art*:

The unhappy academicians of our own day have no lackeys, no critic would dare to praise them, for to do so would be reactionary. When the latest young man hurls a pot of paint in the critic's face, the critic murmurs, as he squeezes the polyvinylacetate out of his whiskers, that he is in no way alienated by what has, he considers, been a total experience in commitment to an environmental situation. To protest would be to commit oneself with the enemies of progress. We fear the judgments of history; our timidity is such that we dare not say boo to a goose for fear that it should turn out to be a swan.

In 1975 the New York journalist Tom Wolfe produced a brilliant survey of contemporary art in *The Painted Word*. Its message was that the critics who then dominated the New York art market had succeeded in enslaving the artists to such an extent that their paintings seemed designed simply as illustrations to the critics' theories. He traced the development of this trend from the Cubists to the Reductionists, going round in ever-decreasing circles, and culminating like the Oozlem Bird by disappearing up its own black hole:

> So it was that in April of 1970 an artist named Lawrence Weiner typed up a work of art that appeared in *Arts Magazine* – as a work of art – with no visual experience before or after whatsoever, and to wit:
>
> 1. The artist may construct the piece
> 2. The piece may be fabricated
> 3. The piece need not be built
>
> Each being equal and consistent with the intent of the artist the decision as to condition rests with the receiver upon the occasion of receivership.   With permission, *Arts Magazine*
>
> And there, at last, it was! No more realism, no more representational objects, no more lines, colors, forms, and contours, no more pigments, no more brushstrokes, no more evocations, no more frames, walls, galleries, museums, no more gnawing at the tortured face of the god Flatness, no more audience required, just a 'receiver' that may or may not be a person or may or may not be there at all, no more ego projected, just 'the artist,' in the third person, who may be anyone or no one at all, for nothing is demanded of him, nothing at all, not even existence, for that got lost in the subjunctive mode – and in that moment of absolutely dispassionate abdication, of insouciant withering away, Art made its final flight, climbed higher and higher in an ever-decreasing tighter-turning spiral until, with one last erg of freedom, one last dendritic synapse, it disappeared up its own fundamental aperture . . . and came out the other side as Art Theory! . . . Art Theory pure and simple, words on a page, literature undefiled by vision, flat, flatter, Flattest, a vision invisible, even ineffable, as ineffable as the Angels and the Universal Souls.

This was not the end. In 1992 a London gallery held an exhibition of works by Michael Craig-Martin. I quote from a review by Geraldine Norman in *The Independent*:

Craig-Martin's own work grows directly out of American Minimal-ism and postulates the collaboration of the viewer in creating a work of art. The viewer is required to think. At the 12 Cork Street gallery he is showing variants on *The Oak Tree* of 1973; it comprised a glass of water on a shelf and a printed interview with himself about his claim that he had 'changed the physical substance of the glass of water into an oak tree'.

In the new works, priced at £12,000 each, the glasses of water on a glass shelf are attached to a canvas painted two different colours. There is also a wall painting – red with a white stripe down the middle at which point the water and shelf are attached to the wall. Here you buy the right to have the work reconstructed in your own house or gallery by the artist, for £20,000.

The corner gallery contains large red paintings patterned with scraped lines allowing the white undercoat to show. The set of nine costs £60,000; single canvases cost £10,000. He has explained that these paintings are 'comparatively unrewarding in all the obvious ways'. Their significance lies in what the viewer makes of them.

Nice work if you can get it!

The *Zeitgeist* is no respecter of intellectual boundaries. It is surely no accident that Reductionism in art was accompanied by Reductionism in biology, through which the Frenchman Jacques Monod sought to show that all biological phenomena derive from the amino-acids. I once sat in on a conference of scientists, including three other Nobel prize-winners, to contest this view at the Rockefeller Study Centre at Bellagio; with Karl Popper there to see fair play, Monod had no chance of winning!

I would like to feel that with Deconstructionism this type of criticism has reached its bitter end. However, now that criticism has been invaded by people who do not enjoy any of the arts, that may be too much to hope.

The ordinary man or woman who does enjoy the arts would do better to read what artists themselves have said, as I have tried to show. Better still, it is worthwhile to be an artist yourself, however imperfectly. I have been deeply moved, as well as surprised, by the number of letters sent by readers of my memoirs, some of which include their own poetry. You can learn more about music by playing an instrument yourself, even if it is only a recorder. And you can learn to use a pencil and brush.

If you are too busy or clumsy to paint, you can take photographs instead. You need only a fraction of a second to take a photograph, as against hours, days, or weeks to paint a picture. That is why I turned to photography when I joined the Labour Party's front bench. At first I developed and printed my own films, even in colour. Nowadays I have no time to process my films, so I take only colour slides; I have amassed some twenty thousand slides from all over the world since 1953.

Modern cameras, with automatic exposure, automatic focusing, and zoom lenses have removed all the technical dificulties from photography. The remaining problem, however, is the most difficult of all – to choose that precise fraction of a second out of a thousand, the precise viewpoint out of a million, the precise combination of speed and aperture, the precise lighting, which will express what you want, and at the same time have artistic merit. At the end of my book *Healey's Eye* I tried to decide whether photography deserves to be called an art:

Since its earliest days people have worried about the status of photography. Is it art or reality? To begin with, a photograph has a direct physical relationship with its subject which none of the arts can claim. The negative is made by light reflected from the subject itself; when Europeans first took their cameras to China a century ago, the Mandarins they photographed saw their portraits as a physical emanation of themselves. The photographer can doctor his negative in various ways when he is developing or printing it; but essentially his job is to choose his position, his lighting and the decisive moment for pressing the button. Then he lets the light *make* the picture – he only *takes* the photograph.

A painter on the other hand actually *makes* the picture himself. However faithfully he aims to represent his subject, he has to choose his medium, mix and lay on the colours; in deciding how to do so he will be influenced by what he knows and feels about the subject as well as what he sees. He must confront his subject for hours, days and even years, learning as he looks and paints, and thinking all the time about what it means to him. Compared with a painting, every photograph is a snapshot even if the shutter is open for a few minutes rather than 1/100 second.

For Cartier-Bresson, taking a photograph should be like firing an arrow in Zen Buddhism – you only hit the target when you do not aim at it. You should never think while you are actually taking the photograph, but 'kiss the joy as it flies'. Other great photographers such as Yousuf Karsh or Edward Weston spent hours arranging their model or waiting for the one moment in the day when the shadows fell exactly as they wanted. But however you approach photography, in the end the picture is made by the light reflected from the subject when the machine opens the shutter.

Then is a photograph more realistic than a painting? Contrary to the old saying, the camera can lie as easily as the paint brush – and more effectively, because so many people believe it reproduces reality. It does not. It reproduces appearance, which, as we all know, is quite a different thing. Philosophers have argued for centuries about the relationship between appearance and reality. Ordinary people know that the appearance of a person depends on all sorts of factors which have nothing to do with reality at all – the mood of the person at the time, the mood of the observer, clothes, make-up, lighting, position and so on. As I have already pointed out, a photograph does not even represent the appearance of an object to the human being who sees it; it reproduces a mechanical image. That is why old photographs have such a fascination for us. As Susan Sontag says, if we could choose between an authentic painting of Shakespeare and a contemporary photograph, most of us would choose the photograph because in this sense at least it is more 'real'. So perhaps the African tribesmen who turned their faces away from my camera and the Arabs who chased me through the Soukh in Damascus were not entirely wrong in seeing a photograph as capturing something of themselves which no one else should have. There is an element of theft in taking a picture – and of aggression too. It is no accident that people talk of shooting pictures. A photographic safari is, after all, a substitute for shooting a lion with a rifle.

Some photographers have attempted to escape from the ambiguous relationship between photography, art and reality, by breaking the link with reality altogether. For example Man Ray and Moholy-Nagy, whom I once invited to talk to the New Oxford Art Society, made pictures by putting objects on sensitive paper and shining light on or through them. Others used photographs as the raw material for fabricated pictures made by sticking bits of different photographs together; this type of 'collage' was used by John Heartfield to great effect for political caricature. Photography has often been used for the surrealistic effects to which it is so well suited, by putting people or objects in unfamiliar or impossible relationships to one another. In fact it lends itself to this type of fantasy better than painting, precisely because its images are 'real'.

Making a hobby of photography does involve risks and temptations – what does not? But you can avoid them providing you keep your humanity. Ansel Adams described his camera as 'an instrument of love and revelation'; his work justifies the phrase. In the photographs he took of his friend Georgia O'Keeffe over thirty years, Alfred Stieglitz produced a work of art as lovely as a sequence of sonnets. The comparison springs naturally to mind; if photography is to be put among the arts, it is as close to poetry as to painting. Its images, like the words in a poem, derive their power from the innumerable associations they bring consciously or subconsciously to mind. It is almost bound to be 'literary' in a way painting is not.

Much as I love photography, I have now started painting again. I think everyone should at least attempt it.

For a serious amateur, Ruskin's booklet on *The Elements of Drawing* is still as useful a guide as any, particularly in a recent illustrated edition with notes by Bernard Dunstan. But for sheer exhilaration, there is nothing to touch Winston Churchill's *Painting as a Pastime*. Churchill taught himself to paint after he left the Admiralty in 1915 following the failure of the Dardanelles campaign – an episode which led my father to saddle me with Winston as my second name. He describes his experience in the following passage:

> Having bought the colours, an easel, and a canvas, the next step was *to begin*. But what a step to take! The palette gleamed with beads of colour; fair and white rose the canvas; the empty brush hung poised, heavy with destiny, irresolute in the air. My hand seemed arrested by a silent veto. But after all the sky on this occasion was unquestionably blue, and a pale blue at that. There could be no doubt that blue paint mixed with white should be put on the top part of the canvas. One really does not need to have had an artist's training to see that. It is a starting-point open to all. So very gingerly I mixed a little blue paint on the palette with a very small brush, and then with infinite precaution made a mark about as big as a bean upon the affronted snow-white shield. It was a challenge, a deliberate challenge; but so subdued, so halting, indeed so cataleptic, that it deserved no response. At that moment the loud approaching sound of a motor-car was heard in the drive. From this chariot there stepped swiftly and lightly none other than the gifted wife of Sir John Lavery. 'Painting! But what are you hesitating about? Let me have a brush – the big one.' Splash into the turpentine, wallop into the blue and the white, frantic flourish on the palette – clean no longer – and then several large, fierce strokes and slashes of blue on the absolutely cowering canvas. Anyone could see that it could not hit back. No evil fate avenged the jaunty violence. The canvas grinned in helplessness before me. The spell was broken. The sickly inhibitions rolled away. I seized

the largest brush and fell upon my victim with Berserk fury. I have never felt any awe of a canvas since.

Yet even in the excitement of learning this new art, Churchill could see its relationship to the role of a politician in government:

> One begins to see, for instance, that painting a picture is like fighting a battle; and trying to paint a picture is, I suppose, like trying to fight a battle. It is, if anything, more exciting than fighting it successfully. But the principle is the same. It is the same kind of problem as unfolding a long, sustained, interlocked argument. It is a proposition which, whether of few or numberless parts, is commanded by a single unity of conception. And we think – though I cannot tell – that painting a great picture must require an intellect on the grand scale. There must be that all-embracing view which presents the beginning and the end, the whole and each part, as one instantaneous impression retentively and untiringly held in the mind.

In fact, politics and art are both part of life. As such, both are capable of infinite variety. And each can enrich the other.

6

NATURE

The world is charged with the grandeur of God.
　　It will flame out, like shining from shook foil;
　　It gathers to a greatness, like the ooze of oil
Crushed. Why do men then now not reck his rod?
Generations have trod, have trod, have trod;
　　And all is seared with trade; bleared, smeared with toil;
　　And wears man's smudge and shares man's smell: the soil
Is bare now, nor can foot feel, being shod.

And, for all this, nature is never spent;
　　There lives the dearest freshness deep down things;
And though the last lights off the black West went
　　Oh, morning, at the brown brink eastward, springs –
Because the Holy Ghost over the bent
　　World broods with warm breast and with ah! bright wings.
　　　　　　　　– 'God's Grandeur', Gerard Manley Hopkins

During my earlier years as a politician, I felt keenly with
Hopkins that urban life risked destroying something essential
in me. Like Landor, 'Nature I loved and next to Nature, Art.' In
the earlier part of my life as a Labour Party official and then as an
MP I was condemned to live in London. I think that it was partly
the difficulty of renewing my contact with nature which led me to
spend so much more of my leisure on the arts. As soon as I could
afford it, I bought a house with a garden in Highgate, close to
Hampstead Heath, where we could take the children on long
walks at the weekend.

Yet with a boyhood spent on Ilkley Moor and in the Yorkshire dales, even that was not enough for me. I bought my first car, a little Hillman Husky estate wagon, when I was thirty-five, so that we could get out into real country at weekends, and go camping abroad on holidays. Those camping holidays with the children were among the happiest times of my life.

In 1955, for the first and last time in my political career, we took a whole five weeks off for our summer holiday. We drove through France and Northern Italy to Yugoslavia, and camped in fields on the coast near Senj, visiting beaches which I had studied ten years earlier, as a soldier looking for places to land. Jenny and Tim slept in the back of the car, while in a tiny pup tent Cressida, then only twelve months old, slept in my army canvas bath next to Edna and me in our sleeping bags. Our children enjoyed it as much as we, and later took our grandchildren camping in the country, at home or abroad. However, as Edna used to remind me, camping for a mother is too often simply house-work in appalling conditions; so they tend now to hire cottages instead.

For me a holiday is a chance to get away from people. I can understand why Henry David Thoreau found even village life too much for him, and spent two years alone on the shore of Walden Pond near Concord, Massachusetts:

I went to the woods because I wished to live deliberately, to front only the essential facts of life, and see if I could not learn what it had to teach, and not, when I came to die, discover that I had not lived. I did not wish to live what was not life, living is so dear; nor did I wish to practise resignation, unless it was quite necessary. I wanted to live deep and suck out all the marrow of life, to live so sturdily and Spartan-like as to put to rout all that was not life, to cut a broad swath and shave close, to drive life into a corner, and reduce it to its lowest terms, and, if it proved to be mean, why then to get the whole and genuine meanness of it, and publish its meanness to the world; or if it were sublime, to know it by experience, and be able to give a true account of it in my next excursion. For most men, it appears to me, are in a strange uncertainty about it, whether it is of the devil or of God, and have *somewhat hastily* concluded that it is the chief end of man here to 'glorify God and enjoy him forever'.

Time is but the stream I go a-fishing in. I drink at it; but while I drink I see the sandy bottom and detect how shallow it is. Its thin current slides away, but eternity remains. I would drink deeper; fish in the sky, whose bottom is pebbly with stars. I cannot count one. I know not the first letter of the alphabet. I have always been regretting that I was not as wise as the day I was born. The intellect is a cleaver; it discerns and rifts its way into the secret of things. I do not wish to be any more busy with my hands than is necessary. My head is hands and feet. I feel all my best faculties concentrated in it. My instinct tells me that my head is an organ for burrowing, as some creatures use their snout and fore-paws, and with it I would mine and burrow my way through these hills. I think that the richest vein is somewhere hereabouts; so by the divining-rod and thin rising vapours I judge; and here I will begin to mine.

Yet Thoreau did not find such solitude sufficient for his needs:

I left the woods for as good a reason as I went there. Perhaps it seemed to me that I had several more lives to live, and could not spare any more time for that one. It is remarkable how easily and insensibly we fall into a particular route, and make a beaten track for ourselves. I had not lived there a week before my feet wore a path from my door to the pond-side; and though it is five or six years since I trod it, it is still quite distinct. It is true, I fear that others may have fallen into it, and so helped to keep it open. The surface of the earth is soft and impressible by the feet of men; and so with the paths which the mind travels. How worn and dusty, then, must be the highways of the world, how deep the ruts of tradition and conformity! I did not wish to take a cabin passage, but rather to go before the mast and on the deck of the world, for there I could best see the moonlight amid the mountains. I do not wish to go below now.

I learned this, at least, by my experiment; that if one advances confidently in the direction of his dreams, and endeavours to live the life which he has imagined, he will meet with a success unexpected in common hours. He will put some things behind, will pass an invisible boundary: new, universal, and more liberal laws will begin to establish themselves around and within him; or the old laws be expanded, and interpreted in his favour in a more liberal sense, and he will live with the licence of a higher order of beings. In proportion as he simplifies his life, the laws of the universe will appear less complex, and solitude will not be solitude, nor poverty poverty, nor weakness weakness. If you have built castles in the air, your work need not be lost; that is where they should be. Now put the foundations under them.

My favourite poets, painters, and musicians have drawn much of their inspiration from nature in the countryside – often content to describe its beauty without attempting to draw any deeper meaning from it. John Clare, the Northamptonshire peasant, did so perfectly:

> I love at early morn from new mown swath
> To see the startled frog his route pursue;
> To mark while, leaping o'er the dripping path,
> His bright sides scatter dew,
> The early lark that from its bustle flies
> To hail his matin new;
> And watch him to the skies:
>
> To note on hedgerow baulks, in moisture sprent,
> The jetty snail creep from the mossy thorn,
> With earnest head, and tremulous intent,
> Frail brother of the morn,
> That from the tiny bent's dew-misted leaves
> Withdraws his timid horn,
> And fearful vision weaves:
>
> Or swallow treed on smoke-tann'd chimney top,
> Wont to be first unsealing morning's eye,
> Ere yet the bee hath glean'd one wayward drop
> Of honey on his thigh;
> To see him seek morn's airy couch to sing,
> Until the golden sky
> Bepaint his russet wings. . . .
>
> But now the evening curdles dank and gray,
> Changing her watchet hue for sombre weed;
> And moping owls, to close the lids of day,
> On drowsy wing proceed;
> While chickering crickets, tremulous and long,
> Light's farewell inly heed,
> And give it parting song.
>
> The pranking bat its flighty circlet makes;
> The glow-worm burnishes its lamp anew
> O'er meadows dew-besprent; and beetle wakes
> Enquiries ever new,
> Teazing each passing ear with murmurs vain,
> As wanting to pursue
> His homeward path again.

*

The spring is coming by a many signs;
The trays are up, the hedges broken down
That fenced the haystack, and the remnant shines
Like some old antique fragment weather'd brown.
And where suns peep, in every shelter'd place,
   The little early buttercups unfold
A glittering star or two – till many trace
The edges of the blackthorn clumps in gold.
And then a little lamb bolts up behind
The hill, and wags his tail to meet the yoe;
And then another, shelter'd from the wind,
Lies all his length as dead – and lets me go
Close by, and never stirs, but baking lies,
With legs stretch'd out as though he could not rise.

*

The nodding oxeye bends before the wind,
The woodbine quakes lest boys their flowers should find,
And prickly dogrose spite of its array
Can't dare the blossom-seeking hand away,
While thistles wear their heavy knobs of bloom
Proud as a warhorse wears its haughty plume,
And by the roadside danger's self defy;
On commons where pined sheep and oxen lie
In ruddy pomp and ever thronging mood
It stands and spreads like danger in a wood,
And in the village street where meanest weeds
Can't stand untouch'd to fill their husks with seeds,
The haughty thistle o'er all danger towers,
In every place the very wasp of flowers.

*

The fir trees taper into twigs and wear
The rich blue green of summer all the year,
Softening the roughest tempest almost calm
And offering shelter ever still and warm
To the small path that towels underneath,
Where loudest winds – almost as summer's breath –
Scarce fan the weed that lingers green below,
When others out of doors are lost in frost and snow.
And sweet the music trembles on the ear
As the wind suthers through each tiny spear,
Makeshifts for leaves; and yet, so rich they show,
Winter is almost summer where they grow.

Clare is extraordinarily accurate in describing the birds and animals of the countryside:

THE FLIGHT OF BIRDS

The crow goes flopping on from wood to wood,
The wild duck wherries to the distant flood,
The starnels hurry o'er in merry crowds,
And overhead whew by like hasty clouds;
The wild duck from the meadow-water plies
And dashes up the water as he flies;
The pigeon suthers by on rapid wing,
The lark mounts upward at the call of spring.
In easy flights above the hurricane
With doubled neck high sails the noisy crane.
Whizz goes the pewit o'er the ploughman's team,
With many a whew and whirl and sudden scream;
And lightly fluttering to the tree just by,
In chattering journeys whirls the noisy pie;
From bush to bush slow swees the screaming jay,
With one harsh note of pleasure all the day.

THE AUTUMN ROBIN

Up on the ditcher's spade thou'lt hop
    For grubs and wreathing worms to search;
Where woodmen in the forest chop,
    Thou'lt fearless on their faggots perch;
Nay, by the gipsies' camp I stop
    And mark thee dwell a moment there
To prune thy wing awhile, then drop,
    The littered crumbs to share.

Domestic bird! thy pleasant face
    Doth well thy common suit commend;
To meet thee in a stranger-place
    Is meeting with an ancient friend.

Shakespeare, another country boy, is as incomparable in describing the countryside as in all other facets of his genius. I think the loveliest lines in English poetry are:

            daffodils,
    that come before the swallow dares, and take
    the winds of March with beauty.

There is a unique freshness about his writing, particularly in his songs:

> When daisies pied and violets blue
>   And lady-smocks all silver white
> And cuckoo-buds of yellow hue
>   Do paint the meadows with delight,
> The cuckoo then, on every tree,
> Mocks married men; for thus sings he,
>   Cuckoo;
> Cuckoo, cuckoo: Oh word of fear,
> Unpleasing to a married ear!
>
> When shepherds pipe on oaten straws,
>   And merry larks are ploughmen's clocks,
> When turtles tread, and rooks, and daws,
>   And maidens bleach their summer smocks,
> The cuckoo then, on every tree,
> Mocks married men; for thus sings he,
>   Cuckoo;
> Cuckoo, cuckoo: Oh word of fear,
> Unpleasing to a married ear!

*

>   When daffodils begin to peer,
>   With heigh! the doxy, over the dale,
>   Why, then comes the sweet o' the year;
>   For the red blood reigns in the winter's pale.
>
> The white sheet bleaching on the hedge,
>   With heigh! the sweet birds, Oh how they sing!
> Doth set my pugging tooth on edge,
>   For a quart of ale is a dish for a king.
>
> The lark, that tirra-lirra chants,
>   With heigh! with heigh! the thrush and the jay,
> Are summer songs for me and my aunts,
>   While we lie tumbling in the hay.

Milton has much the same quality in 'L'Allegro' and 'Lycidas':

> To hear the Lark begin his flight,
> And singing startle the dull night,
> From his watch-towre in the skies,
> Till the dappled dawn doth rise;
> Then to com in spight of sorrow,

And at my window bid good morrow,
Through the Sweet-Briar, or the Vine,
Or the twisted Eglantine,
While the Cock with lively din,
Scatters the rear of darkness thin,
And to the stack, or the Barn dore,
Stoutly struts his Dames before,
Oft list'ning how the Hounds and Horn
Chearly rouse the slumbring morn,
From the side of som Hoar Hill,
Through the high wood echoing shrill.
Som time walking not unseen
By Hedge-row Elms, on Hillocks green,
Right against the Eastern gate,
Where the great Sun begins his state,
Roab'd in flames, and Amber light,
The clouds in thousand Liveries dight,
While the Plowman neer at hand,
Whistles ore the Furrow'd Land,
And the Milkmaid singeth blithe,
And the Mower whets his sithe,
And every Shepherd tells his tale
Under the Hawthorn in the dale.

*

Return *Alpheus*, the dread voice is past,
That shrunk thy streams; Return *Sicilian* Muse,
And call the Vales, and bid them hither cast
Their Bells, and Flourets of a thousand hues.
Ye valleys low where the milde whispers use,
Of shades and wanton winds, and gushing brooks,
On whose fresh lap the swart Star sparely looks,
Throw hither all your quaint enameld eyes,
That on the green terf suck the honied showres,
And purple all the ground with vernal flowres.
Bring the rathe Primrose that forsaken dies.
The tufted Crow-toe, and pale Gessamine,
The white Pink, and the Pansie freakt with jeat,
The glowing Violet.
The Musk-rose, and the well attir'd Woodbine,
With Cowslips wan that hang the pensive head,
And every flower that sad embroidery wears:
Bid *Amarantus* all his beauty shed,
And Daffadillies fill their cups with tears,
To strew the Laureat Herse where *Lycid* lies.

Like most boys, I read only the shorter poems of Milton's youth when I was at school, and enjoyed them above all for their love of nature, a quality which later attracted me to Hopkins. When I first tried Milton's great religious epics, *Paradise Lost* and *Paradise Regained*, I found their theological weight too heavy for me. At Oxford I returned to Milton through his prose works, above all his magnificent defence of free speech, *Areopagitica*, which has remained one of my basic political texts. That lured me back to his later poetry, above all the sonnets and 'Samson Agonistes'. I am still fascinated by the similarity of his evolution to that of Hopkins.

Weather can transform the countryside, as Thomas Hardy wrote:

> This is the weather the cuckoo likes,
>   And so do I;
> When showers betumble the chestnut spikes,
>   And nestlings fly;
> And the little brown nightingale bills his best,
> And they sit outside the 'Traveller's Rest,'
> And maids come forth sprig-muslin drest,
> And citizens dream of the South and West,
>   And so do I.
>
> This is the weather the shepherd shuns,
>   And so do I:
> When beeches drip in browns and duns,
>   And thresh, and ply;
> And hill-hid tides throb, throe on throe,
> And meadow rivulets overflow,
> And drops on gate-bars hang in a row,
> And rooks in families homeward go,
>   And so do I.

I read Thomas Hardy's novels at school, when I was too young to appreciate their grandeur; it was difficult for me to identify with the characters. But I was bowled over by the opening pages of *The Return of the Native*, which describe Egdon Heath with the sombre spaciousness of a tone-poem by Sibelius:

A Saturday afternoon in November was approaching the time of twilight, and the vast tract of unenclosed wild known as Egdon Heath embrowned itself moment by moment. Overhead the hollow stretch of whitish cloud shutting out the sky was as a tent which had the whole heath for its floor.

The heaven being spread with this pallid screen and the earth with the darkest vegetation, their meeting-line at the horizon was clearly marked. In such contrast the heath wore the appearance of an instalment of night which had taken up its place before its astronomical hour was come: darkness had to a great extent arrived hereon, while day stood distinct in the sky. Looking upwards, a furze-cutter would have been inclined to continue work; looking down, he would have decided to finish his faggot and go home. The distant rims of the world and of the firmament seemed to be a division in time no less than a division in matter. The face of the heath by its mere complexion added half an hour to evening; it could in like manner retard the dawn, sadden noon, anticipate the frowning of storms scarcely generated, and intensify the opacity of a moonless midnight to a cause of shaking and dread.

In fact, precisely at this transitional point of its nightly roll into darkness the great and particular glory of the Egdon waste began, and nobody could be said to understand the heath who had not been there at such a time. It could best be felt when it could not clearly be seen, its complete effect and explanation lying in this and the succeeding hours before the next dawn: then, and only then, did it tell its true tale. The spot was, indeed, a near relation of night, and when night showed itself an apparent tendency to gravitate together could be perceived in its shades and the scene. The sombre stretch of rounds and hollows seemed to rise and meet the evening gloom in pure sympathy, the heath exhaling darkness as rapidly as the heavens precipitated it. And so the obscurity in the air and the obscurity in the land closed together in a black fraternization towards which each advanced half-way.

The place became full of a watchful intentness now; for when other things sank brooding to sleep the heath appeared slowly to awake and listen. Every night its Titanic form seemed to await something; but it had waited thus, unmoved, during so many centuries, through the crises of so many things, that it could only be imagined to await one last crisis – the final overthrow.

Francis Kilvert, too, saw his landscape transfigured by a change in the weather. Like Thomas Traherne two centuries earlier, Kilvert was an obscure country parson. HIs diaries are as eloquent of the countryside as those of Dorothy Wordsworth, but were first published eighty years after his death, as the Second World War was breaking out.

I read them just after the war, and return to them constantly for their gentle humanity. He loved his parishioners as much as he loved the countryside round Bredwardine, in the Wye valley:

The afternoon had been stormy but it cleared towards sunset.

Gradually the heavy rain clouds rolled across the valley to the foot of the opposite mountains and began climbing up their sides wreathing in rolling masses of vapour. One solitary cloud still hung over the brilliant sunlit town, and that whole cloud was a rainbow. Gradually it lost its bright prismatic hues and moved away up the Cusop Dingle in the shape of a pillar and of the colour of golden dark smoke. The Black Mountains were invisible, being wrapped in clouds, and I saw one very white brilliant dazzling cloud where the mountains ought to have been. This cloud grew more white and dazzling every moment, till a clearer burst of sunlight scattered the mists and revealed the truth. This brilliant white cloud that I had been looking and wondering at was the mountain in snow. The last cloud and mist rolled away over the mountain tops and the mountains stood up in the clear blue heaven, a long rampart line of dazzling glittering snow so as no fuller on earth can white them. I stood rooted to the ground, struck with amazement and over-whelmed at the extraordinary splendour of this marvellous spec-tacle. I never saw anything to equal it I think, even among the high Alps. One's first involuntary thought in the presence of these magnificent sights is to lift up the heart to God and humbly thank Him for having made the earth so beautiful. An intense glare of primrose light streamed from the west deepening into rose and crimson. There was not a flake of snow anywhere but on the mountains and they stood up, the great white range rising high into the blue sky, while all the rest of the world at their feet lay ruddy rosy brown. The sudden contrast was tremendous, electrifying. I could have cried with the excitement of the overwhelming spec-tacle. I wanted someone to admire the sight with me. A man came whistling along the road riding upon a cart horse. I would have stopped him and drawn his attention to the mountains but I thought he would probably consider me mad. He did not seem to be the least struck by or to be taking the smallest notice of the great sight. But it seemed to me as if one might never see such a sight again. The great white range which had at first gleamed with an intense brilliant yellow light gradually deepened with the sky to the indescribable red tinge that snowfields assume in sunset light, and then the grey cold tinge crept up the great slopes quenching the rosy warmth which lingered still a few minutes on the summits.

Soon all was cold and grey and all that was left of the brilliant gleaming range was the dim ghostly phantom of the mountain rampart scarce distinguishable from the greying sky.

In her descriptive poems Emily Dickinson has an extraordinary capacity to relate birds or bees, or even the weather, to people; indeed she had an almost animistic view of nature:

A prompt – executive Bird is the Jay –
Bold as a Bailiff's Hymn –
Brittle and Brief in quality –
Warrant in every line –

Sitting a Bough like a Brigadier
Confident and straight –
Much is the mien of him in March
As a Magistrate –

*

The Robin is a Gabriel
In humble circumstances –
His Dress denotes him socially,
Of Transport's Working Classes –
He has the punctuality
Of the New England Farmer –
The same oblique integrity,
A Vista vastly warmer –

A small but sturdy Residence,
A self denying Household.
The Guests of Perspicacity
Are all that cross his Threshold –
As covert as a Fugitive,
Cajoling Consternation
By Ditties to the Enemy
And Sylvan Punctuation –

*

Bees are Black, with Gilt Surcingles –
Buccaneers of Buzz.
Ride abroad in ostentation
And subsist on Fuzz.

Fuzz ordained – not Fuzz contingent –
Marrows of the Hill.
Jugs – a Universe's fracture
Could not jar or spill.

*

The Dandelion's pallid tube
Astonishes the Grass,
And Winter instantly becomes
An infinite Alas –

The tube uplifts a signal Bud
And then a shouting Flower, –
The Proclamation of the Suns
That sepulture is o'er.

*

The Sky is low – the Clouds are mean.
A Travelling Flake of Snow
Across a Barn or through a Rut
Debates if it will go –

A Narrow Wind complains all Day
How some one treated him
Nature, like Us is sometimes caught
Without her Diadem.

*

I'll tell you how the Sun rose
A Ribbon at a time –
The Steeples swam in Amethyst –
The news, like Squirrels, ran –
The Hills untied their Bonnets –
The Bobolinks – begun –
Then I said softly to myself –
'That must have been the Sun'!
But how he set – I know not –
There seemed a purple stile
That little Yellow boys and girls
Were climbing all the while –
Till when they reached the other side,
A Dominie in Gray –
Put gently up the evening Bars –
And led the flock away –

*

Blazing in Gold and quenching in Purple
Leaping like Leopards to the Sky
Then at the feet of the old Horizon
Laying her spotted Face to die
Stooping as low as the Otter's Window
Touching the Roof and tinting the Barn
Kissing her Bonnet to the Meadow
And the Juggler of Day is gone

For Wordsworth, poetry was emotion recollected in tranquillity, even when his imagery is most direct as in 'Daffodils' and 'The Prelude':

> I wandered lonely as a cloud
> That floats on high o'er vales and hills,
> When all at once I saw a crowd,
> A host, of golden daffodils;
> Beside the lake, beneath the trees,
> Fluttering and dancing in the breeze.
>
> Continuous as the stars that shine
> And twinkle on the Milky Way,
> They stretched in never-ending line
> Along the margin of a bay:
> Ten thousand saw I at a glance
> Tossing their heads in sprightly dance.
>
> The waves beside them danced; but they
> Out-did the sparkling waves in glee:
> A poet could not but be gay,
> In such a jocund company;
> I gazed – and gazed – but little thought
> What wealth the show to me had brought:
>
> For oft, when on my couch I lie
> In vacant or in pensive mood,
> They flash upon that inward eye
> Which is the bliss of solitude
> And then my heart with pleasure fills,
> And dances with the daffodils.

*

> And in the frosty season, when the sun
> Was set, and visible for many a mile
> The cottage windows blazed through twilight gloom,
> I heeded not their summons: happy time
> It was indeed for all of us – for me
> It was a time of rapture! Clear and loud
> The village clock tolled six, – I wheeled about
> Proud and exulting like an untired horse
> That cares not for his home. All shod with steel,
> We hissed along the polished ice in games
> Confederate, imitative of the chase
> And woodland pleasures, – the resounding horn,

The pack loud chiming, and the hunted hare.
So through the darkness and the cold we flew,
And not a voice was idle; with the din
Smitten, the precipices rang aloud;
The leafless trees and every icy crag
Tinkled like iron; while far distant hills
Into the tumult sent an alien sound
Of melancholy not unnoticed, while the stars
Eastward were sparkling clear, and in the west
The orange sky of evening died away.

Wordsworth, like Milton, is a poet whom I came to appreciate fully only in my later life. As a young man I much preferred Keats and Shelley. The banality of poems like 'Peter Bell' seemed to justify the cruel parody:

Two voices hast thou; one is of the deep,
And one is of a poor dim-witted sheep,
And, Wordsworth, both are thine.

Nowadays, however, I find Wordsworth one of the greatest poets in our language. Any young man will find Wordsworth speaking for him in the first version of 'The Prelude' (Wordsworth produced a sanitized version at the end of his life which has none of the *élan* of the original). He had an extraordinary capacity to convey wisdom as well as feeling in simple and straightforward language. His imagery relied above all on the countryside, from which he drew his deepest inspiration. His sister Dorothy, who lived with him for much of her life, was as eloquent in expressing her love for nature in her prose journals as he in his poetry.

A.E. Housman's recollections were steeped in nostalgia, as much for his lost youth as for the Shropshire countryside:

Into my heart an air that kills
    From yon far country blows:
What are those blue remembered hills,
    What spires, what farms are those?

That is the land of lost content,
    I see it shining plain,
The happy highways where I went
    And cannot come again.

We all have our own 'blue remembered hills'; mine are in Wharfedale and upper Airedale in Yorkshire.

In his prose writings Gerard Manley Hopkins observed nature with astonishing accuracy and objectivity, like the draughtsman he was:

[May 9] This day and May 11 the bluebells in the little wood between the College and the highroad and in one of the Hurst Green cloughs. In the little wood/ opposite the light/ they stood in blackish spreads or sheddings like the spots on a snake. The heads are then like thongs and solemn in grain and grape-colour. But in the clough/ through the light/ they came in falls of sky-colour washing the brows and slacks of the ground with vein-blue, thickening at the double, vertical themselves and the young grass and brake fern combed vertical, but the brake struck the upright of all this with light winged transomes. It was a lovely sight. – The bluebells in your hand baffle you with their inscape, made to every sense: if you draw your fingers through them they are lodged and struggle/ with a shock of wet heads; the long stalks rub and click and flatten to a fan on one another like your fingers themselves would when you passed the palms hard across one another, making a brittle rub and jostle like the noise of a hurdle strained by leaning against; then there is the faint honey smell and in the mouth the sweet gum when you bite them. But this is easy, it is the eye they baffle. They give one a fancy of panpipes and of some wind instrument with stops – a trombone perhaps. The overhung necks – for growing they are little more than a staff with a simple crook but in water, where they stiffen, they take stronger turns, in the head like sheephooks or, when more waved throughout, like the waves riding through a whip that is being smacked – what with these overhung necks and what with the crisped ruffled bells dropping mostly on one side and the gloss these have at their footstalks they have an air of the knights at chess. Then the knot or 'knoop' of buds some shut, some just gaping, which makes the pencil of the whole spike, should be noticed: the inscape of the flower most finely carried out in the siding of the axes, each striking a greater and greater slant, is finished in these clustered buds, which for the most part are not straightened but rise to the end like a tongue and this and their tapering and a little flattening they have make them look like the heads of snakes

Such writing about the countryside, which combines accuracy of observation with audacity of image, has given me intense pleasure throughout my life, particularly at times when I am confined to work in the city.

Much poetry about nature, however, is designed as an offering to the Creator, and derives additional force from its spiritual dimension. Hopkins, in particular, was always concerned in his poetry to relate nature to his God, who in turn is seen as Heraclitean:

Nothing is so beautiful as Spring –
    When weeds, in wheels, shoot long and lovely and lush;
    Thrush's eggs look little low heavens, and thrush
Through the echoing timber does so rinse and wring
The ear, it strikes like lightnings to hear him sing;
    The glassy peartree leaves and blooms, they brush
    The descending blue; that blue is all in a rush
With richness; the racing lambs too have fair their fling.

What is all this juice and all this joy?
    A strain of the earth's sweet being in the beginning
In Eden garden. – Have, get, before it cloy,

    Before it cloud, Christ, lord, and sour with sinning,
Innocent mind and Mayday in girl and boy,
    Most, O maid's child, thy choice and worthy the winning.

*

Summer ends now; now, barbarous in beauty, the stooks rise
Around; up above, what wind-walks! what lovely behaviour
Of silk-sack clouds! has wilder, wilful-wavier
Meal-drift moulded ever and melted across skies?

I walk, I lift up, I lift up heart, eyes,
Down all that glory in the heavens to glean our Saviour;
And, éyes, heárt, what looks, what lips yet gave you a
Rapturous love's greeting of realer, of rounder replies?

And the azurous hung hills are his world-wielding shoulder
Majestic – as a stallion stalwart, very-violet-sweet! –
These things, these things were here and but the beholder
Wanting; which two when they once meet,
The heart rears wings bold and bolder
And hurls for him, O half hurls earth for him off under his feet.

*

Look at the stars! look, look up at the skies!
 O look at all the fire-folk sitting in the air!
 The bright boroughs, the circle-citadels there!
Down in dim woods the diamond delves! the elves'-eyes!
The grey lawns cold where gold, where quickgold lies!
 Wind-beat whitebeam! airy abeles set on a flare!
 Flake-doves sent floating forth at a farmyard scare! –
Ah well! it is all a purchase, all is a prize.
Buy then! bid then! – What? – Prayer, patience, alms, vows.
Look, look: a May-mess, like on orchard boughs!
 Look! March-bloom, like on mealed-with-yellow sallows
These are indeed the barn; withindoors house
The shocks. This piece-bright paling shuts the spouse
 Christ home, Christ and his mother and all his hallows.

*

Glory be to God for dappled things –
 For skies of couple-colour as a brinded cow;
  For rose-moles all in stipple upon trout that swim;
Fresh-firecoal chestnut-falls; finches' wings;
 Landscape plotted and pieced – fold, fallow, and plough;
  And áll trádes, their gear and tackle and trim.
All things counter, original, spare, strange;
 Whatever is fickle, freckled (who knows how?)
  With swift, slow; sweet, sour; adazzle, dim;
 He fathers-forth whose beauty is past change:
  Praise him.

In the same spirit William Blake asked us:

  To see a World in a grain of sand,
  And a heaven in wild flower,
  Hold Infinity in the palm of your hand,
  And Eternity in an hour.

Most of Blake's nature poetry has a religious or mystical dimension:

  'Love seeketh not itself to please,
  Nor for itself hath any care,
  But for another gives its ease,
  And builds a Heaven in Hell's despair.'

So sung a little Clod of Clay,
Trodden with the cattle's feet,
But a Pebble of the brook
Warbled out these metres meet:

'Love seeketh only Self to please,
To bind another to its delight,
Joys in another's loss of ease,
And builds a Hell in Heaven's despite.'

Emily Dickinson also gives mystical meaning to a stone:

How happy is the little Stone
That rambles in the Road alone,
And doesn't care about Careers
And Exigencies never fears –
Whose Coat of elemental Brown
A passing Universe put on,
And independent as the Sun
Associates or glows alone,
Fulfilling absolute Decree
In casual simplicity –

However, she feels so much at one with everything in nature that she is always a little uncertain about the place of God in her universe. She did not find it easy to reconcile her pantheism with the God of Christianity.

It makes no difference abroad –
The Seasons – fit – the same –
The Mornings blossom into Noons –
And split their Pods of Flame –

Wild flowers – kindle in the Woods –
The Brooks slam – all the Day –
No Black bird bates his Banjo –
For passing Calvary –

Auto da Fe – and Judgment –
Are nothing to the Bee –
His separation from His Rose –
To Him – sums Misery –

*

> Our little Kinsmen – after Rain
> In plenty may be seen,
> A Pink and Pulpy multitude
> The tepid Ground upon.
>
> A needless life, it seemed to me
> Until a little Bird
> As to a Hospitality
> Advanced and breakfasted.
>
> As I of He, so God of Me
> I pondered, may have judged,
> And left the little Angle Worm
> With Modesties enlarged.

The love of nature is not necessarily related to the love of God – or man. I suppose that is why some people find nature poetry and landscape painting unsatisfying; they feel it ought to have a theme. Fortunately I am not one of them. I can enjoy a poem by Clare or a painting by Monet without wondering what it means. It is wholly satisfying in itself, and does not require a meaning any more than does the dome of St Paul's Cathedral.

MY OWN LANDSCAPES

I have always been much influenced by my surroundings, at home and abroad, at work and at play. The Brontë sisters described my part of Yorkshire better than anyone else. My first country heaven, when as a little boy I visited my mother's family in Newnham on Severn, has not been celebrated so well. However, A.E. Housman's Shropshire is a good surrogate for my Gloucestershire. 'Bredon Hill' brings back to me Sunday mornings overlooking Newnham and the broad curves of the river Severn from Pleasant Stile.

> In summertime on Bredon
>   The bells they sound so clear;
> Round both the shires they ring them
>   In steeples far and near,
>   A happy noise to hear.

Here of a Sunday morning
   My love and I would lie,
And see the coloured counties,
   And hear the larks so high
   About us in the sky.

The bells would ring to call her
   In valleys miles away:
'Come all to church, good people;
   Good people, come and pray.'
   But here my love would stay.

And I would turn and answer
   Among the springing thyme,
'Oh, peal upon our wedding,
   And we will hear the chime,
   And come to church in time,'

But when the snows at Christmas
   On Bredon top were strown,
My love rose up so early
   And stole out unbeknown
   And went to church alone.

They tolled the one bell only,
   Groom there was none to see,
The mourners followed after,
   And so to church went she,
   And would not wait for me.

The bells they sound on Bredon,
   And still the steeples hum.
'Come all to church, good people,' –
   Oh, noisy bells, be dumb;
   I hear you, I will come.

Fortunately Edna, who as a little girl at Coleford loved that view as much as I, did 'come to church in time'.

Our family holidays, camping in France and Italy, gave us a love of the Alps which remains as keen as ever. For the high Alps, the small towns and villages like Samoens, Chamonix, and Argentière are our favourite centres, as they were for Wordsworth, Ruskin and so many English travellers in the nineteenth century. Ruskin loved Chamonix so much that he tried to buy a house there. Though even then he feared that tourism would ruin the area, it has not changed since he wrote his diary on 26 June 1844:

June 26th. ¼ past 4 morning. Of all the lovely dawns I ever saw on Mont Blanc, this bears the bell. When I woke at ½ past three, its form was scarcely distinguishable through morning mist, which in the lower valley hung in dense white flakes among the trees along the course of the Arve. There were heavy white clouds over the Pavillon, relieved against a threatening black ground which reached the horizon. The outline of the snow was throughout indistinct, with what I thought were wind avalanches, but I believe they must have been evaporating moisture, blowing towards Cormayeur. As the dawn grew brighter, a brown group of cloud formed near the Dôme du Goûté – not on it, but in the sky, blowing also towards Cormayeur. Presently the black threatening part of the horizon grew luminous, and threw out the clouds, before white, as grey dark masses from its body, gradually disappearing itself into the ordinary light of pure horizon. A few minutes afterwards the first rose touched the summit, the mist gradually melting from the higher hills, leaving that in the valley arranged at the top in exquisitely fine horizontal waterlike cirri, separated by little intervals from its chief mass. The light lowered to the Tacul and Dôme and such intense fire I never saw. The colour is deeper in the evening, but far less brilliant. A quarter of an hour afterwards, when it had touched the Aig[uille] du G[oûter] it began to diminish on the summit, which then looked feeble and *green* beside the Tacul and Aig[uille] du G[oûter]. Then the aig[uille] du Midi caught it, but in proportion as it touched the lower height, it was less rosy. It is now intensely white, a little tawny, reaching to base of aig[uille] du G[oûter] on which, as well as on the Breven and top of mont[agne] de la Côte, there is deep fresh snow. The clouds became first brown, then rosy, then melted away, all but one cirrus which yet hangs just over the Dôme. The valley mist is nearly melted, a fleecy flake hangs here and there among the pines; the air is intensely clear, and the meadows white-green with dew. Now another bank of mist has formed down the valley. I never saw anything so exquisite as the view towards Argentière – all the aiguilles of Tour clothed with pure fresh snow, seen through the clear rainy atmosphere. I know not how it is, but the deep snows of the higher Alps scarcely affect me as this sprinkling did; they are too much like iced plumcake, too independent of the hill, undignified in their soft wreathed lines. The Tour aiguilles showed every ridge of rock through their robe, firm as iron, and I am very fond of their forms even without snow to elevate them. Be that as it may, they touched me this morning strangely, and there was a white fishy cloud over the Dru, with edges like amianthus or spun glass, most glorious.

No one can describe the spirit of a landscape better than D.H.Lawrence. I often find that his neurotic personality overpowers his novels and short stories, and prefer to encounter it directly in his letters, where it is less dressed up in portentous philosophizing. But his descriptions of nature in the countryside are always both exact and exhilarating. Moreover many of his landscapes, whether in England, Italy, or Austria, also have a special meaning in my life. The Nottinghamshire mining valley where he was brought up serves well as a surrogate for the country round Keighley: Here he describes it in *The White Peacock*:

> They decided to bury him in our churchyard at Greymede under the beeches; the widow would have it so, and nothing might be denied her in her state.
>
> It was a magnificent morning in early spring when I watched among the trees to see the procession come down the hillside. The upper air was woven with the music of the larks, and my whole world thrilled with the conception of summer. The young pale windflowers had arisen by the wood-gale, and under the hazels, when perchance the hot sun pushed his way, new little suns dawned, and blazed with real light. There was a certain thrill and quickening everywhere, as a woman must feel when she has conceived. A sallow tree in a favoured spot looked like a pale gold cloud of summer dawn; nearer it had poised a golden, fairy busby on every twig, and was voiced with a hum of bees, like any sacred golden bush, uttering its gladness in the thrilling murmur of bees, and in warm scent. Birds called and flashed on every hand; they made off exultant with streaming strands of grass, or wisps of fleece, plunging into the dark spaces of the wood, and out again into the blue.

D.H. Lawrence spent much of his life in Italy, often in places we knew well, like Fiascherino on the southern peninsula of the bay of Spezia, close to Lerici where Shelley was drowned. He describes in one of his letters a Good Friday procession at Tellaro, where we used to stay:

> We went on Good Friday eve to see the procession of Jesus to the tomb. The houses in Tellaro are stuck about on the rocks in a tiny opening. It was a still night with a great moon, but the village deep in shadow, only the moonlight shining out at sea. And on all the window-sills were rows of candles trembling on the still air, long

rows in the square, big windows, very golden in the blue dark shadow under a lighted sky. Then the procession came out of church, the lads running in front clapping wooden clappers, like those they scare birds with at home. Such a din of clappers. And the noise means the grinding of the bones of Judas. Then came the procession – a white bier with drawn curtains, carried high on the shoulders of men dressed all in white, with white cloths on their heads – a weird chanting noise broken by the noise of the sea, and candles fluttering as the white figures moved, and two great gilt rococo lanterns carried above. Then, with all the clatter and the broken mournful chanting and the hoarse wash of the sea, they began to climb the steep staircase between the high dark houses, a white, ghostly winding procession, with the dark-dressed villagers crowding behind. It was gone in a minute. And it made a fearful impression on me. It is the *mystery* that does it – it is Death itself, robbed of its horrors and only Fear and Wonder going humbly behind.

Lake Garda still attracts us whenever we are in the area. Here is Lawrence again on the coming of spring at San Gaudenzio:

The days go by, through the brief silence of winter, when the sunshine is so still and pure, like iced wine, and the dead leaves gleam brown, and water sounds hoarse in the ravines. It is so still and transcendent, the cypress trees poise like flames of forgotten darkness, that should have been blown out at the end of the summer. For as we have candles to light the darkness of night, so the cypresses are candles to keep the darkness aflame in the full sunshine.

Meanwhile, the Christmas roses become many. They rise from their budded, intact humbleness near the ground, they rise up, they throw up their crystal, they become handsome, they are heaps of confident, mysterious whiteness in the shadow of a rocky stream. It is almost uncanny to see them. They are the flowers of darkness, white and wonderful beyond belief.

Then their radiance becomes soiled and brown, they thaw, break, and scatter and vanish away. Already the primroses are coming out, and the almond is in bud. The winter is passing away. On the mountains the fierce snow gleams apricot gold as evening approaches, golden, apricot, but so bright that it is almost frightening. What can be so fiercely gleaming when all is shadowy? It is something inhuman and unmitigated between heaven and earth.

The heavens are strange and proud all the winter, their progress goes on without reference to the dim earth. The dawns come white and translucent, the lake is a moonstone in the dark hills, then across the lake there stretches a vein of fire, then a whole, orange, flashing track over the whiteness. There is the exquisite silent passage of the day, and then at evening the afterglow, a huge incandescence of rose, hanging above and gleaming, as if it were the presence of a host of angels in rapture. It gleams like a rapturous chorus, then passes away, and the stars appear, large and flashing.

Meanwhile, the primroses are dawning on the ground, their light is growing stronger, spreading over the banks and under the bushes. Between the olive roots the violets are out, large, white, grave violets, and less serious blue ones. And looking down the hill, among the grey smoke of olive leaves, pink puffs of smoke are rising up. It is the almond and the apricot trees, it is the Spring.

The most beautiful place we have ever seen, however, is the Yosemite valley in California, where we spent some days during a visit to our daughter in San Francisco. Its beauty defies description in words, though Ansel Adams has captured something of its grandeur in his photographs. John Muir here writes of one of his many climbs in the Yosemite valley:

July 15. – Followed the Mono Trail up the eastern rim of the basin nearly to its summit, then turned off southward to a small shallow valley that extends to the edge of the Yosemite, which we reached about noon, and encamped. After luncheon I made haste to high ground, and from the top of the ridge on the west side of Indian Cannon gained the noblest view of the summit peaks I have ever yet enjóyed. Nearly all the upper basin of the Merced was displayed, with its sublime domes and cannons, dark upsweeping forests, and glorious array of white peaks deep in the sky, every feature glowing, radiating beauty that pours into our flesh and bones like heat rays from fire. Sunshine over all; no breath of wind to stir the brooding calm. Never before had I seen so glorious a landscape, so boundless an affluence of sublime mountain beauty. The most extravagant description I might give of this view to any one who has not seen similar landscapes with his own eyes would not so much as hint its grandeur and the spiritual glow that covered it. I shouted and gesticulated in a wild burst of ecstasy, much to the astonishment of St. Bernard Carlo, who came running up to me, manifesting in his intelligent eyes a puzzled concern that was very ludicrous, which had the effect of bringing me to my senses. A brown bear, too, it would seem, had been a spectator of the show I had made of myself, for I had gone but a few yards when I started one from a thicket of brush. He evidently considered me dangerous, for he ran away very fast, tumbling over the tops of the tangled Manzanita bushes in his haste. Carlo drew back, with his ears depressed as if afraid, and kept looking me in the face, as if expecting me to pursue and shoot, for he had seen many a bear battle in his day.

Following the ridge which made a gradual descent to the south, I came at length to the brow of that massive cliff that stands between Indian Gonñon and Yosemite Falls, and here the far-famed valley came suddenly into view throughout almost its whole extent. The noble walls – sculptured into endless variety of domes and gables, spires and battlements and plain mural precipices – all a-tremble with the thunder tones of the falling water. The level bottom seemed to be dressed like a garden – sunny meadows here and there, and groves of Pine and Oak; the river of Mercy sweeping in majesty through the midst of them and flashing back the sunbeams. The great Tissiack, or Half Dome, rising at the upper end of the valley to a height of nearly a mile, is nobly proportioned and life-like, the most impressive of all the rocks, holding the eye in devout admiration, calling it back again and again from falls or meadows, or even the mountains beyond – marvelous cliffs, marvelous in sheer dizzy depth and sculpture, types of endurance. Thousands of years have they stood in the sky exposed to rain, snow, frost, earthquake and avalanche, yet they still wear the bloom of youth.

I rambled along the valley rim to the westward; most of it is rounded off on the very brink, so that it is not easy to find places where one may look clear down the face of the wall to the bottom. When such places were found, and I had cautiously set my feet and drawn my body erect. I could not help fearing a little that the rock might split off and let me down, and what a down! – more than three thousand feet. Still my limbs did not tremble, nor did I feel the least uncertainty as to the reliance to be placed on them. My only fear was that a flake of the granite, which in some places showed joints more or less open and running parallel with the face of the cliff, might give way. After withdrawing from such places, excited with the view I had got, I would say to myself, 'Now don't go out on the verge again.' But in the face of Yosemite scenery cautious remonstrance is vain; under its spell one's body seems to go where it likes with a will over which we seem to have scarce any control.

After a mile or so of this memorable cliff work I approached Yosemite Creek, admiring its easy, graceful, confident gestures as it comes bravely forward in its narrow channel, singing the last of its mountain songs on its way to its fate – a few rods more over the shining granite, then down half a mile in snowy foam to another world, to be lost in the Merced, where climate, vegetation, inhabitants, all are different. Emerging from its last gorge, it glides in wide lace-like rapids down a smooth incline into a pool where it seems to rest and compose its gray, agitated waters before taking the grand plunge, then slowly slipping over the lip of the pool basin, it descends another glossy slope with rapidly accelerated speed to the brink of the tremendous cliff, and with sublime, fateful confidence springs out free in the air.

Muir is far too little known in Britain. In 1849, after a happy childhood in Scotland, he emigrated to America with his father at the age of ten. John Muir had much in common with Thoreau: he loved nature with a mystical fervour, though his passion was for the mountains and wildernesses of the High Sierra rather than the woods and streams of Massachusetts. It was he who persuaded President Theodore Roosevelt to make Yosemite a national park, and to save the Grand Canyon and the Petrified Forest in Arizona. At the end of his life he travelled to Alaska with the railroad magnate, E.H. Harriman, father of Averell Harriman. When someone mentioned Harriman's great wealth, Muir replied, 'Why, I am richer than Harriman. I have all the money I want and he has not.'

As a politician I have had all too little time to explore the mountains. Once I became a national figure, I had to live in London. That has its compensations too, as even Wordsworth admitted in 'London' and 'Upon Westminster Bridge':

> Rise up, thou monstrous ant-hill on the plain
> Of a too busy world! Before me flow,
> Thou endless stream of men and moving things!
> Thy everyday appearance, as it strikes –
> With wonder heightened, or sublimed by awe –
> On strangers, of all ages; the quick dance
> Of colours, lights and forms; the deafening din;
> The comers and the goers face to face,
> Face after face; the string of dazzling wares,
> Shop after shop, with symbols, blazoned names,
>
> And all the tradesman's honours overhead:
> Here, fronts of houses, like a title-page,
> With letters huge inscribed from top to toe,

Stationed above the door, like guardian saints;
There allegoric shapes, female or male,
Or physiognomies of real men.
Land-warriors, kings, or admirals of the sea,
Boyle, Shakespeare, Newton, or the attractive head
Of some quack-doctor, famous in his day.

Meanwhile the roar continues, till at length,
Escaped as from an enemy, we turn
Abruptly into some sequestered nook,
Still as a sheltered place when winds blow loud!

*

Earth has not anything to show more fair;
Dull would he be of soul who could pass by
A sight so touching in its majesty:
This City now doth like a garment wear
The beauty of the morning; silent, bare,
Ships, towers, domes, theatres, and temples lie
Open unto the fields and to the sky,
All bright and glittering in the smokeless air.
Never did sun more beautifully steep
In his first splendour valley, rock, or hill;
Ne'er saw I, never felt, a calm so deep.
The river glideth at his own sweet will:
Dear God! the very houses seem asleep;
And all that mighty heart is lying still.

Thomas Hardy, though as devoted to the countryside as
Wordsworth, could see the beauty of snow in the suburbs:

Every branch big with it,
Bent every twig with it;
Every fork like a white web-foot;
Every street and pavement mute:
Some flakes have lost their way, and grope back upward, when
Meeting those meandering down they turn and descend again.
The palings are glued together like a wall,
And there is no waft of wind with the fleecy fall.

A sparrow enters the tree,
Whereon immediately
A snow-lump thrice his own slight size
Descends on him and showers his head and eyes.

And overturns him,
And near inurns him,
And lights on a nether twig, when its brush
Starts off a volley of other lodging lumps with a rush.

The steps are a blanched slope,
Up which, with feeble hope,
A black cat comes, wide-eyed and thin;
And we take him in.

The great poet of suburbia was John Betjeman, who lived much of his life, like us, in Highgate, which he describes at length in 'Summoned by Bells'. Before we moved to Highgate, we lived in Kentish Town, not yet a colony of the intelligentsia. So Betjeman's 'Parliament Hill Fields' bridges these two worlds:

Rumbling under blackened girders, Midland, bound for
    Cricklewood,
Puffed its sulphur to the sunset where that Land of Laundries
    stood.
Rumble under, thunder over, train and tram alternate go,
Shake the floor and smudge the ledger, Charrington, Sells, Dale
    and Co,
Nuts and nuggets in the window, trucks along the lines below.

When the Bon Marché was shuttered, when the feet were hot and
    tired,
Outside Charrington's we waited, by the 'STOP HERE IF
    REQUIRED',
Launched aboard the shopping basket, sat precipitately down,
Rocked past Zwanziger the baker's, and the terrace blackish
    brown,
And the curious Anglo-Norman parish church of Kentish Town.

Till the tram went over thirty, sighting terminus again,
Past municipal lawn tennis and the bobble-hanging plane;
Soft the light suburban evening caught our ashlar-speckled spire,
Eighteen-sixty Early English, as the mighty elms retire
Either side of Brookfield Mansions flashing fine French-window fire.

Oh the after-tram-ride quiet, when we heard a mile beyond,
Silver music from the bandstand, barking dogs by Highgate Pond;
Up the hill where stucco houses in Virginia creeper drown –
And my childish wave of pity, seeing children carrying down
Sheaves of drooping dandelions to the courts of Kentish Town.

My constituency in Leeds was yet another world, different of course from London and the South, but different too from Keighley and the Dales. Richard Hoggart has described it as it was before the war in his autobiography, and Alan Bennett has given sympathetic portraits of its people in some of his plays. But for me the most accurate and moving pictures of Leeds are drawn by Tony Harrison, one of the very best of Britain's younger poets. He was born and bred a 'Leeds Loiner'; he read classics at Leeds University on a scholarship from Leeds Grammar School. Then followed a long odyssey of travel, lecturing in Nigeria, Prague, Cuba, Brazil, Senegal and Gambia. In recent years he has written verse libretti for the Metropolitan Opera in New York and verse texts for the National Theatre in London, which recently produced a Greek comic play for him called *The Trackers of Oxyrrynchus* – not all the critics appreciated its outstanding properties! He is married to Teresa Stratas, who sang Violetta in Franco Zeffirelli's film of *La Traviata*, and has recorded the best of all albums of Kurt Weill's cabaret songs. In his poetry Tony Harrison dwells to the point of obsession on his working-class boyhood and youth in Leeds; for example in 'The Allotments' and 'The Queen's English':

> Choked, reverted *Dig for Victory* plots
> Helped put more bastards into Waif Home cots
> Than anywhere, but long before my teens
> The Veterans got them for their bowling greens.
> In Leeds it was never *Who* or *When* but *Where*.
> The bridges of the slimy River Aire,
> Where Jabez Tunnicliffe, for love of God,
> Founded the *Band of Hope* in eighteen odd,
> The cold canal that ran to Liverpool,
> Made hot trickles in the knickers cool
> As soon as flow. The graveyards of Leeds 2
> Were hardly love-nests but they had to do –
> Through clammy mackintosh and winter vest
> And rumpled jumper for a touch of breast.
> Stroked nylon crackled over groin and bum
> Like granny's wireless stuck on Hilversum.
> And after love we'd find some epitaph
> Embossed backwards on your arse and laugh.
> And young, we cuddled by the abattoir,

Faffing with fastenings, never getting far.
Through sooty shutters the odd glimpsed spark
From hooves on concrete stalls scratched at the dark
And glittered in green eyes. Cowclap smacked
Onto the pavings where the beasts were packed.
And offal furnaces with clouds of stench
Choked other couples off the lychgate bench.

*

Last meal together, Leeds, the Queen's Hotel,
that grandish pile of swank in City Square.
Too posh for me! he said (though he dressed well)
If you weren't wi' me now ah'd nivver dare!
I knew that he'd decided that he'd die
not by the way he lingered in the bar,
nor by that look he'd give with one good eye,
nor the firmer handshake and the gruff *ta-ra*,
but when we browsed the station bookstall sales
he picked up *Poems from the Yorkshire Dales* –
'ere tek this un wi' yer to New York
to remind yer 'ow us gaffers used to talk.
It's up your street in't it? ah'll buy yer that!
The broken lines go through me speeding South –
As t'Doctor stopped to oppen woodland yat . . .
and
    wi' skill they putten wuds reet i' his mouth.

When I was Defence Secretary in the sixties we decided we must find ourselves some bolt-hole in the country. Yorkshire was too far from London, so we found a small gatehouse on the Kent-Sussex border. When the children had all left home our house in Highgate was too big for us, so we decided to look for another place in the country to which we could retire when I left the House of Commons, yet which would have room for the whole family at holidays. We found our earthly paradise in the Cuckmere valley just outside Alfriston, with a magnificent view of the downs, and a glimpse of the sea as well.

Glyndebourne and Brighton are both within easy reach. I love Brighton not only for its bookshops, but also for its raffish devotion to pleasure, little changed since Horace Smith described it in Regency times:

Now fruitful autumn lifts his sun-burnt head,
   The slighted Park few cambric muslins whiten,
The dry machines revisit Ocean's bed,
   And Horace quits awhile the town for Brighton.

The Cit foregoes his box at Turnham Green,
   To pick up health and shells with Amphitrite;
Pleasure's frail daughters trip along the Steyne,
   Led by the dame the Greeks call Aphrodite.

Phœbus, the tanner, plies his fiery trade,
   The graceful nymphs ascend Judea's ponies,
Scale the west cliff, or visit the parade,
   While poor papa in town a patient drone is.

Loose trousers snatch the wreath from pantaloons;
   Nankeen of late were worn the sultry weather in;
But now (so with the Prince's Light Dragoons)
   White jean have triumph'd o'er their Indian brethren.

Here with choice food earth smiles and ocean yawns,
   Intent alike to please the London glutton;
This for our breakfast proffers shrimps and prawns,
   That, for our dinner, South-down lamb and mutton.

Yet here, as elsewhere, death impartial reigns,
   Visits alike the cot and the Pavilion,
And for a bribe with equal scorn disdains
   My half-a-crown, and Baring's half a million.

Alas, how short the span of human pride!
   Time flies, and hope's romantic schemes are undone;
Crosweller's coach, that carries four inside,
   Waits to take back th' unwilling bard to London.

Ye circulating novelists, adieu!
   Long envious cords my black portmanteau tighten;
Billiards, begone! avaunt, illegal loo!
   Farewell, old Ocean's bauble, glittering Brighton!

Long shalt thou laugh thine enemies to scorn,
   Proud as Phœnicia, queen of watering places!
Boys yet unbreech'd, and virgins yet unborn,
   On thy bleak downs shall tan their blooming faces.

The main difference today is that pantaloons and Indian wear are
back again, the jeans are blue, and Pleasure has some frail sons as
well as daughters in the Lanes.

The hills of the Cuckmere valley are tawny rather than green, reminding me of my beloved Yorkshire dales. Rudyard Kipling captured the beauty of 'our blunt, bow-headed, whale-backed Downs' in four lines:

> Bare-sloped, where chasing shadows skim,
>   And through the gaps revealed,
> Belt upon belt, the wooded, dim
>   Blue goodness of the Weald.

W.H. Hudson first made his name writing about South America; his novel, *Green Mansions*, inspired Epstein's statue of *Rima* in Hyde Park, which I photographed as a little boy with my Brownie 2A box camera. Nowadays he is better known for his magnificent books on the Sussex countryside. In *Nature in Downland* he paints a picture which any walker on the Downs must have encountered at some time:

The power of the sun and its joy is not felt so early on the downs as on the lower country, and last season it was not until the middle of June that I experienced the blissful sensation and feeling in its fullness. Then a day came that was a revelation; I all at once had a deeper sense and more intimate knowledge of what summer really is to all the children of life; for it chanced that on that effulgent day even the human animal, usually regarded as outside of nature, was there to participate in the heavenly bounty. That I felt the happiness myself was not quite enough, unhuman, or uncivilized, as I generally am, and wish to be. High up the larks were raining down their brightest, finest music; not rising skyward nor falling earthward, but singing continuously far up in that airy blue space that was their home. The little birds that live in the furze, the titlarks, whitethroats, linnets, and stonechats, sprung upwards at frequent intervals and poured out their strains when on the wing. Each bird had its characteristic flight and gestures and musical notes, but all alike expressed the overflowing gladness that summer inspired, even as the flowers seemed to express it in their intense glowing colours, and as the butterflies expressed it in their fluttering dances, and in the rapturous motions of their wings when at rest. There were many rabbits out, but they were not feeding, and when disturbed ran but fifteen or twenty yards away, then sat and looked at me with their big, round, prominent eyes, apparently too contented with life to suspect harm. But I saw no human creature in the course of a long ramble that morning until I was near the sea, when on approaching a coastguard station I all at once came upon some children lying on the grass on the slope of a down. There were five of them, scattered about, all lying on their backs, their arms stretched crossways, straight out, their hands open. It looked as if they had instinctively spread themselves out, just as a butterfly at rest opens wide its wings to catch the beams. The hot sun shone full on their fresh young faces; and though wide awake they lay perfectly still as I came up and walked slowly past them, looking from upturned face to face, each expressing perfect contentment; and as I successively caught their eyes they smiled, though still keeping motionless and silent as the bunnies that had regarded me a while before, albeit without smiling, Brer Rabbit being a serious little beast. Their quietude and composure in the presence of a stranger was unusual, and like the confidence of the wild rabbits on that day was caused by the delicious sensation of summer in the blood. We in our early years are little wild animals, and the wild animals are little children.

It is not only in our early years that we are little wild animals.

7

MEN, WOMEN, AND CHILDREN

That Love is all there is,
Is all we know of Love;
It is enough, the freight should be
Proportioned to the groove.
                        – Emily Dickinson

If he is lucky in his chosen career, much of a man's life is his work. I have described that part of my life in my memoirs. Politics, however, is bound to bring frustration and disappointments which may ruin a man's happiness unless he can live in other worlds as well. I have been able to escape to nature and the arts, either of which could have been sufficient for me on their own if I had not chosen politics. But the main anchor of my equilibrium has been my love for my family. I have always preferred a private life to a social life, which is one reason I have often been regarded as a loner.

I had love affairs before I married Edna – as a student at Oxford and as a soldier in Italy. But once I left the army and got married in December 1945, my love focused on my wife and children – and later my grandchildren. As I grew older I found it easier to love people outside my family, and even people I do not know at all. One of my greatest pleasures nowadays is to watch children from local infant schools playing in the gardens outside our flat in Pimlico – 'moving jewels', every one of them. And I love talking to people of all ages in the street or on a bus or tube.

As a student I wrote a handful of sonnets myself, more to explore my own feelings than as a tribute to my girl-friend. Since then I have relied on greater poets to explain the nature of love. To me, love of one's wife and family is only one example of a wider love which should embrace the whole of the natural world. Love, as Emily Dickinson uses the word, is life itself, and, like the peace of God, passeth all understanding. In this sense, all her poetry is instinct with love.

Yet so far as we know, Emily Dickinson never had a love affair, though she was deeply in love with the Reverend Charles Wadsworth, a preacher in Philadelphia, whom she cannot have met more than three times in her life. It is he who is thought to have inspired her two almost explicit love poems:

> Wild Nights – Wild Nights!
> Were I with thee
> Wild Nights should be
> Our luxury!
>
> Futile – the Winds –
> To a Heart in port –
> Done with the Compass –
> Done with the Chart!
>
> Rowing in Eden –
> Ah, the Sea!
> Might I but moor – Tonight –
> In Thee!

*

> How sick – to wait – in any place – but thine –
> I knew last night – when someone tried to twine –
> Thinking – perhaps – that I looked tired – or alone –
> Or breaking – almost – with unspoken pain –
>
> And I turned – ducal –
> *That* right – was thine –
> *One port* – suffices – for a Brig – like *mine* –
>
> Our's be the tossing – wild though the sea –
> Rather than a Mooring – unshared by thee.
> Our's be the Cargo – *unladen – here* –
> Rather than the 'spicy isles –'
> And thou – not there –

It was probably Wadsworth's departure for California which produced one of Dickinson's best known poems:

> My life closed twice before its close –
> It yet remains to see
> If Immortality unveil
> A third event to me
>
> So huge, so hopeless to conceive
> As these that twice befell.
> Parting is all we know of heaven,
> And all we need of hell.

Throughout the centuries love has inspired people from all walks of life to poetry. Some of the greatest love poems convey their meaning through their music rather than their sense. Here are four which appeal particularly to me.

The first was written by a Scottish farmer's boy in the eighteenth century, the immortal Robert Burns. He wrote love songs, work songs, and drinking songs, as well as satires and letters in verse. His humanity shines through all he wrote; he loved children as well as women, and even put some of his love poetry in the mouths of his sweethearts. Here is one of the best known of all love poems:

> My love is like a red rose
>   That's newly sprung in June:
> My love is like the melodie
>   That's sweetly played in tune.
>
> So fair art thou, my bonny lass,
>   So deep in love am I:
> And I will love thee still, my dear,
>   Till a' the seas gang dry.
>
> Till a' the seas gang dry, my dear,
>   And the rocks melt wi' the sun:
> And I will love thee still, my dear,
>   While the sands o' life shall run.
>
> And fare thee weel, my only love,
>   And fare thee weel awhile!
> And I will come again, my love,
>   Tho' it were ten thousand mile.

My second choice is by a wealthy aristocrat of radical views who more than once leapt into 'an abyss of sensuality', Lord Byron. Notorious for his promiscuity – one of his lovers, Lady Caroline Lamb, described him as 'mad, bad, and dangerous to know' – he found it wise to live abroad for his last eight years. He died of a fever in Greece at the age of thirty-six while helping the Greek struggle for freedom against the Turks. His sexual nature was ambiguous. At Cambridge he had a 'violent, though pure, love and passion' for a chorister, and he wrote his last poems to a Greek boy who acted as his page. His poetry about women is often as cynical in tone as his brilliant satires: *Don Juan* was the title of his greatest work. But one at least of his poems is the essence of romantic love:

> So, we'll go no more a-roving
>   So late into the night,
> Though the heart be still as loving,
>   And the moon be still as bright.
>
> For the sword outwears its sheath,
>   And the soul wears out the breast,
> And the heart must pause to breathe,
>   And love itself have rest.
>
> Though the night was made for loving,
>   And the day returns too soon,
> Yet we'll go no more a-roving
>   By the light of the moon.

My third choice is an early poem by the son of an Irish portrait-painter, who became in the twentieth century one of the greatest poets of our language, William Butler Yeats. This was published in 1889, just before Yeats met the great love of his life, Maude Gonne. Some of its lines are taken from a folk-song he had heard in Sligo:

> Down by the salley gardens my love and I did meet;
> She passed the salley gardens with little snow-white feet.
> She bid me take love easy, as the leaves grow on the tree;
> But I, being young and foolish, with her would not agree.
>
> In a field by the river my love and I did stand,
> And on my leaning shoulder she laid her snow-white hand.
> She bid me take life easy, as the grass grows on the weirs;
> But I was young and foolish, and now am full of tears.

Finally a poem from Wystan Auden, a brilliant young intellectual of the 1930s who loved only his own sex:

> Lay your sleeping head, my love,
> Human on my faithless arm;
> Time and fevers burn away
> Individual beauty from
> Thoughtful children, and the grave
> Proves the child ephemeral:
> But in my arms till break of day
> Let the living creature lie,
> Mortal, guilty, but to me
> The entirely beautiful.
>
> Soul and body have no bounds:
> To lovers as they lie upon
> Her tolerant enchanted slope
> In their ordinary swoon,
> Grave the vision Venus sends
> Of supernatural sympathy,
> Universal love and hope;
> While an abstract insight wakes
> Among the glaciers and the rocks
> The hermit's carnal ecstasy.
>
> Certainty, fidelity
> On the stroke of midnight pass
> Like vibrations of a bell
> And fashionable madmen raise
> Their pedantic boring cry:
> Every farthing of the cost,
> All the dreaded cards foretell,
> Shall be paid, but from this night
> Not a whisper, not a thought,
> Not a kiss nor look be lost.
>
> Beauty, midnight, vision dies:
> Let the winds of dawn that blow
> Softly round your dreaming head
> Such a day of welcome show
> Eye and knocking heart may bless,
> Find our mortal world enough;
> Noons of dryness find you fed
> By the involuntary powers,
> Nights of insult let you pass
> Watched by every human love.

For contrast, here is John Betjeman celebrating the glory of love
'In a Bath Teashop':

> 'Let us not speak, for the love we bear one another –
>   Let us hold hands and look.'
> She, such a very ordinary little woman;
>   He, such a thumping crook;
> But both, for a moment, little lower than the angels
>   In the teashop's ingle-nook.

For most of us when we are young, love is an emotion which
transfigures us by changing another human being into a thing of
beauty we want for our own. Most lyric poetry throughout the
ages has been concerned with this sort of love. The Elizabethan
poets wrote wonderful love songs – and Shakespeare, as usual, was
best of all:

> Oh mistress mine, where are you roaming?
> Oh, stay and hear, your true love's coming,
>   That can sing both high and low.
> Trip no further, pretty sweeting;
> Journeys end in lovers meeting,
>   Every wise man's son doth know.
> What is love? 'Tis not hereafter:
> Present mirth hath present laughter;
>   What's to come is still unsure.
> In delay there lies no plenty;
> Then come kiss me, sweet-and-twenty:
>   Youth's a stuff will not endure.

Campion and Carew were not far behind. The intricate rhythms
of Campion create their own music:

> Kind are her answers,
> But her performance keeps no day;
> Breaks time, as dancers
>   From their own music when they stray:
> All her free favours
> And smooth words wing my hopes in vain.
> O did ever voice so sweet but only feign?
>   Can true love yield such delay,
>   Converting joy to pain?

Lost is our freedom,
   When we submit to women so:
Why do we need them,
   When in their best they work our woe?
   There is no wisdom
Can alter ends, by Fate prefixed.
O why is the good of man with evil mixed?
   Never were days yet call'd two,
   But one night went betwixt.

*

Follow your saint, follow with accents sweet;
   Haste you, sad notes, fall at her flying feet.
   There, wrapped in cloud of sorrow, pity move,
And tell the ravisher of my soul I perish for her love.
   But if she scorns my never-ceasing pain,
Then burst with sighing in her sight, and ne'er return again.

All that I sung still to her praise did tend.
   Still she was first, still she my songs did end.
   Yet she my love and music both doth fly,
The music that her echo is, and beauty's sympathy.
   Then let my notes pursue her scornful flight;
It shall suffice that they were breathed, and died for her delight

The echoing melodies of Carew weave a similar spell:

Ask me no more where Jove bestows,
When June is past, the fading rose;
For in your beauty's orient deep
These flowers, as in their causes, sleep.

Ask me no more whither do stray
The golden atoms of the day;
For in pure love heaven did prepare
Those powders to enrich your hair.

Ask me no more whither doth haste
The nightingale when May is past;
For in your sweet dividing throat.
She winters and keeps warm her note.

Ask me no more where those stars 'light
That downwards fall in dead of night;
For in your eyes they sit, and there
Fixèd become as in their sphere.

Ask me no more if east or west
The phœnix builds her spicy nest;
For unto you at last she flies,
And in your fragrant bosom dies.

Compared with the earlier poets of courtly love, however, the
Elizabethans could analyse their feelings in a very modern way.
Michael Drayton's sonnets have a contemporary air:

Since there's no help, come let us kiss and part:
Nay, I have done; you get no more of me;
And I am glad, yea, glad with all my heart
That thus so cleanly I myself can free.
Shake hands forever; cancel all our vows;
And when we meet at any time again,
Be it not seen in either of our brows
That we one jot of former love retain.
Now at the last gasp of love's latest breath
When, his pulse failing, passion speechless lies,
When faith is kneeling by his bed of death
And innocénce is closing up his eyes;
     Now, if thou would'st, when all have given him over,
     From Death to Life thou might'st him yet recover.

*

You're not alone when you are still alone;
O God! from you that I could private be!
Since you one were, I never since was one,
Since you in me, myself since out of me.
Transported from myself into your being,
Though either distant, present yet to either;
Senseless with too much joy, each other seeing;
And only absent when we are together.
Give me my self, and take your self again!
Devise some means but how I may forsake you!
So much is mine that doth with you remain,
That taking what is mine, with me I take you.
     You do bewitch me! O that I could fly
     From my self you, or from your own self I!

Shakespeare's one hundred and fifty-four sonnets constitute the
most penetrating analysis of love ever written. We do not know to
whom they were addressed. Some were written to 'the dark lady';
but there is no doubt that some were written to a young man.
One at least is quite unambiguous on this:

A Woman's face with nature's owne hand painted,
Hast thou, the Master Mistris of my passion,
A woman's gentle hart but not acquainted
With shifting change as is false women's fashion,
An eye more bright than theirs, lesse false in rowling,
Gilding the object where–upon it gazeth,
A man in hew, all *Hews* in his controwling,
Which steales men's eyes and women's soules amaseth.
And for a woman wert thou first created,

Till nature as she wrought thee fell a dotinge,
And by addition me of thee defeated,
By adding one thing to my purpose nothing.
   But since she prickt thee out for women's pleasure,
   Mine be thy love and thy love's use their treasure.

Yet the moving honesty of another can only be addressed to a woman:

My Mistres eyes are nothing like the Sunne,
Coral is farre more red, than her lips red,
If snow be white, why then her brests are dun:
If haires be wiers, black wiers grow on her head:
I have scene Roses damaskt, red and white,
But no such Roses see I in her cheekes,
And in some perfumes is there more delight,
Than in the breath that from my Mistres reekes.
I love to heare her speake, yet well I know,
That Musicke hath a farre more pleasing sound:
I graunt I never saw a goddesse goe,
My Mistres when shee walkes treads on the ground.
   And yet by heaven I thinke my love as rare,
   As any she beli'd with false compare.

If I were compelled to choose a favourite, I would find myself torn between the following:

Shall I compare thee to a Summer's day?
Thou art more lovely and more temperate:
Rough windes do shake the darling buds of Maie,
And Sommer's lease hath all too short a date:
Sometime too hot the eye of heaven shines,
And often is his gold complexion dimm'd,

And every faire from faire some-time declines,
By chance, or nature's changing course untrim'd:
But thy eternall Sommer shall not fade,
Nor loose possession of that faire thou ow'st,
Nor shall death brag thou wandr'st in his shade,
When in eternall lines to time thou grow'st,
So long as men can breath or eyes can see,
So long lives this, and this gives life to thee.

*

Let me not to the marriage of true mindes
Admit impediments, love is not love
Which alters when it alteration findes,
Or bends with the remover to remove.
O no, it is an ever fixed marke
That lookes on tempests and is never shaken;
It is the star to every wandring barke,
Whose worth's unknowne, although his height be taken.
Lov's not Time's foole, though rosie lips and cheeks
Within his bending sickle's compasse come,
Love alters not with his breefe houres and weekes,
But beares it out even to the edge of doome:
If this be error and upon me proved,
I never writ, nor no man ever loved.

Shakespeare's personal ambiguity about sex may lie behind his treatment of the act of love. We find it in his early poem 'Venus and Adonis', where Venus is a symbol of lust, not love, and tries to rape 'rose cheek'd' Adonis:

And having felt the sweetnesse of the spoile,
With blind fold furie she begins to forage,
Her face doth reeke, and smoke, her blood doth boile,
And careless lust stirs up a desperate courage,
Planting oblivion, beating reason backe,
Forgetting shame's pure blush, and honor's wracke.
. . . She sincketh downe, still hanging on his necke,
He on her belly falls, she on her backe.

Now she is in the verie lists of love,
Her champion mounted for the hot encounter,
All is imaginarie she doth prove,
He will not manage her, although he mount her,
That worse than Tantalus is her annoy,
To clip Elysium, and to lacke her joy.

'The Rape of Lucrece' is of course concerned only with lust. However, Shakespeare is writing of his own self-disgust in this savage, black sonnet:

> Th'expence of Spirit in a waste of shame
> Is lust in action, and till action, lust
> Is perjurd, murdrous, blouddy, full of blame,
> Savage, extreame, rude, cruell, not to trust,
> Injoyd no sooner but dispised straight,
> Past reason hunted, and no sooner had,
> Past reason hated as a swollowed bayt,
> On purpose layd to make the taker mad:
> Mad in pursut and in possession so,
> Had, having, and in quest to have, extreame,
> A blisse in proofe and prov'd, a very wo,
> Before, a joy proposd, behind, a dreame,
> >   All this the world well knowes yet none knowes well,
> >   To shun the heaven that leads men to this hell.

I have always been perplexed by Shakespeare's rejection of sex, as distinct from love. The spiritual dimension is also absent from his writings, which otherwise embrace every aspect of humanity.

Shakespeare's contemporary, Christopher Marlowe, wrote many love songs, including one of the most popular of all time; 'The Passionate Shepherd to his Love':

> Come live with me and be my Love,
> And we will all the pleasures prove
> That hills and valleys, dales and fields,
> Or woods or steepy mountain yields.
>
> And we will sit upon the rocks,
> And see the shepherds feed their flocks
> By shallow rivers, to whose falls
> Melodious birds sing madrigals.
>
> And I will make thee beds of roses
> And a thousand fragrant posies;
> A cap of flowers, and a kirtle
> Embroider'd all with leaves of myrtle.
>
> A gown made of the finest wool
> Which from our pretty lambs we pull;
> Fair-linéd slippers for the cold,
> With buckles of the purest gold.

A belt of straw and ivy-buds
With coral clasps and amber studs:
And if these pleasures may thee move,
Come live with me and be my Love.

The shepherd swains shall dance and sing
For thy delight each May morning:
If these delights thy mind may move,
Then live with me and be my Love.

Sir Walter Raleigh responded with 'The Nymph's Reply to the Shepherd' which adds a dose of realism to Marlowe's romantic pastoral:

If all the world and love were young,
And truth in every Shepherd's tongue,
These pretty pleasures might me move,
To live with thee, and be thy love.

Time drives the flocks from field to fold,
When Rivers rage, and Rocks grow cold,
And Philomel becometh dumb,
The rest complains of cares to come.

The flowers do fade, and wanton fields
To wayward winter reckoning yields,
A honey tongue, a heart of gall,
Is fancy's spring, but sorrow's fall.

Thy gowns, thy shoes, thy beds of Roses,
Thy cap, thy kirtle, and thy posies,
Soon break, soon wither, soon forgotten:
In folly ripe, in reason rotten.

Thy belt of straw and Ivy buds,
Thy Coral clasps and Amber studs,
All these in me no means can move,
To come to thee, and be thy love.

But could youth last, and love still breed,
Had joys no date, nor age no need,
Then these delights my mind might move,
To live with thee, and be thy love.

Raleigh was an outstanding Elizabethan – courtier, politician, poet, adventurer, geographer and historian. The best picture of him is that painted two generations later by the antiquarian John Aubrey in his *Brief Lives*, the first great British work of biography, and one of the most entertaining books I know. It includes a story in which a ghost disappears with 'a most melodious twang'.

Aubrey describes Raleigh as 'a tall, handsome, and bold man – but damnable proud'. He testifies to Raleigh's sexual prowess, saying:

> He loved a wench well: and one time getting up one of the mayds of honor against a tree in a wood ('twas his first lady) who seemed at first boarding to be something fearful of her Honour, and modest, she cryed Sweet Sir Walter, what do you me ask? Will you undoe me? Nay, sweet Sir Walter! Sir Walter! At last, as the danger and the pleasure at the same time grew higher, she cried in the extacey Swisser Swatter! Swisser Swatter! She proved with child and I doubt not but this hero tooke care of them both, as also that the product was more then an ordinary mortall.

Raleigh's son was a true chip off the old block; Aubrey tells us:

> Sir Walter Raleigh being invited to dinner to some great person where his son was to goe with him, he sayd to his son 'Thou art expected to-day at dinner to goe along with me, but thou art such a quarrelsome, affronting . . ., that I am ashamed to have such a beare in my company.' Mr Walter humbled himselfe to his father, and promised he would behave himselfe mighty mannerly. So away they went . . . He sate next to his father and was very demure at least halfe dinner time. Then sayd he, 'I, this morning, not having the feare of God before my eies but by the instigation of the devill, went to a whore. I was very eager of her, kissed and embraced her, and went to enjoy her, but she thrust me from her, and vowed I should not, for your Father lay with me but an hower ago.' Sir Walter being strangely surprized and putt out of his countenance at so great a table, gives his son a damned blow over his face. His son, as rude as he was, would not strike his father, but strikes over the face the gentleman that sate next to him and sayd 'Box about: 'twill come to my father anon.' 'Tis now a common-used proverb.

Unfortunately Raleigh did not express this side of his activities in his verse.

The next generation of English poets, however, had no qualms about describing the sexual activities which accompany love. As they grew older they also wrote religious verse of exceptional power. John Donne, who later became Dean of St Paul's Cathedral and wrote some of the greatest religious poetry and prose, was quite explicit as a young man:

THE SUNNE RISING

Busie old foole, unruly Sunne,
    Why dost thou thus,
Through windowes, and through curtaines call on us?
Must to thy motions lovers seasons run?
        Sawcy pedantique wretch, goe chide
        Late schoole boyes and sowre prentices,
    Goe tell Court-huntsmen, that the King will ride,
    Call countrey ants to harvest offices;
Love, all alike, no season knowes, nor clyme,
Nor houres, dayes, moneths, which are the rags of time.

        Thy beames, so reverend, and strong
        Why shouldst thou thinke?
I could eclipse and cloud them with a winke,
But that I would not lose her sight so long:
        If her eyes have not blinded thine,
        Looke, and to morrow late, tell mee,
    Whether both the'India's of spice and Myne
    Be where thou leftst them, or lie here with mee.
Aske for those Kings whom thou saw'st yesterday,
And thou shalt heare, All here in one bed lay.

        She'is all States, and all Princes, I,
        Nothing else is.
Princes doe but play us; compar'd to this,
All honor's mimique; All wealth alchimie.
        Thou sunne art halfe as happy'as wee,
        In that the world's contracted thus;
    Thine age askes ease, and since thy duties bee
    To warme the world, that's done in warming us.
Shine here to us, and thou art every where;
This bed thy center is, these walls, thy spheare.

TO HIS MISTRIS GOING TO BED

Come, Madam, come, all rest my powers defie,
Until I labour, I in labour lie.
The foe oft-times having the foe in sight,
Is tir'd with standing though he never fight.

Off with that girdle, like heavens Zone glistering,
But a far fairer world incompassing.
Unpin that spangled breastplate which you wear,
That th'eyes of busie fooles may be stopt there.
Unlace your self, for that harmonious chyme,
Tells me from you, that now it is bed time.
Off with that happy busk, which I envie,
That still can be, and still can stand so nigh.
Your gown going off, such beautious state reveals,
As when from flowry meads th'hills shadow steales.
Off with that wyerie Coronet and shew
The haiery Diademe which on you doth grow:
Now off with those shooes, and then safely tread
In this loves hallow'd temple, this soft bed.
In such white robes, heaven's Angels us'd to be
Receavd by men; Thou Angel bringst with thee
A heaven like Mahomets Paradice; and though
Ill spirits walk in white, we easly know,
By this these Angels from an evil sprite,
Those set our hairs, but these our flesh upright.
 Licence my roaving hands, and let them go,
Before, behind, between, above, below.
O my America! my new-found-land,
My kingdome, safeliest when with one man man'd,
My Myne of precious stones, My Emperie,
How blest am I in this discovering thee!
To enter in these bonds, is to be free;
Then where my hand is set, my seal shall be.
 Full nakedness! All joyes are due to thee,
As souls unbodied, bodies uncloth'd must be,
To taste whole joyes. Gems which you women use
Are like Atlanta's balls, cast in mens views,
That when a fools eye lighteth on a Gem,
His earthly soul may covet theirs, not them.
Like pictures, or like books gay coverings made
For lay-men, are all women thus array'd;
Themselves are mystick books, which only wee
(Whom their imputed grace will dignifie)
Must see reveal'd. Then since that I may know;
As liberally, as to a Midwife, shew
Thy self: cast all, yea, this white lynnen hence,
There is no pennance due to innocence.
 To teach thee, I am naked first; why then
What needst thou have more covering than a man.

A generation later Andrew Marvell argued for consummating his love in his most famous poem, 'To His Coy Mistress':

> Had we but world enough, and time,
> This coyness, lady, were no crime.
> We would sit down, and think which way
> To walk, and pass our long love's day.
> Thou by the Indian Ganges' side
> Should'st rubies find: I by the tide
> Of Humber would complain. I would
> Love you ten years before the Flood,
> And you should, if you please, refuse
> Till the conversion of the Jews.
> My vegetable love should grow
> Vaster than empires, and more slow.
> An hundred years should go to praise
> Thine eyes, and on thy forehead gaze:
> Two hundred to adore each breast:
> But thirty thousand to the rest;
> An age at least to every part,
> And the last age should shew your heart.
> For, lady, you deserve this state,
> Nor would I love at lower rate.
>   But at my back I always hear
> Time's wingèd chariot hurrying near:
> And yonder all before us lie
> Deserts of vast eternity
> Thy beauty shall no more be found;
> Nor, in thy marble vault, shall sound
> My echoing song; then worms shall try
> That long-preserv'd virginity:
> And your quaint honour turn to dust,
> And into ashes all my lust.
> The grave's a fine and private place,
> But none, I think, do there embrace.
>   Now, therefore, while the youthful hue
> Sits on thy skin like morning dew,
> And while thy willing soul transpires
> At every pore with instant fires,
> Now let us sport us while we may;
> And now, like amorous birds of prey,
> Rather at once our Time devour,
> Than languish in his slow-chapt power.

Let us roll all our strength and all
Our sweetness up into one ball,
And tear our pleasures with rough strife
Through the iron gates of life.
Thus, though we cannot make our Sun
Stand still, yet we will make him run.

Marvell was an ardent Cromwellian, worked as a secretary to John Milton, and spent nineteen years as Member of Parliament for Hull. His contemporary Robert Herrick, by contrast, was a Cavalier cleric. Yet he preached the same sermon as Marvell in his address 'To the Virgins to make much of Time':

Gather ye rosebuds while ye may,
　　Old Time is still a-flying:
And this same flower that smiles to-day
　　To-morrow will be dying.

The glorious lamp of heaven, the sun,
　　The higher he's a-getting,
The sooner will his race be run,
　　And nearer he's to setting.

That age is best which is the first,
　　When youth and blood are warmer;
But being spent, the worse, and worst
　　Times still succeed the former.

Then be not coy, but use your time,
　　And while ye may, go marry:
For kissing lost but once your prime,
　　You may for ever tarry.

His contemporary John Cleveland, another Cavalier poet, wrote a superb poem against platonic love;

For shame, thou everlasting Woer,
Still saying Grace and ne're fall to her!
Love that's in Contemplation plac't,
Is *Venus* drawn but to the Wast.
Unlesse your Flame confesse its Gender,
And your Parley cause surrender,
Y'are Salamanders of a cold desire,

That live untouch't amid the hottest fire.

What though she be a Dame of stone,
The Widow of *Pigmalion*;
As hard and un-relenting She,
As the new-crusted *Niobe*;
Or what doth more of Statue carry
A Nunne of the Platonick Quarrey?
Love melts the rigor which the rocks have bred,
A Flint will break upon a Feather-bed.

For shame you pretty Female Elves,
Cease for to Candy up your selves;
No more, you Sectaries of the Game,
No more of your calcining flame.
Women Commence by *Cupids* Dart,
As a Kings Hunting dubs a Hart.
Loves Votaries inthrall each others soul,
Till both of them live but upon Paroll.

Vertue's no more in Woman-kind
But the green-sicknesse of the mind.
Philosophy, their new delight,
A kind of Charcoal Appetite.
There is no Sophistry prevails,
Where all-convincing Love assails,
But the disputing Petticoat will Warp,
As skilfull Gamesters are to seek at Sharp.

The souldier, that man of Iron,
Whom Ribs of *Horror* all inviron,
That's strung with Wire, in stead of Veins,
In whose imbraces you're in chains,
Let a Magnetick Girle appear,
Straight he turns *Cupids* Cuiraseer.
Love storms his lips, and takes the Fortresse in,
For all the Brisled Turn-pikes of his chin.

Since Loves Artillery then checks
The Breast-works of the firmest Sex,
Come let us in Affections Riot,
Th' are sickly pleasures keep a Diet.
Give me a Lover bold and free,
Not Eunuch't with Formality;
Like an Embassador that beds a Queen,
With the Nice Caution of a sword between.

I once gave Cleveland's poems to Adlai Stevenson when he was President Kennedy's Ambassador at the United Nations. I told him that I thought 'The Anti-Platonick' applied to politics as well as love; in fact it seemed to explain Stevenson's own failure to win the Presidency himself in 1952 and 1956.

Aubrey describes Cleveland as 'a comely plump man, good curled haire, darke browne'. After the outbreak of the Civil War he left a readership at Cambridge and worked for the King as a propagandist; he was appointed Judge Advocate to the Royalist garrison at Newark. On love, he practised what he preached, as we hear in his 'song of Marke Anthony', with its lilting waltz rhythm:

> When as the Nightingall chanted her Vesper,
>   And the wild Forrester coutch'd on the ground,
> Venus invited me in th' Evening whisper,
> Unto a fragrant field with Roses crown'd:
>   Where she before had sent
>   My wishes complement,
>   Who to my soules content
>   Plaid with me on the Green.
>   Never Marke Anthony
>   Dallied more wantonly
>   With the faire Egyptian Queen.
>
> First on her cherry cheekes I mine eyes feasted,
> Thence feare of surfetting made me retire
> Unto her warmer lips, which, when I tasted,
> My spirits dull were made active as fire.
>   This heate againe to calme
>   Her moyst hand yeilded balme,
>   While we join'd palme to palme
>   As if they one had beene.
>   Never Marke, &c.
>
> Then in her golden hayre I my armes twined,
> Shee her hands in my locks twisted againe,
> As if our hayre had been fetters assigned,
> Great litle Cupids loose captives to chaine.
>   Then we did often dart
>   Each at the others heart,
>   Arrowes that knew no smart;
>   Sweet lookes and smiles between.
>   Never Marke, &c.

Wanting a glasse to pleat those amber trasses,
Which like a bracelet deckt richly mine arme;
Gawdier than *Funo* weares, when as she blesses
Jove with embraces more stately than warme,
    Then did she peepe in mine
    Eyes humour Chrystaline;
    And by reflexive shine
    I in her eye was seene.
        Never Marke, &c.

Mysticall Grammer of amorous glances,
Feeling of pulses, the Phisicke of Love,
Rhetoricall courtings, and Musicall Dances;
Numbring of kisses Arithmeticke prove.
    Eyes like Astronomy,
    Streight limbs Geometry,
    In her arts ingeny
    Our wits were sharpe and keene.
        Never Marke, &c.

None of these love songs eclipses a few anonymous lines from the sixteenth century:

Western wind, when wilt thou blow,
The small rain down can rain?
Christ, if my love were in my arms,
And I in my bed again!

MARRIED LOVE

Far too little was written by poets in those days to celebrate their love for their wives. Queen Elizabeth's godson Sir John Harington was an exception:

THE AUTHOR TO HIS WIFE

Mall, once in pleasant company by chance,
I wished that you for company would dance,
Which you refused, and said, your years require,
Now, Matron-like, both manners and attire.
Well, Mall, if needs thou wilt be matron-like,
Then trust to this, I will a matron like:

Yet so to you my love may never lessen,
  As you for Church, house, bed, observe this lesson.
    Sit in the Church as solemn as a saint.
    No deed, word, thought, your due devotion taint.
    Veil (if you will) your head, your soul reveal
    To him, that only wounded souls can heal.
    Be in my house as busy as a bee,
    Having a sting for everyone but me,
    Buzzing in every corner, gathering honey.
    Let nothing waste, that costs or yieldeth money.
    And when thou seest my heart to mirth incline,
    The tongue, wit, blood, warm with good cheer and wine,
    And that by lawful fancy I am led,
    To climb my nest, thy undefilèd bed
      Then of sweet sports let no occasion 'scape,
      But be as wanton, toying as an ape.

THE AUTHOR TO HIS WIFE, OF A WOMAN'S ELOQUENCE

My Mall, I mark that when you mean to prove me
To buy a velvet gown, or some rich border,
Thou call'st me good sweet heart, thou swear'st to love me,
Thy locks, thy lips, thy looks, speak all in order,
Thou think'st, and right thou think'st, that these do move me,
That all these severally thy suit do further:
  But shall I tell thee what most thy suit advances?
  Thy fair smooth words? no, no, thy fair smooth haunches.

William Blake shared at least some of Harington's views:

What is it men in women do require?
The lineaments of gratified desire.
What is it women in men do require?
The lineaments of gratified desire.

Abstinence sows sand all over
The ruddy limbs and flaming hair,
But Desire gratified
Plants fruits of life and beauty there.

Blake's attitude to marriage was not always as serious as one might assume. In his surrealistic fantasy, *An Island in the Moon*, he gives us this ode to matrimony:

Hail Matrimony, made of Love!
To thy wide gates how great a drove
On purpose to be yok'd do come;
Widows and Maids and Youths also,
That lightly trip on beauty's toe,
Or sit on beauty's bum.

Hail fingerfooted lovely Creatures!
The females of our human natures,
Formed to suckle all Mankind.
'Tis you that come in time of need,
Without you we should never breed,
Or any comfort find.

For if a Damsel's blind or lame,
Or Nature's hand has crook'd her frame,
Or if she's deaf, or is wall-eyed;
Yet, if her heart is well-inclin'd,
Some tender lover she shall find
That panteth for a Bride.

The universal Poultice this,
To cure whatever is amiss
In Damsel or in Widow gay!
It makes them smile, it makes them skip;
Like birds, just cured of the pip,
They chirp and hop away.

Then come, ye maidens! come, ye swains!
Come and be cur'd of all your pains
In Matrimony's Golden Cage –

Blake was always conscious that 'he who bends to himself a joy
Doth the winged life destroy'. So he warns:

Never seek to tell thy love,
  Love that never told can be;
For the gentle wind does move
  Silently, invisibly.

I told my love, I told my love,
  I told her all my heart;
Trembling, cold, in ghastly fears,
  Ah! she did depart!

Soon as she was gone from me,
  A traveller came by,
Silently, invisibly:
  He took her with a sigh.

My hero, Benjamin Franklin, who strongly supported marriage, argued that if a young man would not marry, he should at least choose an old mistress:

My dear Friend,   *June 25. 1745*

I know of no Medicine fit to diminish the violent natural Inclinations you mention; and if I did, I think I should not communicate it to you. Marriage is the proper Remedy. It is the most natural State of Man, and therefore the State in which you are most likely to find solid Happiness. Your Reasons against entring into it at present, appear to me not well-founded. The circumstantial Advantages you have in View by postponing it, are not only uncertain, but they are small in comparison with that of the Thing itself, the being *married and settled*. It is the Man and Woman united that make the compleat human Being. Separate, she wants his Force of Body and Strength of Reason; he, her Softness, Sensibility and acute Discernment. Together they are more likely to succeed in the World. A single Man has not nearly the Value he would have in that State of Union. He is an incomplete Animal. He resembles the odd Half of a Pair of Scissars. If you get a prudent healthy Wife, your Industry in your Profession, with her good Economy, will be a Fortune sufficient.

But if you will not take this Counsel, and persist in thinking a Commerce with the Sex inevitable, then I repeat my former Advice, that in all your Amours you should *prefer old Women to young ones.* You call this a Paradox, and demand my Reasons. They are these:

1. Because as they have more Knowledge of the World and their Minds are better stor'd with Observations, their Conversation is more improving and more lastingly agreable.

2. Because when Women cease to be handsome, they study to be good. To maintain their Influence over Men, they supply the Diminution of Beauty by an Augmentation of Utility. They learn to do a 1000 Services small and great, and are the most tender and useful of all Friends when you are sick. Thus they continue amiable. And hence there is hardly such a thing to be found as an old Woman who is not a good Woman.

3. Because there is no hazard of Children, which irregularly produc'd may be attended with much Inconvenience.

4. Because thro' more Experience, they are more prudent and discreet in conducting an Intrigue to prevent Suspicion. The Commerce with them is therefore safer with regard to your Reputation. And with regard to theirs, if the Affair should happen to be known, considerate People might be rather inclin'd to excuse an old Woman who would kindly take care of a young Man, form his Manners by her good Counsels, and prevent his ruining his Health and Fortune among mercenary Prostitutes.

5. Because in every Animal that walks upright, the Deficiency of the Fluids that fill the Muscles appears first in the highest Part: The Face first grows lank and wrinkled; then the Neck; then the Breast and Arms; the lower Parts continuing to the last as plump as ever: So that covering all above with a Basket, and regarding only what is below the Girdle, it is impossible of two Women to know an old from a young one. And as in the dark all Cats are grey, the Pleasure of corporal Enjoyment with an old Woman is at least equal, and frequently superior, every Knack being by Practice capable of Improvement.

6. Because the Sin is less. The debauching a Virgin may be her Ruin, and make her for Life unhappy.

7. Because the Compunction is less. The having made a young Girl *miserable* may give you frequent bitter Reflections; none of which can attend the making an old Woman *happy*.

8thly and Lastly They are *so grateful!!*

Thus much for my Paradox. But still I advise you to marry directly; being sincerely Your affectionate Friend.

Pastor Bonhoeffer, the anti-Nazi Protestant theologian who was executed for his part in the plot to assassinate Hitler, was as forthright about sex as he was about politics. He was arrested just after becoming engaged; but he had no doubt about his right to earthly love:

To long for the transcendent when you are in your wife's arms is, to put it mildly, a lack of taste and it is certainly not what God expects of us . . . If He pleases to grant us some overwhelming earthly bliss, we ought not to try and be more religious than God Himself.

Stanley J. Sharples puts similar sentiments in the mouth of a modern Sloane Ranger:

'If that's what they call worse than death',
Said Jane, supine on the settee,
'There'll be no moaning at the bar
When I put out to sea.'

Women themselves were not encouraged to write about love and marriage until the eighteenth century, though Ann Bradstreet, a Puritan settler in seventeenth-century Massachusetts, wrote one of the first American poems 'To my Dear and Loving Husband':

If ever two were one, then surely we.
If ever man were loved by wife, then thee;
If ever wife was happy in a man,
Compare with me ye women if you can.
I prize thy love more than whole mines of gold,
Or all the riches that the East doth hold.
My love is such that rivers cannot quench,
Nor ought but love from thee, give recompence.
Thy love is such I can no way repay,
The heavens reward thee manifold I pray.
Then while we live, in love lets so persever,
That when we live no more, we may live ever.

In the Restoration England from which Ann Bradstreet had escaped women were beginning to express themselves very differently about men. In 'The Beaux Stratagem' George Farquhar has Mrs Sullen talk about her husband as follows:

MRS SULLEN: O Sister, Sister! if ever you marry, beware of a sullen, silent Sot, one that's always musing, but never thinks: – There's some Diversion in a talking Blockhead; and since a Woman must wear Chains, I wou'd have the Pleasure of hearing 'em rattle a little. – Now you shall see, but take this by the way; – He came home this Morning at his usual Hour of Four, waken'd me out of a sweet Dream of something else, by tumbling over the Tea-table, which he broke all to pieces, after his Man and he had row'd about the Room like sick Passengers in a Storm . . . he comes flounce into Bed, dead as a Salmon into a Fishmonger's Basket; his Feet cold as Ice, his Breath hot as a Furnace, and his Hands and his Face as greasy as his Flanel Night-cap. – Oh Matrimony! – He tosses up the Clothes with a barbarous swing over his Shoulders, disorders the whole Oeconomy of my Bed,

leaves me half naked, and my whole Night's Comfort is the
tuneable Serenade of that wakeful Nightingale, his Nose. – O
the Pleasure of counting the melancholly Clock by a snoring
Husband!

In 'The Way of the World' William Congreve gives Millamant
and her lover, Mirabell, this delightful dialogue when they discuss
marrying one another:

MILLAMANT: Ah! don't be impertinent. – My dear liberty, shall I
   leave thee? my faithful solitude, my darling contemplation, must
   I bid you then adieu? Ay-h adieu – my morning thoughts,
   agreeable wakings, indolent slumbers, all ye *douceurs, ye sommeils
   du matin*, adieu? – I can't do't, 'tis more than impossible –
   positively, Mirabell, I'll lie abed in a morning as long as I please.
MIRABELL: Then I'll get up in a morning as early as I please.
MILLAMANT: Ah! idle creature, get up when you will – and d'ye
   hear, I won't be called names after I'm married; positively I
   won't be called names.
MIRABELL: Names!
MILLAMANT: Ay, as wife, spouse, my dear, joy, jewel, love, sweetheart, and the rest of that nauseous cant, in which men and their
   wives are so fulsomely familiar – I shall never bear that – good
   Mirabell, don't let us be familiar or fond, nor kiss before folks,
   like my lady Fadler, and sir Francis: nor go to Hyde Park
   together the first Sunday in a new chariot, to provoke eyes and
   whispers, and then never to be seen there together again; as if we
   were proud of one another the first week, and ashamed of one
   another ever after. Let us never visit together, nor go to a play
   together; but let us be very strange and well bred: let us be as
   strange as if we had been married a great while; and as well bred
   as if we were not married at all.
MIRABELL: Have you any more conditions to offer? Hitherto your
   demands are pretty reasonable.
MILLAMANT: Trifles! – As liberty to pay and receive visits to and
   from whom I please; to write and receive letters, without inter-
   rogatories or wry faces on your part; to wear what I please; and
   choose conversation with regard only to my own taste; to have
   no obligation upon me to converse with wits that I don't like,
   because they are your acquaintance; or to be intimate with fools,
   because they may be your relations. Come to dinner when I
   please; dine in my dressing-room when I'm out of humour,
   without giving a reason. To have my closet inviolate; to be sole

empress of my tea-table, which you must never presume to approach without first asking leave. And, lastly, wherever I am, you shall always knock at the door before you come in. These articles subscribed, if I continue to endure you a little longer, I may by degrees dwindle into a wife.

Later Lady Mary Wortley Montagu made the same point more briefly:

> Be plain in dress and sober in your diet;
> In short, my Dearie – kiss me and be quiet.

Virginia Woolf always resented the handicaps which clever women have carried in a society dominated by men, and made a point of drawing attention to the writing of women who might otherwise have been overlooked. Her enthusiasm led me to the memoirs of Marie, Queen of Rumania, who spent much of her childhood at Buckingham Palace, and was always rebuked by her nurse for playing in the gardens there because the grime got her clothes dirty. At the other end of the social scale was the Regency courtesan, Harriet Wilson, whose memoirs begin with the immortal words: 'I shall not say why and how I became, at the age of fifteen, the mistress of the Earl of Craven'; it was Harriet Wilson who provoked the Duke of Wellington's famous reply to her attempt to blackmail him: 'Publish and be damned!' Virginia Woolf also directed me to the fascinating memoirs of a homosexual eighteenth-century actress, Mrs Charlotte Charke, youngest daughter of the playwright Colley Cibber. They were first published in 1755. Virginia herself wrote the anonymous preface when they were republished in the Constable Miscellany in 1929. Her style is unmistakable:

> Ungrammatical, insanely inconsequent, braggart and fantastic, the 'Narrative' is not literature: it has the sudden nakedness of an actress's hurried speech in the wings. Yet an actress still: a shabby Viola, clowning an out-at-elbows Sir Harry Wildair. If the swagger has a quaver in it, it is against her will: barefaced beggar that she is, it is your purse she asks, never your pity: it is the clown's mask, and behind it the eyes of Columbine, courageous and terrified.

The 'Narrative' includes the following account of one of Charlotte's adventures as a little girl:

As I have promis'd to conceal nothing that might raise a Laugh, I shall begin with a small Specimen of my former Madness, when I was but four Years of Age. Having, even then, a passionate Fondness for a Perriwig, I crawl'd out of Bed one Summer's Morning at *Twickenham*, where my Father had Part of a House and Gardens for the Season and, taking it into my small Pate, that by Dint of a Wig and a Waistcoat I should be the perfect Representative of my Sire, I crept softly into the Servants-Hall, where I had the Night before espied all Things in Order, to perpetrate the happy Design I had framed for the next Morning's Expedition. Accordingly I paddled down Stairs, taking with me my Shoes, Stockings, and little Dimity Coat; which I artfully contrived to pin up, as well as I could, to supply the Want of a Pair of Breeches. By the Help of a long Broom, I took down a Waistcoat of my Brother's, and an enormous bushy Tie-wig of my Father's, which entirely enclos'd my Head and Body, with the Knots of the Ties thumping my little Heels as I march'd along, with slow and solemn Pace. The Covert of Hair in which I was conceal'd, with the Weight of a monstrous Belt and large Silver-hilted Sword, that I could scarce drag along, was a vast Impediment in my Procession: And, what still added to the other Inconveniences I labour'd under, was whelming myself under one of my Father's large Beaver-hats, laden with Lace, as thick and broad as a Brickbat.

Being thus accoutred, I began to consider that 'twould be impossible for me to pass for Mr *Cibber* in Girl's Shoes, therefore took an opportunity to slip out of Doors after the Gardener, who went to his Work, and roll'd into a dry Ditch, which was as deep as I was high; and, in this Grotesque Pigmy-State, walk'd up and down the Ditch bowing to all who came by. But, behold, the Oddity of my Appearance soon assembled a Croud about me; which yielded me no small Joy, as I conceiv'd their Risibility on this Occasion to be Marks of Approbation, and walk'd myself into a Fever, in the happy Thought of being taken for the 'Squire.

When the Family arose, 'till which Time I had employ'd myself in this regular March in my Ditch, I was the first Thing enquir'd after, and miss'd; 'till *Mrs Heron*, the Mother of the late celebrated Actress of that Name, happily espied me, and directly call'd forth the whole Family to be Witness of my State and Dignity.

The Drollery of my Figure render'd it impossible, assisted by the Fondness of both Father and Mother, to be angry with me; but, alas! I was borne off on the Footman's Shoulders, to my Shame and Disgrace, and forc'd into my proper Habiliments.

Virginia Woolf also led me to the memoirs of a far greater actress,

Ellen Terry, also a child of the stage. Ellen Terry married the painter G.F. Watts when she was scarcely sixteen, acted with Henry Irving, had a long correspondence with Bernard Shaw, and died in 1928 at the age of eighty. Her life covers almost a century of the English modern stage, of which she can almost claim to be the mother; her son, Gordon Craig, became the leading British stage designer after deciding he could not become a second Irving. Her sister's grandson, John Gielgud, first acted at the Old Vic the year after she died. In 1921 she was much impressed by the performance of a boy at a choir school as Brutus in *Julius Caesar*. 'Already a great actor', she said. The boy was Laurence Olivier.

Ellen Terry's memoirs are not great literature, but they are vastly entertaining. She has a couple of pages on the painter Rossetti's passion for animals – an inconvenient attachment for a man living in Chelsea. He bought a white bull because it had 'eyes like Janie Morris', and had to get rid of it when it destroyed his lawn:

> His next purchase was a white peacock, which, very soon after its arrival, disappeared under the sofa. In vain did Rossetti shoo it out. It refused to budge. This went on for days.
>
> 'The lovely creature won't respond to me,' said Rossetti pathetically to a friend.
>
> The friend dragged out the bird.
>
> 'No wonder! It's *dead*!'
>
> 'Bulls dont like me,' said Rossetti a few days later, 'and peacocks aren't homely.'
>
> It preyed on his mind so much that he tried to repair the failure by buying some white dormice. He sat them up on tiny bamboo chairs, and they looked sweet. When the winter was over, he invited a party to meet them and congratulate them upon waking up from their long sleep.
>
> 'They are awake now,' he said, 'but how quiet they are! How full of repose!'
>
> One of the guests went to inspect the dormice more closely, and a peculiar expression came over his face. It might almost have been thought that he was holding his nose.
>
> 'Wake up, little dormice,' said Rossetti, prodding them gently with a quill pen.
>
> 'They'll never do *that*,' said the guest. 'They're *dead*. I believe they have been dead some days!'
>
> Do you think Rossetti gave up live stock after this? Not a bit of it. He tried armadillos and tortoises.

'How are the tortoises?' he asked his man one day, after a long spell of forgetfulness that he had any.

'Pretty well, sir, thank you . . . That's to say, sir, there aint no tortoises!'

The tortoises, bought to eat the beetles, had been eaten themselves. At least, the shells were found full of beetles.

And the armadillos? 'The air of Chelsea dont suit them,' said Rossetti's servant. They had certainly left Rossetti's house, but they had not left Chelsea. All the neighbours had dozens of them! They had burrowed, and came up smiling in houses where they were far from welcome.

She is of course at her best in describing the stage, and gives a moving description of Sarah Bernhardt at her peak:

How wonderful she looked in those days! She was as transparent as an azalea, only more so; like a cloud, only not so thick. Smoke from a burning paper describes her more nearly! She was hollow-eyed, thin, almost consumptive-looking. Her body was not the prison of her soul, but its shadow.

It is this extraordinary decorative and symbolic quality of Sarah's which makes her transcend all personal and individual feeling on the stage. No one plays a love scene better, but it is a *picture* of love that she gives, a strange exotic picture rather than a suggestion of the ordinary human passion as felt by ordinary human people. She is exotic – well, what else should she be? One does not, at any rate one should not, quarrel with an orchid and call it unnatural because it is not a buttercup or a cowslip.

I have spoken of the face as the chief equipment of the actor. Sarah Bernhardt contradicts this at once. Her face does little for her. Her walk is not much. Nothing about her is more remarkable than the way she gets about the stage without one ever seeing her move. By what magic does she triumph without two of the richest possessions that an actress can have? Eleanora Duse has them. Her walk is the walk of the peasant, fine and free. She has the superb carriage of the head which goes with that fearless movement from the hips. And her face! There is nothing like it, nothing! But it is as the real woman, a particular woman, that Duse triumphs most. Her Cleopatra was insignificant compared with Sarah's. She is not so pictorial.

How futile it is to make comparisons! Better far to thank heaven for both these great actresses.

In my later years I have taken great pleasure in reading such memoirs, usually bought in second-hand bookshops, since so few of those I want are in print these days. I also find myself reading more Dickens, under Edna's guidance. Dickens writes badly about good women – they tend to emerge from his pages insipid and sentimental. Like Shakespeare he was oddly blind to the sexual and spiritual dimensions of life. But he draws brilliant caricatures of every other sort of woman. My favourite grotesque is Sarah Gamp, the midwife in *Martin Chuzzlewit*:

The face of Mrs Gamp – the nose in particular – was somewhat red and swollen, and it was difficult to enjoy her society without becoming conscious of a smell of spirits. Like most persons who have attained to great eminence in their profession, she took to hers very kindly; insomuch that, setting aside her natural predilections as a woman, she went to a lying-in, or a laying-out with equal zest and relish.

'Ah!' repeated Mrs Gamp; for it was always a safe sentiment in cases of mourning. 'Ah, dear! When Gamp was summoned to his long home, and I see him a-lying in Guy's Hospital with a penny-piece on each eye, and his wooden leg under his left arm, I thought I should have fainted away. But I bore up.'

If certain whispers current in the Kingsgate Street circles had any truth in them, she had indeed borne up surprisingly; and had exerted such uncommon fortitude as to dispose of Mr Gamp's remains for the benefit of science. But it should be added, in fairness, that this had happened twenty years before; and that Mr and Mrs Gamp had long been separated on the ground of incompatibility of temper in their drink.

'You have become indifferent since then, I suppose?' said Mr Pecksniff. 'Use is second nature, Mrs Gamp.'

'You may well say second natur, sir,' returned that lady. 'One's first ways is to find sich things a trial to the feelings, and so is one's lasting custom. If it wasn't for the nerve a little sip of liquor gives me (I never was able to do more than taste it), I never could go through with what I sometimes has to do. "Mrs Harris," I says, at the very last case as ever I acted in, which it was but a young person, "Mrs Harris," I says, "leave the bottle on the chimley-piece and don't ask me to take none, but let me put my lips to it when I am so dispoged, and then I will do what I'm engaged to do, according to the best of my ability," "Mrs Gamp," she says, in answer, "if there ever was a sober creetur to be got at eighteen pence a day for working people, and three and six for gentlefolks – night watching," said Mrs Gamp, with emphasis, "being a extra charge – you are that inwallable person." "Mrs Harris," I says to her, "don't name the charge, for it I could afford to lay all my feller creeturs out for nothink, I would gladly do it, sich is the love I bears 'em. But what I always says to them as had the management of matters, Mrs Harris:" here she kept her eye on Mr Pecksniff: "be they gents or be they ladies, is, don't ask me whether I won't take none, or whether I will, but leave the bottle on the chimley-piece, and let me put my lips to it when I am so dispoged."'

However, the ultimate in surrealistic fantasy is Dickens' portrait of Mr F's aunt in *Little Dorrit* – though it is, in fact, all too true to life:

There was a fourth and most original figure in the Patriarchal tent, who also appeared before dinner. This was an amazing little old woman, with a face like a staring wooden doll too cheap for expression, and a stiff yellow wig perched unevenly on the top of her head, as if the child who owned the doll had driven a tack through it anywhere, so that it only got fastened on. Another remarkable thing in this little old woman was, that the same child seemed to have damaged her face in two or three places with some blunt instrument in the nature of a spoon; her countenance, and particularly the tip of her nose, presenting the phenomena of several dints, generally answering to the bowl of that article. A further remarkable thing in this little old woman was, that she had no name but Mr F's Aunt.

The major characteristics discoverable by the stranger in Mr F's Aunt, were extreme severity and grim taciturnity; sometimes interrupted by a propensity to offer remarks in a deep warning voice, which, being totally uncalled for by anything said by anybody, and traceable to no association of ideas, confounded and terrified the mind. Mr F's Aunt may have thrown in these observations on some system of her own, and it may have been ingenious, or even subtle; but the key to it was wanted.

The neatly-served and well-cooked dinner (for everything about the Patriarchal household promoted quiet digestion) began with some soup, some fried soles, a butter-boat of shrimp sauce, and a dish of potatoes. The conversation still turned on the receipt of rents. Mr F's Aunt, after regarding the company for ten minutes with a malevolent gaze, delivered the following fearful remark.

'When we lived at Henley, Barnes's gander was stole by tinkers.'

Mr Pancks courageously nodded his head and said, 'All right, ma'am.' But the effect of this mysterious communication upon Clennam was absolutely to frighten him. And another circumstance invested this old lady with peculiar terrors. Though she was always staring, she never acknowledged that she saw any individual. The polite and attentive stranger would desire, say, to consult her inclinations on the subject of potatoes. His expressive action would be hopelessly lost upon her, and what could he do? No man could say, 'Mr F's Aunt, will you permit me?' Every man retired from the spoon, as Clennam did, cowed and baffled.

Since the last war, I have been fascinated by the number of professional young women who are torn between their work and their desire for a stable relationship with a man. Wendy Cope speaks for many of them as movingly as John Betjeman spoke for his generation. She worked for fifteen years as a primary-school teacher before introducing her first volume, *Making Cocoa for Kingsley Amis*. She sums up her predicament in 'Bloody Men':

> Bloody men are like bloody buses –
> You wait for about a year
> And as soon as one approaches your stop
> Two or three others appear.
>
> You look at them flashing their indicators,
> Offering you a ride.
> You're trying to read the destinations,
> You haven't much time to decide.
>
> If you make a mistake, there is no turning back.
> Jump off, and you'll stand there and gaze
> While the cars and the taxis and lorries go by
> And the minutes, the hours, the days.

I have seen many such young women finally surrender to the words of Chaucer:

> 'Non other lyf', sayd he, 'is worth a bene;
> For wedlock is so esy and so clene'.

Wedlock, however, is not always so easy, particularly in professions which keep man and wife apart for long periods.

MARRIAGE AND POLITICS

Politics can put a great strain on a marriage, as the British press always reminds us when elections come along. Yet some of the busiest politicians have managed, like me, to keep their marriages happy.

Despite one lapse at least, when he had a child by their maidservant, Karl Marx was deeply devoted to his wife, Jenny von Westphalen. They had been married for thirteen years when he wrote her this letter:

My heart's beloved,   *21 June 1856*

I am writing you again, because I am alone and because it troubles me always to have a dialogue with you in my head, without your knowing anything about it or hearing it or being able to answer. Poor as your photograph is, it does perform a service for me, and I now understand how even the 'Black Madonna' [ikon], the most disgraceful portrait of the Mother of God, could find indestructible admirers, indeed even more admirers than the good portraits. In any case, those Black Madonna pictures have never been more kissed, looked at, and adored than your photograph, which, although not black, is morose, and absolutely does not reflect your darling, sweet, kissable *dolce* face. But I improve upon the sun's rays, which have painted falsely, and find that my eyes, so spoiled by lamplight and tobacco, can still paint, not only in dream but also while awake. I have you vivaciously before me, and I carry you on my hands, and I kiss you from head to foot, and I fall on my knees before you, and I groan 'Madame, I love you'. And I truly love you more than the Moor of Venice ever loved . . .

Momentary absence is good, for in constant presence things seem too much alike to be differentiated. Proximity dwarfs even towers, while the petty and commonplace, at close view, grow too big. Small habits, which may physically irritate and take on emotional form, disappear when the immediate object is removed from the eye. Great passions, which through proximity assume the form of petty routine, grow and again take on their natural dimension on account of the magic of distance. So it is with my love. You have only to be snatched away from me even in a mere dream, and I know immediately that the time has only served, as do sun and rain for plants, for growth. The moment you are absent, my love for you shows itself to be what it is, a giant, in which are crowded together all the energy of my spirit and all the character of my heart.

There are actually many females in the world, and some among them are beautiful. But where could I find again a face, whose every feature, even every wrinkle, is a reminder of the greatest and sweetest memories of my life? Even my endless pains, my irreplaceable losses I read in your sweet countenance, and I kiss away the pain when I kiss your sweet face. 'Buried in her arms, awakened by her kisses' – namely, in your arms and by your kisses, and I grant the Brahmins and Pythagoras their doctrine of regeneration and Christianity its doctrine of resurrection ... Goodbye, my sweet heart. I kiss you and the children many thousand times.

Yours,
Karl.

Marx's frenetic political life inevitably created difficulties for their marriage; but in their final years, as my wife Edna has described in her book, *Wives of Fame,* their relationship grew easier. Their daughter Tussy remembered their immense sense of humour:

Assuredly two people never enjoyed a joke more than these two. Again and again – especially if the occasion were demanding decorum and sedateness – have I seen them laugh till the tears ran down their cheeks, and even those inclined to be shocked at such awful levity could not choose but laugh with them. And how often have I seen them not daring to look at one another, each knowing that once a glance was exchanged uncontrollable laughter would result. To see these two with eyes fixed on anything but one another, for all the world like two schoolchildren suffocating with suppressed laughter ... is a memory I would not barter for all the millions I am sometimes accredited with having inherited.

Tussy describes them when Jenny was dying:

Our mother lay in the large front room – Moor in the little room behind and next to it. And they who were so used to each other, whose lives had come to form part of each other, could not be in the same room any longer. Never shall I forget the morning when he felt strong enough to go into mother's room. When they were together they were young again, she a loving girl and he a loving youth, on the threshold of life, not an old man devastated by illness and an old woman parting from each other for life ... She remained fully conscious almost to the last moment and when she could no longer speak she pressed our hands and tried to smile ... but the last word she spoke to Papa was 'good'.

Four months after Jenny's death, Karl Marx himself died, and
Tussy wrote:

> It is no exaggeration to say that Karl Marx could never have been
> what he was without Jenny von Westphalen. Never were the lives
> of two people, both remarkable, so at one, so complementary of
> each other. Of extraordinary beauty — a beauty in which he took
> pleasure and pride to the end, and that wrung admiration from
> men like Heine ... of intellect and wit as brilliant as her beauty,
> Jenny von Westphalen was a woman in a million ... Truly he
> could say of her in Browning's words —
>
> > Therefore she is immortally my bride
> > Chance cannot change my love
> > Nor time impair.

At the other end of the political spectrum, William Gladstone also
had a happy marriage, though he would sometimes tramp the
streets of London after midnight in search of prostitutes whom he
would sometimes bring home for his wife to rescue. Mary
Gladstone, like Jenny Marx, shared her husband's sense of humour.
Her daughter Mary records Mrs Asquith's surprise that Gladstone
had a sufficiently subtle sense of humour to enjoy Heine, and
describes his response to the news that the Cook and the Captain at
her convalescent home were going to be married:

> Apparently he took no notice; seemingly absorbed in his own
> thoughts, he absently stretched out his hand for a sheet of notepaper
> and began to write. 'Oh, of course, you are too full of Homer and
> your old gods and goddesses to care — stupid of me!'
>   For a few minutes he went on writing, then handing her the
> paper — 'There! that's all I can do, your information was so very
> scanty.' And there was a poetic skit in three stanzas entitled:
>
> > THE COOK AND THE CAPTAIN
>
> > The Cook and the Captain determined one day,
> > When worthy Miss Simmons was out of the way,
> > On splicing together a life and a life,
> > The one as a husband the other as wife —
> >   Fol de rol, tol de rol, fol de rol la.

The Captain a subaltern officer made,
But the Cook! *she* was monarch of all she surveyed –
So how could they hit it the marrying day,
If she was to order and he to obey?
    Fol de rol, tol de rol, fol de rol la.

Miss Simmons came home and she shouted, 'Oh dear!
What riot is this? What the d – l is here?
If the Cook and the Captain will not be quiescent,
How can I expect it from each Convalescent?'
    Fol de rol, tol de rol, fol de rol la.

Mr G.W.E. Russell, who visited Hawarden more than once, notices the genial, lighter side of their life as inexpressibly attractive. One of the unexpected incidents which most surprised and pleased him was their custom, in special moments of exhilaration, of standing with arms round each other on the hearthrug, swaying as they sang:

'A ragamuffin husband and a rantipoling wife,
  We'll fiddle it and scrape it through the ups and downs of life.'

Though sex seems to have played no part in it, the writer Virginia Woolf and her politician husband, Leonard, had a supremely happy marriage, which Virginia found a constant source of joy and inspiration. She wrote at one point in her diary: 'I am amazed at my own happiness . . . I have had a good draught of human life, and find much champagne in it. It has not been dull – my marriage; not at all,' and then she describes herself as 'sitting down after dinner, side by side, and saying "are you in your stall, brother, well what can trouble this happiness?"'

It is rare for a marriage without children to be so stable and happy as that of Leonard and Virginia Woolf. Yet, though love for one's children and grandchildren can be as powerful as love for one's wife or husband, comparatively few poets have written about their children. There are exceptions. Coleridge was inspired to one of his best poems, 'Frost at Midnight', by his baby son, Hartley:

Therefore all seasons shall be sweet to thee,
Whether the summer clothe the general earth
With greenness, or the redbreast sit and sing
Betwixt the tufts of snow on the bare branch
Of mossy apple-tree, while the nigh thatch

Smokes in the sun-thaw; whether the eave-drops fall
Heard only in the trances of the blast,
Or if the secret ministry of frost
Shall hang them up in silent icicles,
Quietly shining to the quiet Moon.

Yeats, in his 'Prayer for My Daughter', summed up all he had learned about life, love, and politics:

Once more the storm is howling, and half hid
Under this cradle-hood and coverlid
My child sleeps on. There is no obstacle
But Gregory's wood and one bare hill
Whereby the haystack- and roof-levelling wind,
Bred on the Atlantic, can be stayed;
And for an hour I have walked and prayed
Because of the great gloom that is in my mind.

I have walked and prayed for this young child an hour
And heard the sea-wind scream upon the tower,
And under the arches of the bridge, and scream
In the elms above the flooded stream;
Imagining in excited reverie
That the future years had come,
Dancing to a frenzied drum,
Out of the murderous innocence of the sea.

May she be granted beauty and yet not
Beauty to make a stranger's eye distraught,
Or hers before a looking-glass, for such
Being made beautiful overmuch,
Consider beauty a sufficient end,
Lose natural kindness and maybe
The heart-revealing intimacy
That chooses right, and never find a friend.
Helen being chosen found life flat and dull
And later had much trouble from a fool,
While that great Queen, that rose out of the spray,
Being fatherless could have her way
Yet chose a bandy-leggèd smith for man.
It's certain that fine women eat
A crazy salad with their meat
Whereby the Horn of Plenty is undone.

In courtesy I'd have her chiefly learned;
Hearts are not had as a gift but hearts are earned
By those that are not entirely beautiful;
Yet many, that have played the fool
For beauty's very self, has charm made wise,
And many a poor man that has roved,
Loved and thought himself beloved,
From a glad kindness cannot take his eyes.

May she become a flourishing hidden tree
That all her thoughts may like the linnet be,
And have no business but dispensing round
Their magnanimities of sound,
Nor but in merriment begin a chase,
Nor but in merriment a quarrel.
O may she live like some green laurel
Rooted in one dear perpetual place.

My mind, because the minds that I have loved,
The sort of beauty that I have approved,
Prosper but little, has dried up of late,
Yet knows that to be choked with hate
May well be of all evil chances chief.
If there's no hatred in a mind
Assault and battery of the wind
Can never tear the linnet from the leaf.

An intellectual hatred is the worst,
So let her think opinions are accursed.
Have I not seen the loveliest woman born
Out of the mouth of Plenty's horn,
Because of her opinionated mind
Barter that horn and every good
By quiet natures understood
For an old bellows full of angry wind?

Considering that, all hatred driven hence,
The soul recovers radical innocence
And learns at last that it is self-delighting,
Self-appeasing, self-affrighting,
And that its own sweet will is Heaven's will;
She can, though every face should scowl
And every windy quarter howl
Or every bellows burst, be happy still.

And may her bridegroom bring her to a house
Where all's accustomed, ceremonious;
For arrogance and hatred are the wares
Peddled in the thoroughfares.
How but in custom and in ceremony
Are innocence and beauty born?
Ceremony's a name for the rich horn,
And custom for the spreading laurel tree.

I have never addressed unsolicited advice to my own children, knowing all too well that it would be counterproductive; so I am mightily flattered when they ask me to advise them. Yeats, however, did once take the risk of offering advice to a child – not one of his own, but Anne Gregory, the little granddaughter of his friend Lady Gregory. Forty years later Anne Gregory described the consequences in her account of her childhood at Coole Park, *Me and Nu*:

> Mr Yeats sent a message for me to go up to his sitting-room, and then said that he had written a poem called 'Yellow Hair' and that he had dedicated it to me, and proceeded to read it, in his 'humming' voice. We used to hear his voice 'humming' away for hours while he wrote his verse. He used to hum the rhythm of a verse before he wrote the words, Grandma told us, and that was why his poems are so good to read aloud. That is what Grandma said, but on this occasion I was petrified. I had no idea that he was going to write a poem to me, and had no idea at all what one should say when he had read it aloud.
>
> It was agony! For once, I think I did the right thing. Nearly in tears for fear of doing something silly, 'Read it again,' I pleaded, 'oh do read it to me again.'
>
> Obviously this was all right, for Yeats beamed, put on his pince nez attached to the broad black silk ribbon, and read it through again.

Never shall a young man,
Thrown into despair
By those great honey-coloured
Ramparts at your ear,
Love you for yourself alone
And not your yellow hair.

But I can get a hair-dye
And set such colour there,
Brown or black or carrot,

That young men in despair
Shall love me for myself alone
And not my yellow hair.

I heard an old religious man
But yesternight declare
That he had found a text to prove
That only God, my dear,
Could love you for yourself alone
And not your yellow hair.

This time I was able to stutter: 'Wonderful. Thank you so much. Wonderful. I must go and wash my hair,' and crashed out.

Years later Yeats broadcast some of his works on one of the first radio programmes from Belfast. He announced the next poem, saying it was dedicated to the granddaughter of his old friend Lady Gregory and that she had 'hair like a cornfield in the sun.' This time I was thrilled, and 'Yellow Hair' sounded really rather splendid. I had a couple of boy friends staying and they were very impressed too.

Next morning there was an envelope by my plate, in it was a poem 'To Anne G . . . after WBY.'

I was thrilled. Boy friend coming up to scratch at last, I thought. What Bliss! I opened the envelope, took out the poem and read:

If I was alone on an island,
And only Anne with me there,
I'd make myself cushions and bolsters,
By stuffing her skin with her hair.

Children are indeed often unlike the images which adult poets form of them.

8

AGE

'Therefore my age is as a lusty winter,
Frosty but kindly'
 – *As You Like It*, William Shakespeare

'"Why," said Mr Hennessy, "ye'd give anythin' to be twinty-five agin'." "I widdn't," said Mr Dooley. "Why shud I want to grow old again?"' So wrote Peter Finley Dunne.

Another great American philosopher, Benjamin Franklin, made the same point differently: 'All would live long, yet none would be old.' I suppose Franklin was right. Yet a man is as old as he feels, and Franklin himself never showed any sign of feeling old; he was active until he died at the age of eighty-four.

I am now in my seventy-fifth year. So far, the process of ageing has never troubled me, although I am well aware of the changes it has brought. Greater knowledge and wider experience have changed my views in many ways, and made me less confident that I am always right! I hope it has also given me more wisdom on the underlying issues. The biggest change came when I left the Shadow Cabinet in 1987 and ceased to compete in the political race. The following eighteen months, which I spent in writing my memoirs, gave me time to reflect on my life and to re-assess what I had done. So I suppose I have mellowed with age.

The usual physical changes have also had their effect. I started to wear glasses for reading when I became Defence Secretary at the age of forty-seven. Now I need them for long sight too, so I wear the bifocal lenses which Benjamin Franklin invented in his old age. Even so, I find it infuriatingly difficult to decipher the titles in a bookcase, to read piano music, and to examine paintings in a gallery; even bifocals cannot make up for all the lack of flexibility in my eye-muscles.

Hearing is less of a problem, though certain sounds – particularly the noise of a telephone or door bell – are difficult to catch. But I can hear music perfectly, thank God, and enjoy it more than ever.

My memory has always been exceptionally good, but now it sometimes betrays me; I hear an elusive name go rattling down the grating, and see it glinting there at the bottom, but simply have no way of scraping it up; yet I know it will suddenly jump back into my mind when I no longer need it.

When I was younger I always ran up any flight of stairs. Now I use the lift, if there is one. Edna and I no longer take long walks on our holidays in the Alps. When we came back from a lovely summer holiday last year, I realized that I had never spent so long simply loafing about since I was in the army.

In fact, until the summer of 1991, leaving the Shadow Cabinet had brought me no rest from my labours. For eighteen months I spent every moment of my spare time writing *The Time of my Life*. Once I had finished promoting my book in October 1989, the Berlin Wall collapsed, Eastern Europe won its independence, and Germany was united. I was busier than ever. At the beginning of August 1990 I took Edna across the Channel for a well-earned holiday, feeling I had done my bit. On 2 August Saddam Hussein invaded Kuwait, and I was deeply involved in the Middle East crisis for another year. Those last four years as a backbencher were if anything more tiring than my years as a minister or member of the Shadow Cabinet, since I had no one to work for me except my invaluable secretary, Harriet Shackman.

Nevertheless I managed to get some reading done for pleasure, not politics. I refreshed myself continually by reading once again the poets who had sustained me through the years – particularly Yeats, Traherne, Auden, and Dylan Thomas. I discovered poets new to me, above all Emily Dickinson, and tasted some of the latest verse by Seamus Heaney, Tom Paulin, and Wendy Cope. Until the blessed summer of 1991, however, I had insufficient time and energy left over to read the heavier novels, contenting myself with the latest George V. Higgins and Elmore Leonard, who are serious without requiring undue concentration. And I enjoyed immensely some of the lighter memoirs, particularly Joan Wyndham's books about her youth in wartime.

Meanwhile, like so many women with busy husbands, Edna had waited until all our children had left home before starting her own professional career. She was sixty years old when she published her first book, *Lady Unknown*, about the Victorian philanthropist Angela Burdett-Coutts. Its success led her to write *Wives of Fame* about the wives of Karl Marx, David Livingstone, and Charles Darwin, all remarkable women in their own right. This in turn encouraged her to make two television films in Africa about Mary Livingstone and the Scottish missionary Mary Slessor of Calabar. She then spent seven years writing the history of Coutts & Co. for their tercentenary in 1992. So in old age our writing lives have run parallel; but unlike Donne's loves, though infinite, they often meet.

It is said that as they grow old women either widen or wizen. That applies equally to men – mentally as well as physically. It is all too apparent that I fall into the first category.

Slowing the pace of living makes you enjoy life all the more. One of my role models, along with Benjamin Franklin, is Giuseppe Verdi. Verdi wrote the greatest of his many great works when he was over seventy. He produced his most magical opera, *Falstaff*, when he was eighty. His music for Fenton and Nannetta conveys the essence of young love better than anything by a young composer. When he died at the age of eighty-seven, his close friend and collaborator, the librettist Arrigo Boito, wrote: 'Verdi is dead: he carried away with him an enormous quantity of light and vital warmth. We had all basked in the sunshine of his Olympian old age. He died magnificently, formidable and silent.'

Richard Strauss was eighty-four years old when he wrote his incomparable *Four Last Songs*. 'In Sunset', to words by Eichendorff, describes the composer himself with his wife, Pauline, at the end of their lives facing the prospect of death together with love and resignation, as the larks trill high up in the darkening sky. It is a perfect tribute to a long and happy marriage.

I had the good fortune to know Sir Robert Mayer in his last years. He devoted much of his life to the encouragement of young musicians, and had known Brahms as a boy. When he was a hundred years old, we invited him to dinner, only to be told that he was in America on a lecture tour! Manny Shinwell was also a hundred when I complimented him on looking so fit as he strode down a corridor in the House of Commons. He replied: 'That's all very well, Denis, but you'll find, as I did, that you start slowing down when you're ninety.'

Politics requires exceptional physical and mental stamina; it has killed many men I knew in their fifties – Aneurin Bevan, Hugh Gaitskell, and Iain Macleod among them. But if you survive sixty, you can go on for ever – like Winston Churchill, Konrad Adenauer, and Synghman Ree – not to speak of the leaders of Communist China. I myself have always felt young, although the strains of office exhausted me for a few weeks during the IMF crisis in 1976. On the other hand, I have known people who were born middle-aged, like the steward in *St Joan*, whom Shaw described as 'a man whom age cannot wither because he has never bloomed'.

Many poets, like Keats and Shelley, and some musicians, like Mozart, have died young – and still felt young when they died. Others felt old while still young. Byron had burned his candle at both ends; even so it is surprising to find him celebrating his thirty-sixth birthday at Missolonghi with this melancholy poem to his Greek page:

> Tis time this heart should be unmoved,
> Since others it has ceased to move:
> Yet, though I cannot be beloved,
> Still let me love!
>
> My days are in the yellow leaf;
> The flowers and fruits of love are gone;
> The worm, the canker, and the grief
> Are mine alone!
>
> The fire that on my bosom preys
> Is lone as some volcanic isle;
> No torch is kindled at its blaze –
> A funeral pile!

As a young man Yeats looked forward to his old age with this lovely adaptation of a poem by Ronsard:

> When you are old and grey and full of sleep,
> And nodding by the fire, take down this book,
> And slowly read, and dream of the soft look
> Your eyes had once, and of their shadows deep;

How many loved your moments of glad grace,
And loved your beauty with love false or true,
But one man loved the pilgrim soul in you,
And loved the sorrows of your changing face;

And bending down beside the glowing bars,
Murmur, a little sadly, how Love fled
And paced upon the mountains overhead
And hid his face amid a crowd of stars.

In fact Yeats began to feel old when most of us are in the prime of life; he was under forty-five years of age when he wrote 'The Coming of Wisdom with Time':

Though leaves are many, the root is one;
Through all the lying days of my youth
I swayed my leaves and flowers in the sun;
Now I may wither into the truth.

Yet Yeats began to write some of his best poetry in the years that followed. When he was sixty, another bout of agonizing about his age produced even greater poetry. He asked the question in 'The Tower':

What shall I do with this absurdity –
O heart, O troubled heart – this caricature,
Decrepit age that has been tied to me
As to a dog's tail?
                  Never had I more
Excited, passionate, fantastical
Imagination, nor an ear and eye
That more expected the impossible –
No, not in boyhood when with rod and fly,
Or the humbler worm, I climbed Ben Bulben's back
And had the livelong summer day to spend.
It seems that I must bid the Muse go pack,
Choose Plato and Plotinus for a friend
Until imagination, ear and eye,
Can be content with argument and deal
In abstract things; or be derided by
A sort of battered kettle at the heel.

In 'Sailing to Byzantium' he gave his own answer:

I

That is no country for old men. The young
In one another's arms, birds in the trees
– Those dying generations – at their song,
The salmon-falls, the mackerel-crowded seas,
Fish, flesh, or fowl, commend all summer long
Whatever is begotten, born, and dies.
Caught in that sensual music all neglect
Monuments of unageing intellect.

II

An aged man is but a paltry thing,
A tattered coat upon a stick, unless
Soul clap its hands and sing, and louder sing
For every tatter in its mortal dress,
Nor is there singing school but studying
Monuments of its own magnificence;
And therefore I have sailed the seas and come
To the holy city of Byzantium.

III

O sages standing in God's holy fire
As in the gold mosaic of a wall,
Come from the holy fire, perne in a gyre,
And be the singing-masters of my soul.
Consume my heart away; sick with desire
And fastened to a dying animal
It knows not what it is; and gather me
Into the artifice of eternity.

IV

Once out of nature I shall never take
My bodily form from any natural thing,
But such a form as Grecian goldsmiths make
Of hammered gold and gold enamelling
To keep a drowsy Emperor awake;
Or set upon a golden bough to sing
To lords and ladies of Byzantium
Of what is past, or passing, or to come.

Yet Yeats continued to be so obsessed by the waning of his sexual
powers that he had an operation to restore them – which led
irreverent contemporaries to call him 'the gland old man'. The
quality of his poetry remained as unique as ever. In his last years,
just before the Second World War, he wrote 'An Acre of Grass':

Picture and book remain,
An acre of green grass
For air and exercise,
Now strength of body goes;
Midnight, an old house
Where nothing stirs but a mouse.

My temptation is quiet.
Here at life's end
Neither loose imagination,
Nor the mill of the mind
Consuming its rag and bone,
Can make the truth known.

Grant me an old man's frenzy,
Myself must I remake
Till I am Timon and Lear
Or that William Blake
Who beat upon the wall
Till Truth obeyed his call;

A mind Michael Angelo knew
That can pierce the clouds,
Or inspired by frenzy
Shake the dead in their shrouds;
Forgotten else by mankind,
An old man's eagle mind.

Yeats has been one of the most important inhabitants of my secret planet since I first read him at school. 'The woods of Arcady arc dead, And over is their antique joy' had the same effect on me as Milton's 'Nymphs and Shepherds dance no more' had on A.E. Housman. Yeats was one of the few poets whose work, never less than good, improved steadily as he moved through his life. His style also changed as his thinking grew more profound.

I felt a special affinity with him for many reasons. He was half Irish. His mother's family came from Cornwall and, as I have said, his father's ancestors had come from Yorkshire – a mixture very like my own. To him, poetry was a public activity like politics. He found his involvement in committee work for the Abbey Theatre as necessary and frustrating as mine as a Cabinet minister. Nationalist politics engaged him directly more than once – his first great love, Maud Gonne, was the daughter of an English officer, yet supported terrorism against the English. He became a Senator of the Republic when Ireland finally won independence. Unfortunately the incandescence of his poetic genius was not matched by his judgement as a politician, which burned with a very smoky flame.

Earlier centuries were fascinated by time, but more stoical about growing old. William Shakespeare wrote one of his loveliest sonnets about it:

> That time of year thou mayst in me behold
> When yellow leaves, or none, or few, do hang
> Upon those boughs which shake against the cold,
> Bare ruined choirs, where late the sweet birds sang.
> In me thou see'st the twilight of such day
> As after sunset fadeth in the west,
> Which by and by black night doth take away,
> Death's second self, that seals up all in rest.
> In me thou see'st the glowing of such fire,
> That on the ashes of his youth doth lie,
> As the death-bed whereon it must expire
> Consumed with that which it was nourished by.
> This thou perceiv'st, which makes thy love more strong,
> To love that well which thou must leave ere long.

Sir Walter Raleigh struck a similar note:

> Nature that washed her hands in milk
>   And had forgot to dry them,
> Instead of earth took snow and silk
>   At Love's request to try them,
> If she a mistress could compose
> To please Love's fancy out of those.
>
> Her eyes he would should be of light,
>   A violet breath and lips of jelly,
> Her hair not black, nor over-bright,
>   And of the softest down her belly,
> As for her inside he'd have it
> Only of wantonness and wit.
>
> At Love's entreaty, such a one
>   Nature made, but with her beauty
> She hath framed a heart of stone,
>   So as Love by ill destiny
> Must die for her whom Nature gave him.
> Because her darling would not save him.

But Time which Nature doth despise,
　And rudely gives her love the lie,
Makes Hope a fool, and Sorrow wise,
　His hands doth neither wash, nor dry,
But being made of steel and rust,
Turns snow, and silk, and milk to dust.

The light, the belly, lips and breath,
　He dims, discolours, and destroys,
With those he feeds, but fills not death,
　Which sometimes were the food of joys;
Yea, Time doth dull each lively wit,
And drys all wantonness with it.

Oh cruel Time, which takes in trust
　Our youth, our joys, and all we have,
And pays us but with age and dust,
　Who in the dark and silent grave
When we have wandered all our ways
Shuts up the story of our days.

The idea that a man's role should adjust to increasing age came naturally to the Elizabethans. George Peele wrote 'A Farewell to Arms' to his Queen:

My golden locks Time hath to silver turn'd;
　O Time too swift, O swiftness never ceasing!
My youth 'gainst age, and age 'gainst time, hath spurn'd,
　But spurn'd in vain; youth waneth by increasing:
Beauty, strength, youth, are flowers but fading seen;
Duty, faith, love, are roots, and ever green.

My helmet now shall make an hive for bees,
　And lover's sonnets turn to holy psalms;
A man-at-arms must now serve on his knees,
　And feed on prayers, which are old age his alms:
But though from court to cottage I depart,
My saint is sure of my unspotted heart.

And when I saddest sit in homely cell,
　I'll teach my swains this carol for a song, –
'Blest be the hearts that wish my sovereign well,
　Curst be the souls that think her any wrong!'
Goddess, allow this aged man his right
To be your beadsman now that was your knight.

Peele preceded Shakespeare as a poet and a dramatist. He also wrote the first known script for the Lord Mayor's Show in London – 'Device of the Pageant Borne before Woolstone Dixi'. A generation later Ben Jonson, the greatest Elizabethan dramatist after Shakespeare, emphasized the quality, rather than the length, of life in a poem I learned by heart at school:

> It is not growing like a tree
> In bulk, doth make men better be;
> Or standing long an oak, three hundred year,
> To fall a log at last, dry, bald, and sere:
> A lily of a day
> Is fairer far in May
> Although it fall and die that night;
> It was the plant and flower of light.
> In small proportions we just beauties see;
> And in short measures life may perfect be.

I have found that a happy marriage is the best recipe for a happy old age. So did Burns, who wrote:

> John Anderson my jo, John,
> When we were first acquent,
> Your locks were like the raven,
> Your bonnie brow was brent;
> But now your brow is beld, John,
> Your locks are like the snow;
> But blessings on your frosty pow,
> John Anderson my jo.
>
> John Anderson my jo, John,
> We clamb the hill thegither,
> And mony a canty day, John,
> We've had wi' ane anither:
> Now we maun totter down, John,
> But hand in hand we'll go,
> And sleep thegither at the foot,
> John Anderson my jo.

Hartley Coleridge was less accommodating:

> If I were young as I have been,
> And you were only gay sixteen,

I would address you as a goddess,
Write loyal cantos to your bodice,
Wish that I were your cap, your shoe,
Or anything that's near to you.
But I am old, and you, my fair,
Are somewhat older than you were.
A lover's language in your hearing
Would sound like irony and jeering.
Once you were fair to all that see,
Now you are only fair to me.

Tennyson in his old age wrote a beautiful poem to his wife, Emily, on their forty-first wedding anniversary:

There on the top of the down,
The wild heather round me and over me June's high blue,
When I look'd at the bracken so bright and the heather so brown,
I thought to myself I would offer this book to you,
This and my love together,
To you that are seventy-seven,
With a faith as clear as the heights of the June-blue heaven,
And a fancy as summer-new
As the green of the bracken amid the gloom of the heather.

In the eighteenth century Walter Pope felt he could grow old happily even without a wife:

If I live to grow old, for I find I go down,
Let this be my fate: – in a country town
May I have a warm house, with a stone at the gate,
And a cleanly young girl to rub my bald pate.
May I govern my passions with absolute sway,
And grow wiser and better as strength wears away,
Without gout or stone, by a gentle decay.

With a courage undaunted may I face my last day;
And when I am dead may the better sort say,
In the morning when sober, in the evening when mellow,
'He's gone, and has left not behind him his fellow:
For he governed his passions with absolute sway,
And grew wiser and better as strength wore away,
Without gout or stone, by a gentle decay.'

Benjamin Franklin quoted this poem with strong approval in a letter he wrote in 1785, when he was 'rising (or more properly falling) 80'. The letter covered everything from annihilation to bifocals, with an excursion to the Foundling Hospital in Paris, whose population had recently tripled. Franklin attacked 'the monstrous deficiency of natural affection' in the mothers responsible with his usual broad humour:

> A Surgeon I met with here excused the Women of Paris, by saying, seriously, that they *could not* give suck; '*Car*,' dit il, '*elles n'ont point de tetons.*' He assur'd me it was a Fact, and bade me look at them, and observe how flat they were on the Breast; 'they have nothing more there,' said he, 'than I have upon the Back of my hand.' I have since thought that there might be some Truth in his Observation, and that, possibly, Nature, finding they made no use of Bubbies, had left off giving them any. Yet, since Rousseau, with admirable Eloquence, pleaded for the Rights of Children to their Mother's Milk, the Mode has changed a little; and some Ladies of Quality now suckle their Infants and find Milk enough. May the Mode descend to the lower Ranks, till it becomes no longer the Custom to pack their Infants away, as soon as born, to the *Enfants Trouvés*, with the careless Observation, that the King is better able to maintain them.

Thomas Hardy suffered the same pangs about ageing as did Yeats:

> I look into my glass,
> And view my wasting skin,
> And say, 'Would God it came to pass
> My heart had shrunk as thin!'
>
> For then, I, undistrest
> By hearts grown cold to me,
> Could lonely wait my endless rest
> With equanimity.
>
> But Time, to make me grieve,
> Part steals, lets part abide;
> And shakes this fragile frame at eve
> With throbbings of noontide.

Hardy finally came to terms with old age through his love for nature:

When the present has latched its postern behind my tremulous
    stay,
    And the May month flaps its glad green leaves like wings,
Delicate filmed as new-spun silk, will the neighbours say,
    'He was a man who used to notice such things'?

If it be in the dusk when, like an eyelid's soundless blink,
    The dewfall-hawk comes crossing the shades to alight
Upon the wind-warped upland thorn, a gazer may think,
    'To him this must have been a familiar sight'.

If I pass during some nocturnal blackness, mothy and warm,
    When the hedgehog travels furtively over the lawn,
One may say, 'He strove that such innocent creatures should come
    to no harm,
    But he could do little for them; and now he is gone'.

If, when hearing that I have been stilled at last, they stand at the
    door,
    Watching the full-starred heavens that winter sees,
Will this thought rise on those who will meet my face no more,
    'He was one who had an eye for such mysteries';

And will any say when my bell of quittance is heard in the gloom,
    And a crossing breeze cuts a pause in its outrollings,
Till they rise again, as they were a new bell's boom,
    'He hears it not now, but used to notice such things'?

I do not believe, however, that is is possible to come to terms with
old age if it brings a serious mental deterioration. John Clare spent
the last twenty-three years of his life in an asylum, suffering bouts
of extreme depression. Yet he was still able to express himself in
verse:

I am: yet what I am none cares or knows,
    My friends forsake me like a memory lost;
I am the self-consumer of my woes,
    They rise and vanish in oblivious host,
Like shades in love and death's oblivion lost;
And yet I am, and live with shadows tost
Into the nothingness of scorn and noise,
    Into the living sea of waking dreams,
Where there is neither sense of life nor joys,
    But the vast shipwreck of my life's esteems;
And e'en the dearest – that I loved the best –
Are strange – nay, rather stranger than the rest.

I long for scenes where man has never trod,
   A place where woman never smiled or wept;
There to abide with my Creator, God,
   And sleep as I in childhood sweetly slept:
Untroubling and untroubled where I lie,
The grass below — above the vaulted sky.

My mother died at the age of ninety-nine. Until the last few weeks she could enjoy her life, even when her memory began to fail. Once she had to go to a nursing home for permanent medical attention, she faded fast. I sat with her in her final hours until the end had come, but doubt if she even knew I was there. So I find 'Ward 14' by Charles Causley unbearably moving:

Today, incredibly, the nurse
Attempts to reason with her —
The mother with the brain three quarters struck away

By apoplexy, and other
Assorted fevers and indignities as the body
Slides slowly, O so slowly, to harbour.

'Wake up!' orders the nurse, kindly.
'Open your eyes.'
The mother does so.
'Your son is here,' says the nurse:
A razor-voice stained momentarily with a little sugar.

'You mustn't cry
When your son is here.
Mothers don't cry
When their sons are here.
Now be a good girl;
That's a good girl.'

Puzzled, the mother stares at her:
Wonder creasing the face.
'You're going to be a good girl
Now that your son is here
Aren't you?'
'Yes,' says the mother rapidly,
Wide-eyed, astounded.

Her task accomplished, the nurse
Clops purposefully away down the ward

Like a fractious charger
After a small battle.

As soon as she has gone, the mother
Breaks once more into swift, unceasing tears
Of pain, misery, frustration.
The other visitors look at the son
With a compassionate air;
Rather less so at the patient.

Weep on, mother!
It is your right.
It is your due.
Helpless at the foot of your crucifixion
He is not going to deny you that.

9

DEATH

> 'That undiscovered country from whose bourne
> No traveller returns.'
> — *Hamlet*, William Shakespeare

During the war it was impossible to forget that 'in the midst of life we are in death'. But, though uncertain whether I would survive, I was never, like Webster as T.S. Eliot described him, 'much obsessed by death'. I did not 'see the skull beneath the skin'.

In recent years, I find more and more familiar names in the obituary columns. But fortunately through most of my life death has never taken my nearest and dearest. A century ago most children had to endure the death of a brother or sister, and most adults lost their mother or father before they themselves were forty. I have been exceptionally lucky in my generation. Even in the war none of my closest friends were killed.

I was Chancellor of the Exchequer when my father died, and used to visit him daily at Whipps Cross Hospital in his last days. Though he was then ninety-two years old and his body was quite worn out, his mind was clear to the end. I felt his death keenly, and had difficulty getting through my farewell address at his funeral service. My mother wept for the first time for many years when we got back to her house.

A few years later, when I had already passed my statutory three score years and ten, I was deeply distressed by the death of my best friend, Dave Linebaugh, in Washington. He had spent his last twenty years badly crippled by a broken back. Yet he had contrived to continue working for disarmament in the State Department and other organizations, and even made one visit to Moscow. I last saw him on a life-support machine in Georgetown Hospital just before he died.

The loss I felt most bitterly followed shortly afterwards, when my mother died at the age of ninety-nine. Except in these three cases, my grief at the deaths of friends or relatives was more for those they left behind them than for themselves.

On 28 March 1941, Leonard Woolf found the following letter from his wife on the sitting-room mantelpiece at his home, Monk's House, in Rodmell:

> *Dearest,*
> I feel certain that I am going mad again. I feel we can't go through another of those terrible times. And I shan't recover this time.
> I begin to hear voices, and I can't concentrate. So I am doing what seems the best thing to do. You have given me the greatest possible happiness. You have been in every way all that anyone could be. I don't think two people could have been happier till this terrible disease came. I can't fight any longer. I know that I am spoiling your life, that without me you could work. And you will I know. You see I can't even write this properly. I can't read. What I want to say is I owe all the happiness of my life to you. You have been entirely patient with me and incredibly good. I want to say that — everybody knows it. If anybody could have saved me it would have been you. Everything has gone from me but the certainty of your goodness. I can't go on spoiling your life any longer.
> I don't think two people could have been happier than we have been.
>
> *V.*

In fact Virginia had drowned herself in the River Ouse, close to their home. When her body was finally recovered, Leonard planned, as they had agreed, to have the Cavatina from Beethoven's B flat quartet played at her cremation. In the event, he was too distraught to arrange it, so instead they played the music of the Blessed Spirits from Gluck's *Orfeo*. Leonard returned to their home at Monk's House in the evening and played the Cavatina on his gramophone. He wrote:

I buried Virginia's ashes at the foot of the great elm tree on the bank of the great lawn in the garden, called the Croft, which looks out over the field and the water-meadows. There were two great elms there with boughs interlaced which we always called Leonard and Virginia. In the first week of January 1943, in a great gale one of the elms was blown down.

I too have always sought consolation for the death of a loved one in music. When my father died, I had the 'Pie Jesu' from Fauré's Requiem played at his cremation. For my mother's cremation I chose the 'Lacrimosa' from Mozart's Requiem Mass. Such music can lift me above all earthly cares.

However, I think I owe my comparatively philosophical attitude towards death above all to some of the poets and writers I have read.

Francis Bacon told us that 'men fear death as children fear to go in the dark'. Yet he also told us:

There is no passion in the mind of man so weak, but it mates and masters the fear of death. And therefore death is no such terrible enemy, when a man hath so many attendants about him that can win the combat of him. Revenge triumphs over death; love slights it: honour aspireth to it; grief flieth to it.

Shakespeare tended to dwell on the physical consequences of death, as in Hamlet's soliloquy over the skull of poor Yorick, and on the terrors of Hell, as in Claudio's words:

> Ay, but to die, and go we know not where;
> To lie in cold obstruction and to rot;
> This sensible warm motion to become
> A kneaded clod; and the delighted spirit
> To bathe in fiery floods, or to reside
> In thrilling region of thick-ribbèd ice;
> To be imprisoned in the viewless winds,
> And blown with restless violence round about
> The pendent world; or to be worse than worst
> Of those that lawless and incertain thought
> Imagine howling! 'Tis too horrible!
> The weariest and most loathèd worldly life
> That age, ache, penury, and imprisonment
> Can lay on nature is a paradise
> To what we fear of death.

Yet he could treat death very differently in his songs, like the dirge from *Cymbeline*:

> Fear no more the heat o'the sun,
>   Nor the furious winter's rages;
> Thou thy worldly task hast done,
>   Home art gone, and ta'en thy wages.
> Golden lads and girls all must,
> As chimney-sweepers, come to dust.
>
> Fear no more the frown o' the great,
>   Thou art past the tyrant's stroke;
> Care no more to clothe and eat,
>   To thee the reed is as the oak.
> The sceptre, learning, physic, must
> All follow this, and come to dust.
>
> Fear no more the lightning-flash,
>   Nor the all-dreaded thunder-stone;
> Fear not slander, censure rash;
>   Thou hast finished joy and moan.
> All lovers young, all lovers must
> Consign to thee, and come to dust.
>
> No exorciser harm thee!
> Nor no witchcraft charm thee!
> Ghost unlaid forbear thee!
> Nothing ill come near thee!
> Quiet consummation have,
> And renownèd be thy grave!

He shows the same resignation in his sonnet:

> No longer mourn for me when I am dead
> Than you shall hear the surly sullen bell
> Give warning to the world that I am fled
> From this vile world, with vilest worms to dwell:
> Nay, if you read this line, remember not
> The hand that writ it; for I love you so,
> That I in your sweet thoughts would be forgot,
> If thinking on me then should make you woe.
> O, if, I say, you look upon this verse
> When I perhaps compounded am with clay,
> Do not so much as my poor name rehearse,

But let your love even with my life decay;
　　Lest the wise world should look into your moan,
　　And mock you with me after I am gone.

Others escaped the fear of death through reason, as in Donne's great sonnet:

Death, be not proud, though some have callèd thee
Mighty and dreadful, for thou art not so:
For those whom thou think'st thou dost overthrow
Die not, poor Death; nor yet canst thou kill me.
From Rest and Sleep, which but thy pictures be,
Much pleasure, then from thee much more must flow;
And soonest our best men with thee do go —
Rest of their bones and soul's delivery!
Thou'rt slave to fate, chance, kings, and desperate men,
And dost with poison, war, and sickness dwell;
And poppy or charms can make us sleep as well
And better than thy stroke. Why swell'st thou then?
　　One short sleep past, we wake eternally,
　　And Death shall be no more: Death, thou shalt die!

Death as the great leveller produced many tributes, like James Shirley's:

The glories of our blood and state
　　Are shadows, not substantial things;
There is no armour against Fate;
　　Death lays his icy hand on kings:
　　　　Sceptre and Crown
　　　　Must tumble down,
　　And in the dust be equal made
With the poor crooked scythe and spade.

Some men with swords may reap the field,
　　And plant fresh laurels where they kill:
But their strong nerves at last must yield;
　　They tame but one another still:
　　　　Early or late
　　　　They stoop to fate,
And must give up their murmuring breath
When they, pale captives, creep to death.

The garlands wither on your brow;
    Then boast no more your mighty deeds!
Upon Death's purple altar now
    See where the victor-victim bleeds.
        Your heads must come
        To the cold tomb:
Only the actions of the just
Smell sweet and blossom in their dust.

Francis Beaumont gives the same warning in his poem 'On the Tombs in Westminster Abbey':

Mortality, behold and fear!
What a change of flesh is here!
Think how many royal bones
Sleep within this heap of stones:
Here they lie had realms and lands,
Who now want strength to stir their hands:
Where from their pulpits sealed with dust
They preach, 'In greatness is no trust'.
Here's an acre sown indeed
With the richest, royalest seed
That the earth did e'er suck in
Since the first man died for sin;
Here the bones of birth have cried –
'Though gods they were, as men they died.'
Here are sands, ignoble things,
Dropped from the ruined sides of kings;
Here's a world of pomp and state,
Buried in dust, once dead by fate.

Thomas Nashe treats life after death as more certain than life on earth in his song from 'Summer's Last Will and Testament':

Adieu, farewell earth's bliss,
This world uncertain is;
Fond are life's lustful joys,
Death proves them all but toys,
None from his darts can fly.
I am sick, I must die.
        Lord have mercy on us!

Rich men, trust not in wealth,
Gold cannot buy you health;
Physic himself must fade,
All things to end are made.
The plague full swift goes by;
I am sick, I must die.
      Lord have mercy on us!

Beauty is but a flower
Which wrinkles will devour:
Brightness falls from the air,
Queens have died young and fair,
Dust hath closed Helen's eye.
I am sick, I must die.
      Lord have mercy on us!

Strength stoops unto the grave,
Worms feed on Hector brave,
Swords may not fight with fate.
Earth still holds ope her gate;
Come! come! the bells do cry.
I am sick, I must die.
      Lord have mercy on us!

Wit with his wantonness
Tasteth death's bitterness;
Hell's executioner
Hath no ears for to hear
What vain art can reply.
I am sick, I must die.
      Lord have mercy on us!

Haste, therefore, each degree,
To welcome destiny.
Heaven is our heritage,
Earth but a player's stage;
Mount we unto the sky.
I am sick, I must die.
      Lord have mercy on us!

In the seventeenth century, religion was the main source of consolation, as in Donne's triumphant Holy Sonnet:

At the round earths imagin'd corners, blow
Your trumpets, Angells, and arise, arise

From death, you numberlesse infinities
Of soules, and to your scattred bodies goe,
All whom the flood did, and fire shall o'erthrow,
All whom warre, dearth, age, agues, tyrannies,
Despaire, law, chance, hath slaine, and you whose eyes,
Shall behold God, and never tast deaths woe.
But let them sleepe, Lord, and mee mourne a space,
For, if above all these, my sinnes abound,
'Tis late to aske abundance of thy grace,
When wee are there; here on this lowly ground,
Teach mee how to repent; for that's as good
As if thou'hadst seal'd my pardon, with thy blood.

George Herbert is gentler but no less compelling, in 'Virtue':

Sweet day, so cool, so calm, so bright!
The bridal of the earth and sky –
The dew shall weep thy fall to-night;
    For thou must die.

Sweet rose, whose hue angry and brave
Bids the rash gazer wipe his eye,
Thy root is ever in its grave,
    And thou must die.

Sweet spring, full of sweet days and roses,
A box where sweets compacted lie,
My music shows ye have your closes.
    And all must die.

Only a sweet and virtuous soul,
Like season'd timber, never gives;
But though the whole world turn to coal,
    Then chiefly lives.

Love, as Bacon said, can triumph over death. In 1641 Lady Catherine Dyer had this poem inscribed on a monument to her dead husband:

My dearest dust, could not thy hasty day
Afford thy drowszy patience leave to stay
One hower longer: so that we might either
Sate up, or gone to bedd together?
But since thy finisht labour hath possest

Thy weary limbs with early rest,
Enjoy it sweetly: and thy widdowe bride
Shall soone repose her by thy slumbring side.
Whose business, now, is only to prepare
My nightly dress, and call to prayre:
Mine eyes wax heavy and ye day growes old.
The dew falls thick, my belovd growes cold.
Draw, draw ye closed curtaynes: and make roome:
My dear, my dearest dust; I come, I come.

Among Wordsworth's most moving poems are those about a little girl he made friends with in Lakeland – Lucy Gray:

She dwelt among the untrodden ways
    Beside the springs of Dove,
A maid whom there were none to praise
    And very few to love:

A Violet by a mossy stone
    Half hidden from the eye!
– Fair as a star, when only one
    Is shining in the sky.

She lived unknown, and few could know
    When Lucy ceased to be;
But she is in her grave, and oh,
    The difference to me!

*

A slumber did my spirit seal;
    I had no human fears:
She seem'd a thing that could not feel
    The touch of earthly years.

No motion has she now, no force;
    She neither hears nor sees,
Roll'd round in earth's diurnal course,
    With rocks, and stones, and trees.

Dylan Thomas produced a magnificent epitaph to Ann Jones, an old woman, who died when he was a child, in 'After the Funeral':

After the funeral, mule praises, brays,
Windshake of sailshaped ears, muffle-toed tap
Tap happily of one peg in the thick

Grave's foot, blinds down the lids, the teeth in black,
The spittled eyes, the salt ponds in the sleeves,
Morning smack of the spade that wakes up sleep,
Shakes a desolate boy who slits his throat
In the dark of the coffin and sheds dry leaves,
That breaks one bone to light with a judgment clout,
After the feast of tear-stuffed time and thistles
In a room with a stuffed fox and a stale fern,
I stand, for this memorial's sake, alone
In the snivelling hours with dead, humped Ann
Whose hooded, fountain heart once fell in puddles
Round the parched worlds of Wales and drowned each sun
(Though this for her is a monstrous image blindly
Magnified out of praise; her death was a still drop;
She would not have me sinking in the holy
Flood of her heart's fame; she would lie dumb and deep
And need no druid of her broken body).
But I, Ann's bard on a raised hearth, call all
The seas to service that her wood-tongued virtue
Babble like a bellbuoy over the hymning heads,
Bow down the walls of the ferned and foxy woods
That her love sing and swing through a brown chapel,
Bless her bent spirit with four, crossing birds.
Her flesh was meek as milk, but this skyward statue
With the wild breast and blessed and giant skull
Is carved from her in a room with a wet window
In a fiercely mourning house in a crooked year.
I know her scrubbed and sour humble hands
Lie with religion in their cramp, her threadbare
Whisper in a damp word, her wits drilled hollow,
Her fist of a face died clenched on a round pain;
And sculptured Ann is seventy years of stone.
These cloud-sopped, marble hands, this monumental
Argument of the hewn voice, gesture and psalm,
Storm me forever over her grave until
The stuffed lung of the fox twitch and cry Love
And the strutting fern lay seeds on the black sill.

Yeats echoed John Donne in his poem on death:

> Nor dread nor hope attend
> A dying animal;
> A man awaits his end
> Dreading and hoping all;

Many times he died,
Many times rose again.
A great man in his pride
Confronting murderous men
Casts derision upon
Supersession of breath;
He knows death to the bone –
Man has created death.

In modern times the Polish poet Anna Kamienska has written a poem to a victim of Auschwitz which gives us one chilling glimpse of the tragedy of the concentration camps. Edith Stein was a Catholic convert from Judaism, who took the name Sister Theresa Benedicta of the Cross when she became a Carmelite nun:

Dr Edith Stein of Wroclaw
flew through the Auschwitz chimney
on the ninth day of August in the one thousand
nine hundred and forty second year of Our Lord

She went up to the sky huge and straight
like a pillar of smoke from Abel's offering

She was silent
Husserl's best pupil
who understood even before the master
that one must stop philosophising
when God comes near

She went in silence
the wise Sister Theresa Benedicta of the Cross
when two brown archangels
knocked at the gates of the convent shouting
Doctor Edith Stein

Did a brief sob break out of her breast
when they tore the black veil off her
the bride of the Lamb

Great Sister
there are so many questions I have to ask you
especially when the grace of sense
abandons the pages of days
and even the leaves of wise books

Why do you persistently answer me
with a straight pillar of smoke
and I am still afraid to understand.

(Translated from the Polish by Tomasz P.
Krzeszowski and Desmond Graham.)

I find Emily Dickinson the most penetrating commentator on death, as on so many other things. Almost a third of her nearly eighteen hundred poems contain reflections on death, which she saw essentially as an interruption, perhaps permanent, of all contact with a loved one. When she was thirteen she witnessed the death of a friend, Sophia Holland, and described the experience in a letter two years later:

I have never lost but one friend near my age & with whom my thoughts & her own were the same. It was before you came to Amherst. My friend was Sophia Holland . . . I visited her often in sickness & watched over her bed. But at length Reason fled and the physician forbid any but the nurse to go into her room. Then it seemed to me I should die too if I could not be permitted to watch over her or even to look at her face. At length the doctor said she must die & allowed me to look at her a moment through the open door. I took off my shoes and stole softly to the sick room. There she lay mild and beautiful as in health & her pale features lit up with an unearthly smile. I looked as long as friends would permit & when they told me I must look no longer I let them lead me away. I shed no tear, for my heart was too full to weep, but after she was laid in her coffin & I felt I could not call her back again I gave way to a fixed melancholy. I told no one the cause of my grief, though it was gnawing at my very heart strings. I was not well & I went to Boston & stayed a month & my health improved so that my spirits were better.

Sometimes she could treat calmly of death, as in one of her best known poems:

Because I could not stop for Death –
He kindly stopped for me –
The Carriage held but just Ourselves –
And Immortality.

We slowly drove – He knew no haste
And I had put away
My labor and my leisure too,
For His Civility –

We passed the School, where Children strove
At Recess – in the Ring –
We passed the Fields of Gazing Grain –
We passed the Setting Sun –

Or rather – He passed Us –
The Dews drew quivering and chill –
For only Gossamer, my Gown –
My Tippet – only Tulle –

We paused before a House that seemed
A Swelling of the Ground –
The Roof was scarcely visible –
The Cornice – in the Ground –

Since then – 'tis Centuries – and yet
Feels shorter than the Day
I first surmised the Horses' Heads
Were toward Eternity –

Sometimes she could be philosophical:

All but Death, can be Adjusted –
Dynasties repaired –
Systems – settled in their Sockets –
Citadels – dissolved –

Wastes of Lives – resown with Colors
By Succeeding Springs –
Death – unto itself – Exception –
Is exempt from Change –

*

This quiet Dust was Gentlemen and Ladies
And Lads and Girls –
Was laughter and ability and Sighing
And Frocks and Curls.

This Passive Place a Summer's nimble mansion
Where Bloom and Bees
Exists an Oriental Circuit
Then cease, like these –

But sometimes she conveyed the pain of seeing death more directly:

> After great pain, a formal feeling comes –
> The Nerves sit ceremonious, like Tombs –
> The stiff Heart questions was it He, that bore,
> And Yesterday, or Centuries before?
>
> The Feet, mechanical, go round –
> Of Ground, or Air, or Ought –
> A Wooden way
> Regardless grown,
> A Quartz contentment, like a stone –
>
> This is the Hour of Lead –
> Remembered, if outlived,
> As Freezing persons, recollect the Snow –
> First – Chill – then Stupor – then the letting go –

*

> That after Horror – that 'twas *us* –
> That passed the mouldering Pier –
> Just as the Granite Crumb let go –
> Our Savior, by a Hair –
>
> A second more, had dropped too deep
> For Fisherman to plumb –
> The very profile of the Thought
> Puts Recollection numb –
>
> The possibility – to pass
> Without a Moment's Bell –
> Into Conjecture's presence –
> Is like a Face of Steel –
> That suddenly looks into ours
> With a metallic grin –
> The Cordiality of Death –
> Who drills his Welcome in –

She could imagine the death of those she never knew, and even of herself:

> He scanned it – staggered –
> Dropped the Loop
> To Past or Period –
> Caught helpless at a sense as if
> His Mind were going blind –

Groped up, to see if God was there –
Groped backward at Himself
Caressed a Trigger absently
And wandered out of Life.

*

I heard a Fly buzz – when I died –
The Stillness in the Room
Was like the Stillness in the Air –
Between the Heaves of Storm –

The Eyes around – had wrung them dry –
And Breaths were gathering firm
For that last Onset – when the King
Be witnessed – in the Room –

I willed my Keepsakes – Signed away
What portion of me be
Assignable – and then it was
There interposed a Fly –

With Blue – uncertain stumbling Buzz –
Between the light – and me –
And then the Windows failed – and then
I could not see to see –

The act of composing poetry tends to filter and organize emotion. Emily Dickinson's raw feelings emerge more directly in her letters. I find her letter to her cousins about her father's death overwhelming with its sense of a human being distracted by grief almost to madness:

To Louise and Frances Norcross   *Summer 1874*

You might not remember me, dears. I cannot recall myself. I thought I was strongly built, but this stronger has undermined me.

We were eating our supper the fifteenth of June, and Austin came in. He had a despatch in his hand, and I saw by his face we were all lost, though I didn't know how. He said that father was very sick, and he and Vinnie must go. The train had already gone. While horses were dressing, news came he was dead.

Father does not live with us now – he lives in a new house. Though it was built in an hour it is better than this. He hasn't any garden because he moved after gardens were made, so we take him the best flowers, and if we only knew he knew, perhaps we could stop crying. . . . The grass begins after Pat has stopped it.

I cannot write any more, dears. Though it is many nights, my mind never comes home. Thank you each for the love, though I could not notice it. Almost the last tune that he heard was, 'Rest from thy loved employ.'

Emily.

My wife, Edna, was only fourteen when her father died, and did not care to talk about what was one of the most searing experiences of her life. Sixty years later she was persuaded to describe her feelings in an interview with Danny Danziger in *The Independent*:

My father's death was the worst blow. Shakespeare says it all about the finality of death, when King Lear learns of the death of Cordelia:

> *Thou'lt come no more,*
> *Never, never, never, never, never.*

We were five children, I was the last but one. I was Nin, short for nincompoop, and I have always been Nin — I still am at home.

We lived in Coleford, a small country town in Gloucestershire. He was very much a Gloucestershire man, my father, he came from the heart of the Forest of Dean, from a place called Park End, where his mother and father were buried.

Well, we were very close. He was a very gentle, sensitive man, very musical, he played all sorts of instruments in the village band, and conducted, too.

He was very careful of his appearance, very nicely dressed when he went out, and he always wore a pansy in his buttonhole; when he and my mother were young and courting, the courtesies were observed, and he always wore white gloves.

I remember he had a wonderful turn of phrase: 'He was as happy as a bee in a snomper' — a snomper is a foxglove — and when we saw people walking down the road he would make little observations: 'Here she comes, hold my head for my behind is coming.'

He was very keen I should study — the great threat if I didn't do my homework was that I would be sent to the pin factory in the town, so he was very insistent that I should work at my books.

He had a genius for finding out where the wildflowers were, and he knew the places where we could find orchids, and after chapel we would all go for a long walk through the woods, and if we were lucky, we would find butterfly orchids, which were very heavily scented: you don't see them now.

People walked everywhere in those days, and it was two or three miles to the waterworks where he was employed. On my fourteenth birthday I decided I would get up and walk to work with him, and that should be my treat. The night before I said: 'I am coming to work with you this morning,' and I know he was pleased. He said: 'Bet you don't.' But I got up very early that morning because he would leave at something like half past six.

And so I walked with him until we got to the top of a very steep hill, and I stood and watched him going down the winding path through the orchard and on to the quarry, and I waited, and, now a tiny figure, he waved goodbye. Somehow that morning is absolutely clear, every minute of it.

And then he got pneumonia six months later. The agony of hearing him struggling for breath and coughing was the most awful thing, and my sister and I were sent out on all sorts of errands that weren't necessary, just to get us out of the house. They put straw down in the street outside, which is what people did in those days to deaden the sound of the traffic.

I made his pillow comfortable for him, and he'd hold my hand and say: 'Ah, that's a bed of roses.' I remember looking at his hands, although it was a workman's hands, he had long sensitive fingers.

He was not a moaner at all, but at the last it was impossible to be cheerful, his groanings for breath rang through the house.

It was nearly his birthday, and I remember going to the chemist, and I got him a tin of brilliantine, and then I went to the grocer and bought some pears, which he couldn't possibly have eaten.

And then he died. He was only 46.

We were out of the house, we had been sent to a neighbour who had given us cocoa with skin on top, and when we came back, we didn't need to be told what had happened. My mother was desperately distressed. It was by now late in the year, and bitterly cold, and I remember her saying: 'I can't bear him to be put in the cold ground.'

I think about him a great deal; he was a great gardener, and every time I dig the garden and I put my foot on the spade, I see him with his foot on a spade watching the robins.

I do remember him a great deal, much more than I would have thought.

He would be jolly pleased at the way I have got on, that I followed my books and I didn't go to the pin factory, he'd be pleased about that.

Virginia Woolf was similarly affected by her mother's death when she was fifteen. She touched on it indirectly in describing the death of Mrs Ramsay in *To the Lighthouse*, but did not feel able to face her own feelings at the time until she wrote *A Sketch of the Past* just before her own death forty years later:

George took us down to say goodbye. My father staggered from the bedroom as we came. I stretched out my arms to stop him, but he brushed past me, crying out something I could not catch; distraught. And George led me in to kiss my mother, who had just died. . . .

Led by George with towels wrapped round us and given each a drop of brandy in warm milk to drink, we were taken into the bedroom. I think candles were burning; and I think the sun was coming in. At any rate I remember the long looking-glass; with the drawers on either side; and the washstand; and the great bed on which my mother lay. I remember very clearly how even as I was taken to the bedside I noticed that one nurse was sobbing, and a desire to laugh came over me, and I said to myself as I have often done at moments of crisis since, 'I feel nothing whatever'. Then I stooped and kissed my mother's face. It was still warm. She [had] only died a moment before. Then we went upstairs into the day nursery.

Perhaps it was the next evening that Stella took me into the bedroom to kiss mother for the last time. She had been lying on her side before. Now she was lying straight in the middle of her pillows. Her face looked immeasurably distant, hollow and stern. When I kissed her, it was like kissing cold iron. Whenever I touch cold iron the feeling comes back to me – the feeling of my mother's face, iron cold, and granulated. I started back. Then Stella stroked her cheek, and undid a button on her nightgown. 'She always liked to have it like that,' she said. When she came up to the nursery later she said to me, 'Forgive me. I saw you were afraid.' She had noticed that I had started. When Stella asked me to forgive her for having given me that shock, I cried – we had been crying off and on all day – and said, 'When I see mother, I see a man sitting with her.' Stella looked at me as if I had frightened her. Did I say that in order to attract attention to myself? Or was it true? I cannot be sure, for certainly I had a great wish to draw attention to myself. But certainly it was true that when she said: 'Forgive me,' and thus made me visualize my mother, I seemed to see a man sitting bent on the edge of the bed.

'It's nice that she shouldn't be alone', Stella said after a moment's pause.

Of course the atmosphere of those three or four days before the funeral was so melodramatic, histrionic and unreal that any hallucination was possible. We lived through them in hush, in artificial light. Rooms were shut. People were creeping in and out. People were coming to the door all the time. We were all sitting in the drawing room round father's chair sobbing. The hall reeked of flowers. They were piled on the hall table. The scent still brings back those days of astonishing intensity.

After these agonies it is a relief to turn to Virginia Woolf again, this time exorcising her personal tragedy by describing 'The Death of a Moth':

Moths that fly by day are not properly to be called moths; they do not excite that pleasant sense of dark autumn nights and ivy-blossom which the commonest yellow-underwing asleep in the shadow of the curtain never fails to rouse in us. They are hybrid creatures, neither gay like butterflies nor sombre like their own species. Nevertheless the present specimen, with his narrow hay-coloured wings, fringed with a tassel of the same colour, seemed to be content with life. It was a pleasant morning, mid-September, mild, benignant, yet with a keener breath than that of the summer months. The plough was already scoring the field opposite the window, and where the share had been, the earth was pressed flat and gleamed with moisture. Such vigour came rolling in from the fields and the down beyond that it was difficult to keep the eyes strictly turned upon the book. The rooks too were keeping one of their annual festivities; soaring round the tree tops until it looked as if a vast net with thousands of black knots in it had been cast up into the air; which, after a few moments sank slowly down upon the trees until every twig seemed to have a knot at the end of it. Then, suddenly, the net would be thrown into the air again in a wider circle this time, with the utmost clamour and vociferation, as though to be thrown into the air and settle slowly down upon the tree tops were a tremendously exciting experience.

The same energy which inspired the rooks, the ploughmen, the horses, and even, it seemed, the lean bare-backed downs, sent the moth fluttering from side to side of his square of the window-pane. One could not help watching him. One was, indeed, conscious of a queer feeling of pity for him. The possibilities of pleasure seemed that morning so enormous and so various that to have only a moth's part in life, and a day moth's at that, appeared a hard fate, and his zest in enjoying his meagre opportunities to the full, pathetic. He flew vigorously to one corner of his compartment, and, after waiting there a second, flew across to the other. What remained for him but to fly to a third corner and then to a fourth? That was all he could do, in spite of the size of the downs, the width of the sky, the far-off smoke of houses, and the romantic voice, now and then, of a steamer out at sea. What he could do he did. Watching him, it seemed as if a fibre, very thin but pure, of the enormous energy of the world had been thrust into his frail and diminutive body. As often as he crossed the pane, I could fancy that a thread of vital light became visible. He was little or nothing but life.

Yet, because he was so small, and so simple a form of the energy that was rolling in at the open window and driving its way through so many narrow and intricate corridors in my own brain and in those of other human beings, there was something marvellous as well as pathetic about him. It was as if someone had taken a tiny bead of pure life and decking it as lightly as possible with down and feathers, had set it dancing and zigzagging to show us the true nature of life. Thus displayed one could not get over the strangeness of it. One is apt to forget all about life, seeing it humped and bossed and garnished and cumbered so that it has to move with the greatest circumspection and dignity. Again, the thought of all that life might have been had he been born in any other shape caused one to view his simple activities with a kind of pity.

After a time, tired by his dancing apparently, he settled on the window ledge in the sun, and, the queer spectacle being at an end, I forgot about him. Then, looking up, my eye was caught by him. He was trying to resume his dancing, but seemed either so stiff or so awkward that he could only flutter to the bottom of the window-pane; and when he tried to fly across it he failed. Being intent on other matters I watched these futile attempts for a time without thinking, unconsciously waiting for him to resume his flight, as one waits for a machine, that has stopped momentarily, to start again without considering the reason of its failure. After perhaps a seventh attempt he slipped from the wooden ledge and fell, fluttering his wings, on to his back of the window sill. The helplessness of his attitude roused me. It flashed upon me that he was in difficulties; he could no longer raise himself; his legs struggled vainly. But, as I stretched out a pencil, meaning to help him to right himself, it came over me that the failure and awkwardness were the approach of death. I laid the pencil down again.

The legs agitated themselves once more. I looked as if for the enemy against which he struggled. I looked out of doors. What had happened there? Presumably it was midday, and work in the fields had stopped. Stillness and quiet had replaced the previous animation.

The birds had taken themselves off to feed in the brooks. The horses stood still. Yet the power was there all the same, massed outside indifferent, impersonal, not attending to anything in particular. Somehow it was opposed to the little hay-coloured moth. It was useless to try to do anything. One could only watch the extraordinary efforts made by those tiny legs against an oncoming doom which could, had it chosen, have submerged an entire city, not merely a city, but masses of human beings; nothing, I knew, had any chance against death. Nevertheless after a pause of exhaustion the legs fluttered again. It was superb this last protest, and so frantic that he succeeded at last in righting himself. One's sympathies, of course, were all on the side of life. Also, when there was nobody to care or to know, this gigantic effort on the part of an insignificant little moth, against a power of such magnitude, to retain what no one else valued or desired to keep, moved one strangely. Again, somehow, one saw life, a pure bead. I lifted the pencil again, useless though I knew it to be. But even as I did so, the unmistakable tokens of death showed themselves. The body relaxed, and instantly grew stiff. The struggle was over. The insignificant little creature now knew death. As I looked at the dead moth, this minute wayside triumph of so great a force over so mean an antagonist filled me with wonder. Just as life had been strange a few minutes before, so death was now as strange. The moth having righted himself now lay most decently and uncomplainingly composed. O yes, he seemed to say, death is stronger than I am.

The most fitting conclusion for this chapter is the epitaph which Benjamin Franklin wrote for himself when he was twenty-two years old:

> The Body of
> B. Franklin,
> Printer;
> Like the Cover of an old Book,
> Its Contents torn out,
> And stript of its Lettering and Gilding,
> Lies here, Food for Worms.
> But the Work shall not be wholly lost:
> For it will, as he believ'd, appear once more,
> In a new & more perfect Edition,
> Corrected and amended
> By the Author.
> He was born Jan. 6. 1706.
> Died   17

10

THE SPIRIT

A deep, but dazzling darkness
– Henry Vaughan

Organized religion has never had much appeal for me. When I
was a little boy in Keighley we used to walk every Sunday
to the Congregational Church in Utley for the morning service –
not because my parents were religious, but because the chairman
of my father's Technical College was an active Congregationalist.
The hymns and prayers meant nothing to me. I remember my
father complaining when I was about seven years old that my
school report put me bottom in scripture. He gave me a
tremendous clout when I replied: 'Why do you care? You don't
believe in God.'

At that time, my picture of God was very much that of
Heinrich Heine, who wrote:

> I recollect once seeing God in a dream far above in the most distant
> firmament. He was looking contentedly out of a little window in
> the sky, a devout hoary-headed being with a small Jewish beard,
> and he was scattering forth myriads of seed-corns, which, as they
> fell from heaven, burst open in the infinitude of space, and expanded
> to vast dimensions till they became actual, radiant, blossoming,
> peopled worlds, each one as large as our own globe. I could never
> forget this countenance, and often in dreams I used to see the

cheerful-looking old man sprinkling forth the world-seeds from his little window in the sky; once I even saw him clucking like our maid when she threw down for the hens their barley. I could only see how the falling seed-corns expanded into great shining orbs: but the great hens that may by chance have been waiting about with eager open bills to be fed with the falling orbs I could not see.

By the time I reached the sixth form my views were better reflected by Byron in the opening of 'The Vision of Judgment':

I

Saint Peter sat by the celestial gate:
   His keys were rusty, and the lock was dull,
So little trouble had been given of late;
   Not that the place by any means was full,
But since the Gallic era 'eighty-eight'
   The devils had ta'en a longer, stronger pull,
And 'a pull altogether,' as they say
At sea – which drew most souls another way.

II

The angels all were singing out of tune,
   And hoarse with having little else to do,
Excepting to wind up the sun and moon,
   Or curb a runaway young star or two,
Or wild colt of a comet, which too soon
   Broke out of bounds o'er the ethereal blue.
Splitting some planet with its playful tail,
As boats are sometimes by a wanton whale.

It was T.S. Eliot who first awakened me as a student at Balliol to the fact that an intelligent man could be a Christian. This was something which Leonard and Virginia Woolf, like the rest of the Bloomsbury set, simply could not understand; they regarded Eliot's conversion as a sign that his mind was going. But while I admired and respected Eliot's faith as expressed in his poetry, I have never been able to accept the theology and dogma of the Church. I preferred the ethical Christianity of Tolstoy's last years; so I was able to satisfy my own spiritual needs simply by believing in the brotherhood of man. This has always been the mainspring of my Socialism, as it was of my moral commitment to Communism at Oxford.

My years in the army deepened my interest in the spiritual nature of man. After the war I was much impressed by Christian theologians such as the Protestant Reinhold Niebuhr and the Orthodox Nicolas Berdyaev. They confirmed my belief in democratic Socialism and rooted it firmly in realism about human nature and society. But they did not persuade me to believe in a personal God. Through my Polish friends I came to know some of the Jesuit priests in Farm Street. They soon gave up their attempt to convert me to Roman Catholicism, although I have many good friends in the Catholic Church.

As I grew older, I developed a deep interest in the life of the spirit as expressed in literature, painting, and music. It is not possible fully to appreciate the poetry of Herbert, the novels of Dostoevsky, the painting of Mantegna, the sculpture of Michelangelo or the music of Bach without sharing in their spiritual dimension. I remember arguing at Königswinter during an Anglo-German Conference about the importance of the spirit. My opponents were three Labour colleagues – Dick Crossman, John Strachey and Tony Crosland. The debate ended when I described Strachey as a 'spiritual imbecile'.

I suspect that this argument gave Dick Crossman a lasting suspicion of me as not philosophically correct. He later told a colleague that I was receiving instruction for admission to the Catholic Church. When I challenged him on this, it turned out that he had seen me in the Central Lobby of Parliament with a dark-faced man wearing a black cassock, whom he took to be Father Martin D'Arcy, the well-known Jesuit proselytiser of intellectuals. In fact it was my dear friend Ernie Southcott, the Anglican vicar of Halton in my constituency. If anyone could have converted me, it would have been he, the most numinous man I have ever known.

My spiritual path has been well trodden by millions of others. Sir Walter Raleigh, whose love poetry and sexual promiscuity I have already quoted, was a free thinker in his thirties; he was even accused of keeping a 'School of Atheism'. For many years he was a favourite of Queen Elizabeth, and led expeditions for her to America, where he discovered tobacco, an achievement on which opinion is still divided.

In the second half of his life his fortune changed. When the Virgin Queen discovered he had married in secret, she put him for a time in the Tower of London. A few years later he was sentenced to death for plotting against her successor, King James I. His sentence was suspended, but he was consigned again to the Tower for thirteen years. After being released for two years, he was finally executed in 1616, at the age of sixty-four. While in prison he wrote a superb religious poem, 'The Passionate Man's Pilgrimage – Supposed to be Written by One at the Point of Death':

> Give me my scallop shell of quiet,
> My staff of faith to walk upon,
> My scrip of joy, immortal diet,
> My bottle of salvation:
> My gown of glory, hope's true gage,
> And thus i'll take my pilgrimage.
>
> Blood must be my body's balmer,
> No other balm will there be given,
> Whilst my soul like a white Palmer
> Travels to the land of heaven,
> Over the silver mountains,
> Where spring the Nectar fountains:
> And there i'll kiss
> The bowl of bliss,
> And drink my eternal fill
> On every milken hill.
> My soule will be a-dry before,
> But after it, will ne'er thirst more.
>
> And by the happy blisful way
> More peaceful pilgrims I shall see,
> That have shook off their gowns of clay,
> And go apparelled fresh like me.
> I'll bring them first
> To slake their thirst,
>
> And then to tast those nectar suckets
> At the clear wells
> Where sweetness dwells,
> Drawn up by Saints in crystal buckets.
>
> And when our bottles and all we,
> Are filled with immortality:
> Then the holy paths we'll travel
> Strewed with rubies thick as gravel,
> Ceilings of diamonds, saphire floors,
> High walls of coral and pearl bowers.

From thence to heaven's bribeless hall
Where no corrupted voices brawl,
No conscience molten into gold,
Nor forg'd accusers bought and sold,
No cause deferd, nor vain spent jorney,
For there Christ is the King's Attourney:
Who pleads for all without degrees,
And he hath Angels, but no fees.

When the grand twelve million jury,
Of our sinns with sinful fury,
Gainst our souls black verdicts give,
Christ pleads his death, and then we live,
Be thou my speaker, taintless pleader,
Unblotted lawyer, true proceeder,
Thou movest salvation even for alms:
Not with a bribèd lawyers palms.

And this is my eternal plea,
To him that made heaven, earth and sea,
Seeing my flesh must die so soon,
And want a head to dine next noon,
Just at the stroke when my veins start and spread
Set on my soul an everlasting head.
Then am I ready like a palmer fit,
To tread those blest paths which before I writ.

His younger contemporary, John Donne, spent his youth like
Raleigh as an adventurer and womanizer. In middle age he was
ordained and later became the Dean of St Paul's Cathedral. His
religious poetry has immense power; he loved God as he had once
loved women:

Batter my heart, three person'd God; for, you
As yet but knocke, breathe, shine, and seeke to mend;
That I may rise, and stand, o'erthrow mee, 'and bend
Your force, to breake, blowe, burn and make me new.
I, like an usurpt towne, to'another due,
Labour to'admit you, but Oh, to no end,
Reason your viceroy in mee, mee should defend,
But is captiv'd, and proves weake or untrue.
Yet dearely' I love you,' and would be loved faine,
But am betroth'd unto your enemie:
Divorce mee,' untie, or breake that knot againe,

Take mee to you, imprison mee, for I
Except you' enthrall mee, never shall be free,
Nor ever chast, except you ravish mee.

Herrick and Marvell also followed their love poetry with distinguished religious verse. The greatest period of English religious
poetry, however, came a few years later with the so-called
'metaphysical' poets who impressed me first at Balliol – Quarles,
Crashaw, Herbert, Vaughan – and above all Milton, who stands in
a class of his own.

Among the metaphysicals, my favourite is Henry Vaughan, for
whom God was a transcendental light in the darkness:

There is in God (some say)
A deep, but dazzling darkness; as men here
Say it is late and dusky, because they
See not all clear;
O for that night! where I in him
Might live invisible and dim.

In 'The World' Vaughan puts love, politics, business, and pleasure
in the scales against God, and finds them all wanting:

I saw Eternity the other night,
Like a great ring of pure and endless light,
All calm, as it was bright;
And round beneath it, Time, in hours, days, years,
Driven by the spheres,
Like a vast shadow moved; in which the world
And all her train were hurl'd.

The doting Lover in his quaintest strain
Did there complain;
Near him, his lute, his fancy, and his slights,
Wit's sour delights;

With gloves and knots, the silly snares of pleasure;
Yet his dear treasure
All scatter'd lay, while he his eyes did pour
Upon a flower.
The darksome Statesman hung with weights and woe,
Like a thick midnight-fog, moved there so slow,
He did not stay, nor go;

Condemning thoughts – like sad eclipses – scowl
      Upon his soul,
And clouds of crying witnesses without
      Pursued him with one shout;

Yet digg'd the mole, and lest his ways be found,
      Work'd under ground,
Where he did clutch his prey; but One did see
      That policy;
Churches and altars fed him; perjuries
      Were gnats and flies;
It rain'd about him blood and tears, but he
      Drank them as free.

The fearful Miser on a heap of rust
Sate pining all his life there; did scarce trust
      His own hands with the dust;
Yet would not place one piece above, but lives
      In fear of thieves:
Thousands there were as frantic as himself,
      And hugg'd each one his pelf.

The down-right Epicure placed heaven in sense,
      And scorn'd pretence;
While others, slipped into a wide excess,
      Said little less;
The weaker sort, slight, trivial wares enslave,
      Who think them brave;
And poor, despisèd Truth sat counting by
      Their victory.

Yet some, who all this while did weep and sing,
And sing, and weep, soar'd up into the ring;
      But most would use no wing.
O fools – said I – thus to prefer dark night
      Before true light!
To live in grots, and caves, and hate the day
      Because it shews the way: –
The way, which from this dead and dark abode
      Leads up to God;
A way where you might tread the Sun, and be
      More bright than he!
But as I did their madness so discuss,
      One whisper'd thus, –
This ring the Bride-groom did for none provide
      But for His Bride.

One of Vaughan's poems gave the title to Aldous Huxley's only play, *The World of Light*, which had moved me greatly as a schoolboy when I saw it at Bradford Civic Theatre:

> They are all gone into the world of light!
>   And I alone sit ling'ring here;
> Their very memory is fair and bright,
>   And my sad thoughts doth clear.
>
> It glows and glitters in my cloudy breast
>   Like stars upon some gloomy grove,
> Or those faint beams in which this hill is dress'd,
>   After the sun's remove.
>
> I see them walking in an air of glory,
>   Whose light doth trample on my days:
> My days, which are at best but dull and hoary,
>   Mere glimmering and decays.
>
> O holy hope! and high humility,
>   High as the Heavens above!
> These are your walks, and you have show'd them me
>   To kindle my cold love,
>
> Dear, beauteous death! the Jewel of the Just,
>   Shining nowhere, but in the dark;
> What mysteries do lie beyond thy dust;
>   Could man outlook that mark!

The crystalline simplicity of Henry Vaughan is echoed in an 'Epitaph for a godly man's tomb' by Robert Wild:

> Here lies a piece of Christ; a star in dust;
> A vein of gold; a china dish that must
> Be used in heaven, when God shall feast the just.

With Milton's great religious works, *Paradise Lost* and *Paradise Regained*, poetry began to argue about God, and even with God. Vaughan's light began to wane. There is a hint of this in Milton's famous sonnet 'On his Blindness':

> When I consider how my light is spent,
>   Ere half my days, in this dark world and wide,
>   And that one talent which is death to hide

> Lodg'd with me useless, though my soul more bent
> To serve therewith my Maker, and present
>   My true account, lest he returning chide;
>   'Doth God exact day-labour, light deni'd?'
>   I fondly ask: but Patience, to prevent
> That murmur, soon replies, 'God doth not need
>   Either man's work, or his own gifts; who best
>   Bear his mild yoke, they serve him best: his state
> Is kingly; thousands at his bidding speed,
>   And post o'er land and ocean without rest;
>   They also serve who only stand and wait.'

Towards the end of the eighteenth century the Enlightenment, the French Revolution, and the advance of science all cast doubt on the truth of the Bible and shook confidence in Christianity itself. Such scepticism was a hallmark of the nineteenth century. Two hundred years earlier Isaac Newton had been able to reconcile his science with his religion. But Charles Darwin, who embarked on the voyage of the *Beagle* as a candidate for holy orders, was driven by his researches on the origin of man into agnosticism.

The poets of the Romantic Revival reflected this process. Even Wordsworth, who was more obviously religious than Keats and Shelley, occasionally expressed a deep spiritual disillusionment:

> From low to high doth dissolution climb,
> And sink from high to low, along a scale
> Of awful notes, whose concord shall not fail;
> A musical but melancholy chime,
> Which they can hear who meddle not with crime,
> Nor avarice, nor over-anxious care.
> Truth fails not; but her outward forms that bear
> The longest date do melt like frosty rime
> That in the morning whiten'd hill and plain
> And is no more; drop like the tower sublime
> Of yesterday, which royally did wear
> His crown of weeds, but could not even sustain
> Some casual shout that broke the silent air,
> Or the unimaginable touch of Time.

He began to hanker after some earlier religion:

The world is too much with us. Late and soon,
Getting and spending, we lay waste our powers.
Little we see in Nature that is ours:
We have given our hearts away, a sordid boon.
This Sea that bares her bosom to the moon,
The winds that will be howling at all hours
And are up-gathered now like sleeping flowers –
For this, for everything, we are out of tune:
It moves us not. – Great God! I'd rather be
A Pagan, suckled in a creed outworn,
So might I, standing on this pleasant lea,
Have glimpses that would make me less forlorn:
Have sight of Proteus rising from the sea,
Or hear old Triton blow his wreathèd horn.

With Hopkins, who had chosen a religious vocation, such disillusionment was replaced by despair. In Dublin at the end of his life he fell prey to a terrible sense of desolation, for which he found it impossible not to blame his God:

Thou art indeed just, Lord, if I contend
With thee; but sir, so what I plead is just.
Why do sinners' ways prosper? and why must
Disappointment all I endeavour end?
Wert thou my enemy, O thou my friend,
How wouldst thou worse, I wonder, than thou dost
Defeat, thwart me? Oh, the sots and thralls of lust
Do in spare hours more thrive than I that spend,

Sir, life upon thy cause. See, banks and brakes
Now, leavèd how thick! lacèd they are again
With fretty chervil, look, and fresh wind shakes

Them; birds build – but not I build; no, but strain,
Time's eunuch, and not breed one work that wakes.
Mine, O thou lord of life, send my roots rain.

*

I wake and feel the fell of dark, not day.
What hours, O what black hoürs we have spent
This night! what sights you, heart, saw; ways you went!
And more must, in yet longer light's delay.

With witness I speak this. But where I say
Hours I mean years, mean life. And my lament
Is cries countless, cries like dead letters sent
To dearest him that lives alas! away.

I am gall, I am heartburn. God's most deep decree
Bitter would have me taste: my taste was me;
Bones built in me, flesh filled, blood brimmed the curse.
Selfyeast of spirit a dull dough sours. I see
The lost are like this, and their scourge to be
As I am mine, their sweating selves; but worse.

*

No worst, there is none. Pitched past pitch of grief,
More pangs will, schooled at forepangs, wilder wring.
Comforter, where, where is your comforting?
Mary, mother of us, where is your relief?
My cries heave, herds-long; huddle in a main, a chief-
woe, world-sorrow; on an age-old anvil wince and sing –
Then lull, then leave off. Fury had shrieked 'No ling-
ering! Let me be fell: force I must be brief'.
O the mind, mind has mountains; cliffs of fall
Frightful, sheer, no-man-fathomed. Hold them cheap
May who ne'er hung there. Nor does long our small
Durance deal with that steep or deep. Here! creep,
Wretch, under a comfort serves in a whirlwind: all
Life death does end and each day dies with sleep.

*

Not, I'll not, carrion comfort, Despair, not feast on thee;
Not untwist – slack they may be – these last strands of man
In me ór, most weary, cry *I can no more*. I can;
Can something, hope, wish day come, not choose not to be.
But ah, but O thou terrible, why wouldst thou rude on me

Thy wring-world right foot rock? lay a lionlimb against me? scan
With darksome devouring eyes my bruisèd bones? and fan,
O in turns of tempest, me heaped there; me frantic to avoid thee
    and flee?

Why? That my chaff might fly; my grain lie, sheer and clear.
Nay in all that toil, that coil, since (seems) I kissed the rod,
Hand rather, my heart lo! lapped strength, stole joy, would laugh,
    chéer.
Cheer whom though? the hero whose heaven-handling flung me,
    fóot tród
Me? or me that fought him? O which one? is it each one?
      That night, that year
Of now done darkness I wretch lay wrestling with (my God!)

Hopkins could wrestle with his God, but never doubted that God did exist as He is defined in Jesuit theology.

William Blake was no less deeply religious, but found it impossible to accept Christianity as preached by the Church. He would call God as seen, for example, by the child Heine, 'Nobodaddy', even writing a rude poem against Klopstock, a German religious poet, in which 'old Nobodaddy aloft Farted and Belched and coughed'. He explained his reason for rejecting conventional Christianity in 'The Marriage of Heaven and Hell':

Without Contraries is no progression. Attraction and Repulsion, Reason and Energy, Love and Hate, are necessary to Human existence.

From these contraries spring what the religious call Good and Evil. Good is the passive that obeys Reason. Evil is the active springing from Energy.

Good is Heaven. Evil is Hell.

THE VOICE OF THE DEVIL

All Bibles or sacred codes have been the causes of the following Errors:-

1. That Man has two real existing principles, viz. a Body and a Soul.

2. That Energy, call'd Evil, is alone from the Body; and that Reason, call'd Good, is alone from the Soul.

3. That God will torment Man in Eternity for following his Energies.

But the following Contraries to these are True:-

1. Man has no Body distinct from his Soul; for that call'd Body is a portion of Soul discern'd by the five Senses, the chief inlets of Soul in this age.

2. Energy is the only life, and is from the Body; and Reason is the bound or outward circumference of Energy.

3. Energy is Eternal Delight.

His belief that man must contain opposites produced some of his most memorable proverbs, like: 'Eternity is in love with the productions of time'; 'Prudence is a rich, ugly old maid courted by incapacity'; 'Damn braces. Bless relaxes.'

He states his faith again in his long poem, 'Jerusalem':

They know not why they love nor wherefore they sicken and die,
Calling that holy love, which is envy, revenge, and cruelty,
Which separated the stars from the mountains, the mountains from
  man,
And left man, a little grovelling root, outside of himself.
Negations are not contraries: contraries mutually exist:
But negations exist not: exceptions and objections and unbeliefs
Exist not; nor shall they ever be organized for ever and ever.

The epilogue to 'Jerusalem' is addressed 'To the Accuser who is
the God of this World':

> Truly, my Satan, thou art but a dunce,
> And dost not know the garment from the man;
> Every harlot was a virgin once,
> Nor canst thou ever change Kate into Nan.

> Tho' thou art worshipp'd by the names divine
> Of Jesus and Jehovah, thou art still
> The son of morn in weary night's decline,
> The lost traveller's dream under the hill.

This rejection of conventional religion did not damage Blake's
faith. He could convey mystical feeling as powerfully as did
Traherne:

> How do you know but ev'ry Bird that cuts the airy way,
> Is an immense World of Delight, clos'd by your senses five?

He ends 'A Vision of the Last Judgment' with the words:

> 'What,' it will be Question'd, 'When the sun rises, do you not see a
> round disk of fire somewhat like a Guinea?' 'O no, no, I see an
> Innumerable company of the Heavenly host crying, Holy, Holy,
> Holy is the Lord God Almighty'. I question not my Corporeal or
> Vegetative Eye any more than I would Question a Window
> concerning a Sight. I look thro' it and not with it.

Blake rejected science and politics as vehemently as he rejected
conventional Christianity:

Titus! Constantine! Charlemaine!
O Voltaire! Rousseau! Gibbon! Vain
Your Grecian mocks and Roman sword
Against this image of his Lord!

For a tear is an intellectual thing;
And a sigh is the sword of an angel king;
And the bitter groan of a martyr's woe
Is an arrow from the Almighty's bow.

*

Mock on, mock on, Voltaire, Rousseau;
Mock on, mock on; 'tis all in vain!
You throw the sand against the wind,
And the wind blows it back again.

And every sand becomes a gem
Reflected in the beams divine;
Blown back they blind the mocking eye,
But still in Israel's paths they shine.

The Atoms of Democritus
And Newton's Particles of Light
Are sands upon the Red Sea shore,
Where Israel's tents do shine so bright.

Emily Dickinson had Blake's intensity of vision, and shared his difficulty in accepting conventional religion. She believed in the immortality of the soul:

It is an honorable Thought
And makes One lift One's Hat
As One met sudden Gentlefolk
Upon a daily Street
That We've immortal Place
Though Pyramids decay
And Kingdoms, like the Orchard
Flit Russetly away

*

This World is not Conclusion.
A Species stands beyond –
Invisible, as Music –
But positive, as Sound –
It beckons, and it baffles –
Philosophy – don't know –
And through a Riddle, at the last –

Sagacity, must go –
To guess it, puzzles scholars –
To gain it, Men have borne
Contempt of Generations
And Crucifixion, shown –
Faith slips – and laughs, and rallies –
Blushes, if any see –
Plucks at a twig of Evidence –
And asks a Vane, the way –
Much Gesture, from the Pulpit –
Strong Hallelujahs roll –
Narcotics cannot still the Tooth
That nibbles at the soul –

She found the God of Christianity too jealous and censorious:

God is indeed a jealous God –
He cannot bear to see
That we had rather not with Him
But with each other play.

*

The Bible is an antique Volume –
Written by faded Men
At the suggestion of Holy Spectres –
Subjects – Bethlehem –
Eden – the ancient Homestead –
Satan – the Brigadier –
Judas – the Great Defaulter –
David – the Troubadour –
Sin – a distinguished Precipice
Others must resist –
Boys that 'believe' are very lonesome –
Other Boys are 'lost' –
Had but the Tale a warbling Teller –
All the Boys would come –
Orpheus' Sermon captivated –
It did not condemn –

Yet she longed for the security given by religion:

Those – dying then,
Knew where they went –
They went to God's Right Hand –

That Hand is amputated now
And God cannot be found –

The abdication of Belief
Makes the Behavior small –
Better an ignis fatuus
Than no illume at all –

Sometimes she slipped into a despair which recalls that of Hopkins:

The Soul has Bandaged moments –
When too appalled to stir –
She feels some ghastly Fright come up
And stop to look at her –

Salute her – with long fingers –
Caress her freezing hair –
Sip, Goblin, from the very lips
The Lover – hovered – o'er –
Unworthy, that a thought so mean
Accost a Theme – so – fair –

The soul has moments of Escape –
When bursting all the doors –
She dances like a Bomb, abroad,
And swings upon the Hours,

As do the Bee – delirious borne –
Long Dungeoned from his Rose –
Touch Liberty – then know no more,
But Noon, and Paradise –

The Soul's retaken moments –
When, Felon led along,
With shackles on the plumed feet,
And staples, in the Song,

The Horror welcomes her, again,
These, are not brayed of Tongue –

Emily Brontë expresses a mystical experience very like Dickinson's in one of her 'Gondal' poems. It is worth remembering when you read it that in her daily life Emily was a practical, realistic Yorkshire woman who did most of the cooking, the household ironing, and made all the bread for the family. Mrs Gaskell says that anyone passing by the kitchen door might have seen her studying German out of an open book propped up in front of her as she kneaded the dough. She also played Mozart and Haydn on Charlotte's little piano with brilliance and precision. Yet she was equally capable of writing this:

'He comes with western winds, with evening's wandering airs,
'With that clear dusk of heaven that brings the thickest stars;

'Winds take a pensive tone and stars a tender fire
'And visions rise and change which kill me with desire –

'Desire for nothing known in my maturer years
'When joy grew mad with awe at counting future tears;
'When, if my spirit's sky was full of flashes warm,
'I knew not whence they came, from sun or thunderstorm;

'But first a hush of peace, a soundless calm descends;
'The struggle of distress and fierce impatience ends;
'Mute music soothes my breast – unuttered harmony
'That I could never dream till earth was lost to me.

'Then dawns the Invisible, the Unseen its truth reveals;
'My outward sense is gone, my inward essence feels –
'Its wings are almost free, its home, its harbour found;
'Measuring the gulf it stoops and dares the final bound!

'Oh dreadful is the check – intense the agony
'When the ear begins to hear and the eye begins to see;
'When the pulse begins to throb, the brain to think again;
'The soul to feel the flesh and the flesh to feel the chain!

'Yet I would lose no sting, would wish no torture less:
'The more that anguish racks the earlier it will bless
'And robed in fires of Hell, or bright with heavenly shine
'If it but herald Death, the vision is divine!'

Yeats was moved to a similar spiritual ecstasy in a Lyons Corner House:

My fiftieth year had come and gone,
I sat, a solitary man
In a crowded London shop,
An open book and empty cup
On the marble table top.
While on the shop and street I gazed
My body of a sudden blazed;
And twenty minutes more or less
It seemed, so great my happiness,
That I was blessèd, and could bless.

Yeats never accepted Christianity, though he was moved by its symbols, such as 'the uncontrollable mystery on the bestial floor'. Throughout his life he was attracted by the occult. In his youth he moved from the fairies of his native Ireland to theosophy and Madame Blavatsky. In his old age he was fascinated by the religions of the Far East. After Maude Gonne's daughter, Iseult, had refused him, he married George Hyde-Lees and was delighted to find that she could receive communications in automatic writing. This led him to construct his own mystical philosophy out of symbols and emblems he had used for years, as a means of 'uniting the sleeping and waking mind'. Yet he regarded his system not as literal truth, but as 'stylistic arrangements of experience comparable to the cubes in the drawing of Wyndham Lewis and to the ovoids in the sculpture of Brancusi . . . . They have helped me to hold in a single thought reality and justice.'

Dostoevsky, on the other hand, though always torn between the demands of reason, emotion, and religion, was a Christian who believed in the brotherhood of man. He was more attracted, however, by mysticism than by organized religion. In *The Brothers Karamazov* Alyosha's explosion of love after the funeral of father Zossima must reflect something in Dostoevsky's own life:

He did not stop on the steps either, but went quickly down; his soul, overflowing with rapture, yearned for freedom, space, openness. The vault of heaven, full of soft, shining stars, stretched vast and fathomless above him. The Milky Way ran in two pale streams from the zenith to the horizon. The fresh, motionless, still night enfolded the earth. The white towers and golden domes of the cathedral gleamed out against the sapphire sky. The gorgeous autumn flowers, in the beds round the house, were slumbering till morning. The silence of earth seemed to melt into the silence of the heavens. The mystery of earth was one with the mystery of the stars. . . .

Alyosha stood, gazed, and suddenly threw himself down on the earth. He did not know why he embraced it. He could not have told why he longed so irresistibly to kiss it, to kiss it all. But he kissed it weeping, sobbing and watering it with his tears, and vowed passionately to love it, to love it for ever and ever. 'Water the earth with the tears of your joy and love those tears,' echoed in his soul.

What was he weeping over?

Oh! In his rapture he was weeping even over those stars, which were shining to him from the abyss of space, and 'he was not ashamed of that ecstasy'. There seemed to be threads from all those innumerable worlds of God, linking his soul to them, and it was trembling all over 'in contact with other worlds'. He longed to forgive everyone and for everything, and to beg forgiveness. Oh, not for himself but for all men, for all and for everything. 'And others are praying for me too,' echoed again in his soul. But with every instant he felt clearly and, as it were, tangibly that something firm and unshakable as that vault of heaven had entered into his soul. It was as though some idea had seized the sovereignty of his mind – and it was for all his life and for ever and ever. He had fallen on the earth a weak boy, but he rose up a resolute champion, and he knew and felt it suddenly at the very moment of his ecstasy. And never, never, all his life long, could Alyosha forget that minute.

'Someone visited my soul in that hour,' he used to say afterwards, with implicit faith in his words.

The type of mystical experience described here by Dostoevsky is found in people of very different faiths and personalities, and often expressed in very similar words. Besides the metaphysical poets and Traherne, and the more recent poets like Blake, Dickinson, and Yeats, whom I have quoted, it is found in the Journal of George Fox, the Quaker:

> Now was I come up in spirit through the flaming sword into the Paradise of God. All things were new: and all the Creation gave another smell unto me than before.

Even the Olympian genius of Goethe, who in maturity passed far away from the Pietism of his childhood to reconcile, in his words, the Dionysian with the Apollonian, told his disciple Eckermann:

> Often before dawn I am awake, and lie down by the open window to enjoy the splendour of the three planets at present visible together, and to refresh myself with the increasing brilliance of the morning-red. I then pass almost the whole day in the open air, and hold spiritual communion with the tendrils of the vine, which say good things to me, and of which I could tell you wonders.

Reflecting now on my life-long love of that art which deals with Blake's 'sunrise of eternity', I realize how powerfully my views have been moulded by studying Kant and other philosophers at Oxford. Any attempt to approach the transcendental through the propositions of scientific logic is bound to fail; but in failing, as Kant said, it 'abolishes knowledge to make possible belief'. Theology by itself, like all metaphysics, is as likely to destroy faith as to fortify it.

I conclude this exploration of the spirit as it moves in me with two works from very different authors which convey the same message – a short story from *Sketches from a Huntsman's Album*, an early work by Ivan Turgenev, and a poem by Thomas Traherne.

Turgenev was the son of a wealthy Russian landowner, but spent much of his adult life in Western Europe. On one of his several visits to England he stayed in the New Forest with the parents of Florence Nightingale, was proposed for membership of the Athenaeum Club by Monckton Milnes, and spent a morning at the House of Commons. He admired the 'strength, durability and efficiency' of the British and above all their tolerance, describing them as 'in spite of everything the best people on earth'.

He was deeply interested in politics throughout his life, and four of his novels are concerned with the struggle against reaction in Russia and Eastern Europe. He first sketched out his greatest work, *Fathers and Children*, at Ventnor on the Isle of Wight. Though he had many friends among the revolutionaries, in France and Germany as well as Russia, he was deeply opposed to the use of violence. As a Westernizer and a liberal, he found himself caught in the crossfire between reaction and revolution. His sensitivity, balance, and psychological penetration led Henry James to call him 'the only real beautiful genius'.

As a young man I preferred Tolstoy and Dostoevsky, but nowadays I turn increasingly to Turgenev. My mother read all his novels three times when she was over ninety, though I am not certain she fully understood them; I once overheard her telling my aunt, who was ten years younger, that Dmitri was the Russian word for Mister!

However, I never read *Sketches from a Huntsman's Album* until I was on holiday last year. The title had made me imagine it must be concerned with blood-sports, and the idea of a Russian Jorrocks did not appeal to me. When in 1964 Bob McNamara showed me the Soviet-American hot line in the bowels of the White house, I was only mildly interested to see that while the Americans typed out pieces from the *Encyclopedia Britannica* to test if it was working, their Soviet counterparts used extracts from Turgenev's *Sketches*. When I finally read the book the contrast was far more striking; it was difficult to reconcile the choice of these Russian soldiers with the cultural stagnation under Brezhnev.

For, although Turgenev bases his sketches on his expeditions into the countryside to shoot game, they have almost nothing to say about killing animals; instead, they are among the most magical evocations of country life and landscape ever written. Even so, they led to his arrest and subsequent exile from Moscow to his estate, since one or two of them reflect on the cruelty and injustice of serfdom, which was not abolished in Russia until 1861. *Living Relic*, however, is an ennobling fragment of humanity with no political content whatever, though its epigraph is two lines from the poet Tyuchev:

> O native land of long suffering –
> Land of the Russian people.

It starts with the author sheltering from heavy rain in an empty cottage:

The next day I awoke pretty early. The sun had only just risen and the sky was cloudless. All around glistened with a strong, two-fold brilliance: the brilliance of the youthful rays of morning light and of yesterday's downpour. While a little cart was being got ready for me, I set off to wander a little way through the small, once fruit-bearing but now wild, orchard, which pressed up on all sides against the cottage with its richly scented, luxuriantly fresh under-growth. Oh, how delightful it was to be in the open air, under a clear sky in which larks fluttered, whence poured the silver beads of their resonant song! On their wings they probably carried drops of dew, and their singing seemed to be dew-sprinkled in its sweetness. I even removed my cap from my head and breathed in joyfully, lungfuls at a time . . . On the side of a shallow ravine, close by the wattle fencing, a bee-garden could be seen; a small path led to it, winding like a snake between thick walls of weeds and nettles, above which projected – God knows where they had come from – sharp-tipped stalks of dark-green hemp.

I set off along this path and reached the bee-garden. Next to it there stood a little wattle shed, a so-called *amshanik*, where the hives are put in winter. I glanced in through the half-open door: it was dark, silent and dry inside, smelling of mint and melissa. In a corner boards had been fixed up and on them, covered by a quilt, a small figure was lying. I turned to go out at once.

'Master, but master! Pyotr Petrovich!' I heard a voice say, as faintly, slowly and hoarsely as the rustling of marsh sedge.

I stopped.

'Pyotr Petrovich! Please come here!' the voice repeated. It came to me from the corner, from those very boards which I had noticed.

I drew close and froze in astonishment. In front of me there lay a live human being, but what kind of human being was it?

The head was completely withered, of a uniform shade of bronze, exactly resembling the colour of an ancient icon painting; the nose was as thin as a knife-blade; the lips had almost disappeared – only the teeth and eyes gave any gleam of light, and from beneath the kerchief wispy clusters of yellow hair protruded on to the temples. At the chin, where the quilt was folded back, two tiny hands of the same bronze colour slowly moved their fingers up and down like little sticks. I looked more closely and I noticed that not only was the face far from ugly, it was even endowed with beauty, but it seemed awesome none the less and incredible. And the face seemed all the more awesome to me because I could see that a smile was striving to appear on it, to cross its metallic cheeks – was striving and yet could not spread.

'Master, don't you recognize me?' the voice whispered again: it was just like condensation rising from the scarcely quivering lips. 'But how would you recognize me here! I'm Lukeria ... Remember how I used to lead the dancing at your mother's, at Spasskoye ... and how I used to be the leader of the chorus, remember?'

'Lukeria!' I cried. 'Is it you? Is it possible?'

'It's me, master – yes, it's me, Lukeria.'

I had no notion what to say, and in a state of shock I gazed at this dark, still face with its bright, seemingly lifeless eyes fixed upon me. Was it possible? This mummy was Lukeria, the greatest beauty among all the maid servants in our house, tall, buxom, white-skinned and rosy-cheeked, who used to laugh and sing and dance! Lukeria, talented Lukeria, who was sought after by all our young men, after whom I myself used to sigh in secret, I – a sixteen-year-old boy!

'Forgive me, Lukeria,' I said at last, 'but what's happened to you?'

'Such a calamity overtook me! Don't feel squeamish, master, don't turn your back on my misfortune – sit down on that little barrel, bring it closer, so as you'll be able to hear me ... See how talkative I've become! . . . Well, it's glad I am I've seen you! How ever did you come to be in Alekseyevka?'

Lukeria spoke very quietly and faintly, but without pausing.

'Yermolay the hunter brought me here. But go on with what you were saying . . .'

'About my misfortune, is it? If that's what you wish, master. It happened to me long, long ago, six or seven years ago. I'd just then been engaged to Vasily Polyakov – remember him, such a fine upstanding man he was, with curly hair, and in service as wine butler at your mother's house. But by that time you weren't here in the country any longer – you'd gone off to Moscow for your schooling. We were very much in love, Vasily and I. I couldn't get him out of my mind; it all happened in the springtime. One night – it wasn't long to go till dawn – I couldn't sleep, and there was a nightingale singing in the garden so wonderfully sweetly! I couldn't bear it, and I got up and went out on to the porch to listen to it. He was pouring out his song, pouring it out . . . and suddenly I imagined I could hear someone calling me in Vasya's voice, all quiet like: "Loosha! . . ." I glanced away to one side and, you know, not awake properly, I slipped right off the porch step and flew down – bang! – on to the ground. And, likely, I hadn't hurt myself so bad, because – soon I was up and back in my own room. Only it was just like something inside – in my stomach – had broken . . . Let me get my breath back . . . Just a moment, master.'

Lukeria fell silent, and I gazed at her with astonishment. What amazed me was the almost gay manner in which she was telling her story, without groans or sighs, never for a moment complaining or inviting sympathy.

'Ever since that happened,' Lukeria continued, 'I began to wither and sicken, and a blackness came over me, and it grew difficult for me to walk, and then I even began to lose control of my legs – I couldn't stand or sit, I only wanted to lie down all the time. And I didn't feel like eating or drinking: I just got worse and worse. Your mother, out of the goodness of her heart, had medical people to look at me and sent me to hospital. But no relief for me came of it all. And not a single one of the medicals could even say what kind of an illness it was I had. The things they didn't do to me, burning my spine with red-hot irons and sitting me in chopped-up ice – and all for nothing. In the end I got completely stiff . . . So the masters decided there was no good in trying to cure me any more, and because there wasn't room for a cripple in their house . . . well, they sent me here – because I have relations here. So here I'm living, as you see.'

Lukeria again fell silent and again endeavoured to smile.

'But this is horrible, this condition you're in!' I exclaimed, and not knowing what to add, I asked: 'What about Vasily Polyakov?' It was a very stupid question.

Lukeria turned her eyes a little to one side.

'About Polyakov? He grieved, he grieved – and then he married someone else, a girl from Glinnoye. Do you know Glinnoye? It's not far from us. She was called Agrafena. He loved me very much, but he was a young man – he couldn't be expected to remain a bachelor all his life. And what sort of a companion could I be to him? He's found himself a good wife, who's a kind woman, and they've got children now. He's steward on the estate of one of the neighbours: your mother released him with a passport, and things are going very well for him, praise be to God.'

'And you can't do anything except lie here?' I again inquired.

'This is the seventh year, master, that I've been lying like this. When it's summer I lie here, in this wattle hut, and when it begins to get cold – then they move me into a room next to the bath-house. So I lie there, too.'

'Who comes to see you? Who looks after you?'

'There are kind people here as well. They don't leave me by myself. But I don't need much looking after. So far as feeding goes, I don't eat anything, and I have water – there it is in that mug: it always stands by me full of pure spring water. I can stretch out to the mug myself, because I've still got the use of one arm. Then there's a little girl here, an orphan; now and then she drops by, and I'm grateful to her. She's just this minute gone . . . Did you meet her? She's so pretty, so fair-skinned. She brings me flowers – I'm a great one for them, flowers, I mean. We haven't any garden flowers. There used to be some here, but they've all disappeared. But field flowers are pretty too, and they have more scent than the garden flowers. Lilies-of-the-valley now – there's nothing lovelier!'

'Aren't you bored, my poor Lukeria, don't you feel frightened?'

'What's a person to do? I don't want to pretend – at first, yes, I felt very low, but afterwards I grew used to it, I learnt to be patient – now it's nothing. Others are much worse off.'

'How do you mean?'

'Some haven't even got a home! And others are blind or dumb! I can see perfectly, praise be to God, and I can hear everything, every little thing. If there's a mole digging underground, I can hear it. And I can smell every scent, it doesn't matter how faint it is! If the buckwheat is just beginning to flower in the field or a lime tree is just blossoming in the garden, I don't have to be told: I'm the first to smell the scent, if the wind's coming from that direction. No, why should I make God angry with my complaints? Many are worse off than I am. Look at it this way: a healthy person can sin very easily, but my sin has gone out of me. Not long ago Father Aleksey, the priest, was beginning to give me communion and he said: "There can't be any need to hear your confession, for how can you sin in your condition?" But I answered him: "What about a sin of the mind, father?" "Well," he said and laughed, "that kind of sin's not very serious."'

'And, it's true, I'm not really sinful even with sins of the mind,' Lukeria went on, 'because I've learned myself not to think and, what's more, not even to remember. Time passes quicker that way.'

This surprised me, I must admit.

'You are so much by yourself, Lukeria, so how can you prevent thoughts from entering your head? Or do you sleep all the time?'

'Oh, no, master! Sleep's not always easy for me. I may not have big pains, but something's always gnawing at me, right there inside me, and in my bones as well. It doesn't let me sleep as I should. No . . . I just lie like this and go on lying here, not thinking. I sense that I'm alive, I breathe – and that's all there is of me. I look and I smell scents. Bees in the apiary hum and buzz, then a dove comes and sits on the roof and starts cooing, and a little brood-hen brings her chick in to peck crumbs; then a sparrow'll fly in or a butterfly – I enjoy it all very much. The year before last swallows made a nest over there in the corner and brought up their young. Oh, how interesting that was! One of them would fly in, alight on the little nest, feed the young ones – and then off again. I'd take another look and there'd be another swallow there in place of the first. Sometimes it wouldn't fly in but just go past the open door, and then the baby birds'd start chirping and opening their little beaks . . . The next year I waited for them, but they say a hunter in these parts shot them with his gun. Now what good could he have got from doing that? After all, a swallow's no more harm than a beetle. What wicked men you are, you hunters!'

'I don't shoot swallows,' I hastened to point out.

'And one time,' Lukeria started to say again, 'there was a real laugh! A hare ran in here! Yes, really! Whether dogs were chasing him or not, I don't know, only he came running straight in through the door! He sat down quite close and spent a long time sniffing the air and twitching his whiskers – a regular little officer he was! And he took a look at me and realized that I couldn't do him any harm. Eventually he upped and jumped to the door and looked all round him on the doorstep – he was a one, he was! Such a comic!'

Lukeria glanced up at me, as if to say: wasn't that amusing? To please her, I gave a laugh. She bit her dried-up lips.

'In the winter, of course, things are worse for me. I'm left in the dark, you see – it's a pity to light a candle and anyhow what'd be the good of it? I know how to read and was always real keen on reading, but what's there to read here? There are no books here, and even if there were, how would I be able to hold it, the book, I mean? Father Aleksey brought me a church calendar so as to distract me, but he saw it wasn't any use and picked it up and took it away again. But even though it's dark, I've always got something to listen to – maybe a cricket'll start chirruping or a mouse'll begin scratching somewhere. That's when it's good not to be thinking at all!'

After a short rest, Lukeria continued: 'Or else I say prayers. Only I don't know many of them, of those prayers. And why should I start boring the Lord God with my prayers? What can I ask him for? He knows better than I do what's good for me. He sent me a cross to carry, which means he loves me. That's how we're ordained to understand our suffering. I say Our Father, and the prayer to the Blessed Virgin, and I sing hymns for all who sorrow – and then I lie still without a single thought in my mind. Life's no bother to me!'

Two minutes went by. I did not break the silence and I did not stir on the narrow barrel which served as a place for me to sit. The cruel, stony immobility of the unfortunate living being who lay before me affected me also, and I became literally rigid.

'Listen, Lukeria,' I began finally. 'Listen to what I want to propose to you. Would you like it if I arranged for you to be taken to a hospital, a good town hospital? Who knows, but maybe they can still cure you? At least you won't be by yourself . . .'

Lukeria raised her brows ever so slightly.

'Oh, no, master,' she said in an agitated whisper, 'don't send me to a hospital, let me alone. I'll only have to endure more agony there. There's no good in trying to cure me! Once a doctor came here and wanted to have a look at me. I said to him, begging him: "Don't disturb me for Christ's sake!" What good was it! He started turning me this way and that, straightening and bending my legs and arms and telling me: "I'm doing this for learning, that's why. I'm one who serves, a scientist! And don't you try to stop me, because they've pinned a medal on me for my contributions to science and it's for you, you dolts, that I'm working so hard." He pulled me about and pulled me about, named what was wrong with me – and a fine name it was! – and with that he left. But for a whole week afterwards my poor bones were aching. You say I'm alone, all the time by myself. No, not all the time. People come to see me. I'm quiet and I'm not a nuisance to anyone. The peasant girls come sometimes for a chat. Or a holy woman will call in on her wanderings and start telling me about Jerusalem and Kiev and the holy cities. I'm not frightened of being by myself. Truly it's better, truly it is! Let me alone, master, don't move me to hospital. Thank you, you're a good man, only leave me alone, my dear.'

'Just as you wish, as you wish, Lukeria. I was only suggesting it for your own good . . .'

'I know, master, it was for my own good. But, master, my dear one, who is there that can help another person? Who can enter into another's soul? People must help themselves! You won't believe it, but sometimes I lie by myself like I am now – and it's just as if there was no one on the whole earth except me. And I'm the only living person! And a wondrous feeling comes over me, as if I'd been visited by some thought that seizes hold of me – something wonderful it is.'

'What do you think about at such times, Lukeria?'

'It's quite impossible to say, master – you can't make it out. And afterwards I forget. It comes out like a cloud and pours its rain through me, making everything so fresh and good, but what the thought was really you can never understand! Only it seems to me that if there were people round me – none of that would have happened and I'd never feel anything except my own misfortune.'

Lukeria sighed with difficulty. Like the other parts of her body, her breast would not obey her wishes.

'As I look at you now, master,' she began again, 'you feel very sorry for me. But don't you pity me too much, don't you do that! See, I'll tell you something: sometimes even now I . . . You remember, don't you, what a gay one I was in my time? One of the girls! . . . D'you know something? I sing songs even now.'

'Songs? You really sing?'

'Yes, I sing songs, the old songs, roundelays, feast songs, holy songs, all kinds! I used to know many of them, after all, and I haven't forgotten them. Only I don't sing the dancing songs. In my present state that wouldn't be right.'

'How do you sing them – to yourself?'

'To myself and out loud. I can't sing them loudly, but they can still be understood. I was telling you that a little girl comes to visit me. An orphan, that's what she is, but she understands. So I've been teaching her and she's picked up four songs already. Don't you believe me? Wait a moment, I'll show you . . .'

Lukeria drew upon all her reserves of energy. The idea that this half-dead being was preparing to sing aroused in me a spontaneous feeling of horror. But before I could utter a word, a long-drawn, scarcely audible, though clear sound, pitched on the right note, began to quiver in my ears, followed by another, then a third. Lukeria was singing 'I walked in the meadows of green grieving for my life'. She sang without altering the expression on her petrified face, even gazing fixedly with her eyes. But so touchingly did this poor, forced, wavering little voice of hers resound, rising like a wisp of smoke, that I ceased to feel horror: an indescribable piteousness compressed my heart.

'Oh, I can't any more!' she uttered suddenly. 'I've no strength left . . . I've rejoiced so very much already at seeing you.'

She closed her eyes.

I placed my hands on her tiny cold fingers. She looked up at me and her dark eyelids, furred with golden lashes like the lids of ancient statuary, closed again. An instant later they began to glisten in the semi-darkness. Tears moistened them.

As before, I did not stir.

'Silly of me!' Lukeria uttered suddenly with unexpected strength and, opening her eyes wide, attempted to blink away the tears. 'Shouldn't I be ashamed? What's wrong with me? This hasn't happened to me for a long time – not since the day Vasya Polyakov visited me last spring. While he was sitting with me and talking it was all right. But when he'd gone – how I cried then all by myself! Where could so many tears come from! For sure a woman's tears cost nothing. Master,' Lukeria added, 'if you have a handkerchief, don't be finicky, wipe my eyes.'

I hastened to do what she asked, and left the handkerchief with her. She tried to refuse at first, as if she were asking why she should be given such a present. The handkerchief was very simple, but clean and white. Afterwards she seized it in her feeble fingers and did not open them again. Having grown accustomed to the darkness which surrounded us both, I could clearly distinguish her features and could even discern the delicate flush which rose through the bronze of her face and could make out in her face – or so at least it seemed to me – traces of her past beauty.

'Just now you were asking me, master,' Lukeria started saying again, 'whether I sleep. I certainly don't sleep often, but every time I have dreams – wonderful dreams! I never dream that I'm ill. In my dreams I'm always so young and healthy . . . I've only one complaint: when I wake up, I want to have a good stretch and yet here I am, just as if I were bound in fetters. Once I had such a marvellous dream! Would you like me to tell it to you? Well, listen. I dreamt of myself standing in a field, and all around me there was rye, so tall and ripe, like gold . . . And there was a little rust-red dog with me, wickedly vicious it was, all the time trying to bite me. And I had a sickle in my hand, and it wasn't a simple sickle, but it was the moon when the moon has the shape of a sickle. And with the moon itself I had to reap the rye until it was all cut. Only I grew very tired from the heat, and the moon blinded me, and a languor settled on me; and all around me cornflowers were growing – such big ones! And they all turned their little heads towards me. And I thought I would pick these cornflowers, because Vasya had promised to come, so I'd make myself a garland first of all and then still have time to do the reaping. I began to pluck the cornflowers, but they started to melt away through my fingers, to melt and melt, no matter what I did! And I couldn't weave myself a garland. And then I heard someone coming towards me, coming close up to me and calling: "Loosha! Loosha!" Oh dear, I thought, I'm too late! It doesn't matter, though, I thought, because I can put the moon on my head instead of the cornflowers. So I put the moon on my head, and it was just like putting on one of those tall bonnets – at once I glowed with light from head to foot and lit up all the field around me. I looked, and there, through the very tips of the heads of rye, someone was smoothly approaching ever so quickly – only it wasn't Vasya, it was Christ Himself! And why I knew it was Christ I can't say – He's never depicted as I saw Him – but it was Him! He was beardless, tall, young, clad all in white, except for a belt of gold, and He put out a hand to me and said: "Fear not, for thou art My chosen bride, come with Me. In My heavenly kingdom thou shalt lead the singing and play the songs of paradise." And how firmly I pressed my lips to His hand. Then my little dog seized me by the legs, but at once we ascended up into the heavens, He leading me, and His wings stretched out to fill the heavens, as long as the wings of a gull – and I followed after Him! And the little dog had to leave go of me. It was only then that I understood that the little dog was my affliction and that there was no place for my affliction in the Kingdom of Heaven.'

Lukeria fell silent for a minute.

'But I also had another dream,' she began again, 'or perhaps it was a vision I had – I don't know which. It seemed that I was lying in this very wattle hut and my dead parents – my mother and my father – came to me and bowed low to me, but without saying anything. And I asked them: "Why do you, my mother and father, bow down to me?" And they answered and said: "Because thou hast suffered so greatly in this world, thou hast lightened not only thine own soul but hast also lifted a great weight from ours. And for us in our world the way has been made easier. Thou hast already done with thine own sins and art now conquering ours." And, having said this, my parents again bowed low to me – and then I couldn't see them any longer: all I could see were the walls. Afterwards I was very full of doubt whether such a thing had happened to me. I told the priest of it, only he said it couldn't have been a vision, because visions are vouchsafed only to those of ecclesiastical rank.

'Then there was yet another dream I had,' Lukeria continued. 'I saw myself sitting beside a big road under a willow, holding a whittled stick, with a bag over my shoulders and my head wrapped in a kerchief, just like a holy wanderer! And I had to go somewhere far, far away on a pilgrimage, offering prayers to God. And the holy wanderers, the pilgrims, were continually going past me; they were walking quietly past me, as if unwillingly, all the time going in the same direction; and their faces were all sad and very much alike. And I saw that weaving and hurrying among them was one woman, a whole head taller than all the others, and she wore a special kind of dress, not our kind, not like a Russian dress. And her face was also of a special kind, stern and severe, like the face of one used to fasting. And it seemed that all the others made way for her; and then she suddenly turned and came straight towards me. She stopped and looked at me. Her eyes were like the eyes of a falcon, yellow and big and bright as could be. And I asked her: "Who are you?" And she said to me: "I am your death." I should've been frightened, but instead I was happy as a child, I swear to God I was! And this woman, my death, said to me: "I am sorry for you, Lukeria, but I cannot take you with me. Farewell!" O Lord, what sorrow there was for me then! "Take me," I cried, "beloved mother, dear one, take me!" And my death turned to face me and began to speak . . . And I understood that she was appointing the hour when I should die, but I couldn't quite grasp it, it wasn't clear, except that it would be some time after Saint Peter's Day . . . Then I woke up. Such surprising dreams I've been having!'

Lukeria raised her eyes to the ceiling and grew reflective.

'Only I have this one trouble, that a whole week may pass and I never once go to sleep. Last year there was a lady who came by, saw me and gave me a little bottle with some medicine to make me sleep. She told me to take ten drops each time. That was a great help to me, and I slept. Only now that little bottle's long ago finished. Do you know what that medicine was and how to get it?'

The lady who came by obviously gave Lukeria opium. I promised to procure such a little bottle for her and again could not restrain myself from remarking aloud at her patience.

'Oh, master!' she protested. 'What d'you mean by that? What sort of patience? Now Simon Stilites' patience was really great: he spent thirty years on a pillar! And there was another of God's servants who ordered himself to be buried in the ground up to his chest, and the ants ate his face . . . And here's something else that an avid reader of the Bible told me: there was a certain country, and that country was conquered by the Hagarenes, and they tortured and killed all who lived therein; and no matter what those who lived there did, they could in no way free themselves. And there appeared among those who dwelt in that country a holy virgin; she took a mighty sword and arrayed herself in heavy armour and went out against the Hagarenes and did drive them all across the sea. But when she had driven them away, she said to them: "Now it is time that you should burn me, for such was my promise, that I should suffer a fiery death for my people." And the Hagarenes seized her and burned her, but from that time forward her people were freed for ever! Now that's a really great feat of suffering! Mine's not like that!'

I wondered to myself in astonishment at the distance the legend of Joan of Arc had travelled and the form it had taken, and after a brief silence I asked Lukeria how old she was.

'Twenty-eight . . . or twenty-nine. I'm not thirty yet. What's the good of counting them, the years, I mean! I'll tell you something else . . .'

Lukeria suddenly coughed huskily and gave a groan.

'You are talking a great deal,' I remarked to her, 'and it could be bad for you.'

'That's true,' she whispered, hardly audible. 'Our little talk's got to end, no matter what happens! Now that you'll be going I'll be quiet as long as I wish. I've unburdened my heart to the full . . .'

I began to take leave of her, repeating my promise to send her the medicine and imploring her again to give careful thought to my question whether there was anything that she needed.

'I don't need anything, I'm quite content, praise God,' she uttered with the greatest of effort, but moved by my concern. 'God grant everyone good health! And you, master, tell your mother that, because the peasants here are poor, she should take a little less in rent from them! They haven't enough land, there isn't an abundance of anything . . . They'd give thanks to God for you if you did that . . . But I don't need a thing – I'm quite content.'

I gave Lukeria my word that I would fulfil her request and was already on the way to the door when she called to me again.

'Remember, master,' she said, and something wondrous glimmered in her eyes and on her lips, 'what long tresses I had? Remember, they reached right down to my knees! For a long time I couldn't make up my mind . . . Such long hair! . . . But how could I comb it out? In my state, after all! . . . So I cut it all off . . .

Yes, that's what I did ... Well, master, forgive me! I can't go on any more ...'

That very day, before setting out for the hunt, I had a talk about Lukeria with the farm overseer. I learned from him that she was known in the village as the 'Living Relic' and that, in this regard, there had never been any trouble from her; never a murmur was to be heard from her, never a word of complaint. 'She herself asks for nothing, but, quite to the contrary, is thankful for everything; a quiet one, if ever there was a quiet one, that's for sure. Struck down by God, most likely for her sins,' the overseer concluded, 'but we don't go into that. And as, for instance, for passing judgement on her – no, we don't pass judgement. Let her alone!'

A few weeks later I learned that Lukeria had died. Her death had come for her, as she thought – 'after Saint Peter's Day'. There were rumours that on the day of her death she heard a bell ringing all the time, although from Alekseyevka to the church is a matter of three miles or more and it was not a Sunday. Lukeria, however, said that the ringing did not come from the church, but 'from above'. Probably she did not dare to say that it came from heaven.

I have set against this story by Turgenev a poem by the obscure country parson Thomas Traherne; it was written just after the English Civil War in a small Herefordshire town, but remained unknown and unpublished for more than two centuries. Like most of his writing, 'The Preparative' celebrates Traherne's joy in everything that lives and moves. It echoes the pantheism of Blake and Dickinson, as of Turgenev's Lukeria:

My body being dead, my limbs unknown;
    Before I skill'd to prize
    Those living stars, mine eyes;
Before my tongue or cheeks were to me shewn,
    Before I knew my hands were mine,
Or that my sinews did my members join;
    When neither nostril, foot, nor ear,
As yet was seen, or felt, or did appear;
    I was within
A house I knew not, newly cloth'd with skin.
Then was my Soul my only all to me,
    A living endless eye,
    Scarce bounded with the sky,
Whose power, whose act, whose essence was to see:

I was an inward sphere of light,
Or an interminable orb of sight,
        An endless and a living day,
A vital sun that round about did ray:
                All life, all sense,
A naked, simple, pure intelligence.

I then no thirst nor hunger did perceive;
            No dull necessity,
            No want was known to me:
Without disturbance then I did receive
        The fair ideas of all things,
And had the honey even without the stings.
        A meditating inward eye
Gazing at quiet did within me lie,
                And every thing
Delighted me that was their heavenly king.

For sight inherits beauty; hearing, sounds;
        The nostril, sweet perfumes,
        All tastes have hidden rooms
Within the tongue; the feeling feeling wounds
        With pleasure and delight: but I
Forgot the rest, and was all sight or eye,
        Unbody'd and devoid of care,
Just as in heav'n the holy angels are:
                For simple sense
Is lord of all created excellence.

A disentangled and a naked sense,
        A mind that's unpossess'd,
        A disengaged breast,
An empty and a quick intelligence
        Acquainted with the golden mean,
An even spirit, pure, and serene,
        Is that where beauty, excellence
And pleasure keep their court of residence.
                My soul retire,
Get free, and so thou shalt even all admire.

Being thus prepar'd for all felicity;
            Not prepossess'd with dross,
            Nor basely glued to gross
And dull materials that might ruin me,
            Not fetter'd by an iron fate,
With vain affections in my earthy state,

To anything that might seduce
My sense, or else bereave it of its use;
        I was as free
As if there were nor sin nor misery.

Pure empty powers that did nothing loathe,
        Did, like the fairest glass
        Or spotless polish'd brass,
Themselves soon in their object's image clothe:
        Divine impressions, when they came,
Did quickly enter and my soul inflame.
        'Tis not the object, but the light,
That maketh heav'n: 'tis a truer sight.
        Felicity
Appears to none but them that purely see.

This book has been much concerned to explore those realities which escape capture by scientific reason. Those words of Traherne express my feelings best:

'Tis not the object, but the light,
That maketh heav'n.

EPILOGUE

A book like this is never finished. Every time I look at a page I wish I had added something new. In recent years our understanding of the world outside Western Europe has been expanded by a series of great writers from Latin America such as Borges and Marquez, and by writers from tropical Africa and Asia. The first cultural thaw in Moscow under Khrushchev allowed Yevtushenko and Solzhenitsyn to reveal something of Soviet life as it really was. Now the end of the Cold War has released a flood of great writing from Eastern Europe as well as the Soviet Union, of which I have most enjoyed some of the Polish poets and the magical short stories of the Russian Tatyana Tolstoya.

However, this is not a collection of my favourite writings, but of writings which have influenced or reflected my own life. Even limiting it in this way faced me with difficult choices. I have also had to consider a question I had not cared to confront before. What is the relationship between art and life? So I was forced back to the issue raised by that passage in Kant which had most baffled me at Oxford. How do we explain our consciousness of ourselves as human beings?

When I had completed the last chapter I read the whole book through again with as cold an eye as I could muster; I then realized how difficult I found it in later life to see myself as I really was as a boy, or a student, or a soldier. My memory was inevitably coloured by everything that has happened to me since, and perhaps by a preference for dwelling on the happier aspects of my past. Children are not in their own eyes the 'moving jewels' which Traherne describes; indeed I quoted his own admission that when he was only four years old he had moments of dejection and rebellion against the lot which God had given him.

Youth, too, rarely lives up in practice to the romantic claims of popular song and of advertising copy. In retrospect, however, we tend to see it in a rosier glow. Wordsworth said that 'poetry takes its origin from emotion recollected in tranquillity'. Yet that tranquillity in itself is bound to lead to a reshaping of the original emotion − which is why Wendy Cope confesses: 'Sometimes poetry is emotion recollected in a highly emotional state'.

Memory is bound to distort reality; poetry and painting add to the distortion by turning the original reality into words and sounds with rhyme and rhythm, or into lines and colours with shapes which form a pattern. And when we read a poem for the second or third time after an interval of years it will mean something different to us; we will interpret it afresh in the light of our own experience since we read it first. That is why a great poem, or novel, or painting, or piece of music is a source of never-ending delight. Every time we encounter it, we learn something new about ourselves as well. It enables us to confront reality in a different way, in the light of our own experience as well that of the poet or artist. We examine what is left in us of our past as a child or student, or lover, or soldier − or indeed as a politician.

Besides being a source of infinite enjoyment, reading is a tool for understanding ourselves and the world around us. It is not possible to express that understanding in the sort of propositions which are used by science, or to confine them in the straitjacket of logical analysis.

Nature, the arts, and human relations are all worlds which transcend the world of the scientist. And each of them has its own infinite variety. These worlds can include contradictions, opposites, or contraries, as Blake called them, in ways which are abhorrent to science. They can be explored directly, and through the work of painters, musicians, and writers. I hope that in reading this book you too will discover that quality which Thomas Traherne described as 'Insatiableness':

This busy, vast, enquiring Soul
Brooks no Controul,
No limits will endure,
Nor any Rest: It will all see,
Not Time alone, but ev'n Eternity.

'Tis mean Ambition to desire
A single World:
To many I aspire,
Tho one upon another hurl'd:
Nor will they all, if they be all confin'd
Delight my mind.

This busy, vast enquiring Soul
Brooks no Controul;
'Tis hugely curious too.
Each one of all those Worlds must be
Enricht with infinite Variety
And Worth; or 'twill not do.

POSTSCRIPT

A GUIDE TO FURTHER READING

I have tried wherever possible to give the source of my quotations where they occur. Most of the books from which I have quoted are easily available in bookshops and libraries. Most poets of the nineteenth century and earlier, including Traherne, Cleveland and Hopkins, have been reprinted by the Oxford University Press, while Faber & Faber have published much of the twentieth-century poetry. Penguin have republished selections from many modern poets, as well as some excellent anthologies. I found the poem of Anna Kamienska in the autumn 1991 issue of that invaluable magazine *Poetry Review*, which has published many translations of poetry from Eastern Europe and Russia.

There are many first-rate anthologies which include lesser-known poets. The Oxford Books of English Verse cover most centuries and many themes; in recent years I have much enjoyed the New Oxford Books of English Verse, which have republished fascinating poetry which has never been printed since its first editions – particularly the *New Oxford Book of Eighteenth Century Verse* and the *New Oxford Book of Women's Verse*. Most of my poems about the Second World War are drawn from the excellent volumes published by the Everyman Library of selections made by the Salamander Oasis Trust.

Wherever possible, I like to read contemporary editions of the poets; so I have been a hopeless addict of second-hand bookshops since my schooldays. In recent years market forces have brought an increasing torrent of closures, since most second-hand booksellers cannot afford the rents and taxes imposed on their shops; if they continue at all, they tend to work from home and by post. It is difficult to find an accurate and up-to-date guide to second-hand booksellers; probably the best is the *Skoob Directory of Second-Hand Bookshops in the British Isles*. (Skoob Publishing Ltd, 15 Sicilian Avenue, London WC1A 2QH.) It is periodically updated.

I particularly cherish two editions, now alas available only second-hand – the Nonesuch Press, which produced exquisitely bound and printed volumes of Donne, Milton, Blake, Shelley and Coleridge in the thirties and forties, and the older Muses' Library, which published some of the lesser-known poets such as Campion, Beddoes and Clough. They are well worth looking out for.

A special word now about some of my favourites.

Emily Dickinson

The first complete edition of Emily Dickinson's poems was edited by Thomas H. Johnson and published in America in 1955. Faber & Faber now publish it in England. Johnson also published her letters, in three volumes, and an indispensable selection of the letters in 1971. They are published by the Belknap Press of Harvard University. By far the best book on Dickinson's life is also by Johnson – *Emily Dickinson, an Interpretive Biography*. I have found it quite indispensable as a guide to the work of a poet who is often very difficult to understand. It is now available from Atheneum Publishers, New York, a subsidiary of Macmillan, and is well worth much effort to obtain. A much fuller biography by Richard B. Sewell, *The Life of Emily Dickinson*, is published by Farrar, Strauss and Giroux, New York.

Gerard Manley Hopkins

Besides his collected poems, his notebooks and letters repay careful reading. The last year has produced two good lives of Hopkins – *A Very Private Life* by Robert Bernard Martin is probably the better, and already available as a Flamingo paperback. Since much of his poetry is as difficult as Dickinson's, it is worth getting *A*

Reader's Guide to Gerard Manley Hopkins by Norman H. Mackenzie (Thames and Hudson, 1981).

William Butler Yeats

His poetry and plays are now available in good paperback editions; you will also enjoy much of his prose, of which Pan Books published a good selection in 1980. His biography by Norman Jeffares (Hutchinson, 1988) is indispensable; there are also two entertaining volumes of *Interviews and Recollections* edited by E.H. Mikhail (Macmillan, 1977). I doubt if any modern writer has attracted such an avalanche of critical studies; many of them are well worth reading. In my view the best are two books by Richard Ellman, *Yeats, the Man and the Masks* and *The Identity of Yeats.*

Rudyard Kipling

Kipling's poems and stories are easily obtained. Angus Wilson has written a brilliant biography, *The Strange Ride of Rudyard Kipling: His Life and Works*, published by Secker & Warburg.

Virginia Woolf

Her novels are now all published in paperback. Penguin have published her diaries in five volumes, Chatto and Windus her letters in six. Her essays, reviews, and occasional writings are still appearing, volume by volume. Though I love her novels, I find the rest of her work even more enjoyable – especially the diaries and letters. If you find the complete sets too daunting, the Hogarth Press has published good selections of the diaries in *A Moment's Liberty*, and of the letters in *Congenial Spirits*.

Leonard Woolf's memoirs are also published by the Hogarth Press, in five volumes. They constitute one of the best chronicles of the first seventy years of the twentieth century. The Woolfs wrote so well about themselves that others can add little worthwhile. However, Virginia's nephew, Quentin Bell, wrote one of the best biographies of our time about his aunt, explaining some of the things which his subject took for granted or did not care to disclose. *Virginia Woolf* is now published in paperback by Triad Paladin Grafton Books. Quentin Bell has also written a sympathetic yet penetrating account of the Bloomsbury set as a whole, in *Bloomsbury*, Futura Publications.

Dylan Thomas

Though his poems are his best work, much of his prose has the same boisterous vitality – particularly the pieces in *A Prospect of the Sea*. His radio play *Under Milk Wood* is unique, and best listened to in the recording with Richard Burton. Constantine FitzGibbon has edited his letters and written his life – a sad story made even sadder by the memoir of his widow, Caitlin, *Leftover Life to Kill*.

Plato

Benjamin Jowett, the nineteenth-century Master of Balliol, produced the best translation of Plato's *Dialogues*. All are worth reading. The *Republic* gives the best picture of Plato's political philosophy and The *Phaedo* gives an unforgettable account of the death of Socrates.

Kant

The best advice on reading Kant was given in a letter by the poet Coleridge:

> I enquired after all the more popular writings of Kant – read them with delight. I then read the prefaces of several of his systematic works, as the Prolegomena etc; here too every part I understood – and that was nearly the whole – was replete with sound and plain tho' bold and novel truths to me; and I followed Socrates' adage respecting Heraclitus – all I understand is excellent; and I am bound to presume that the rest is at least worth the trouble of trying whether it be not equally so.

When I was totally lost in the tortuous anfractuosities of Kant's greatest work, the *Critique of Pure Reason*, I went back to his *Prolegomena to Any Future Metaphysics*, edited in English by Dr Paul Carus, published by Kegan Paul, Trench and Trubner in 1909. All was in fact made plain. Apart from Kant's own words, which were here so much clearer than in his masterpiece, there was an essay by Carus on Kant's philosophy and a series of essays by other scholars. Above all there were Heine's remarks on Kant, which I have quoted.

Heine

Heine's poetry is untranslatable, though brave attempts have been made. His prose, however, has been brilliantly selected, edited, and translated by Frederic Ewen, together with an eloquent study of the man, in *Heinrich Heine: Self Portrait and Other Prose Writings* (Citadel Press, Secaucus, New Jersey). I have quoted a great deal from this selection, because Heine is both an education and a pleasure to read on any subject.

Benjamin Franklin

Far too much excellent writing published in the United States is difficult to find in Britain. The best collection of Benjamin Franklin is a beautifully printed volume of over fifteen hundred pages published by the Library of America in 1987, which I picked up for twenty-two dollars at a second-hand bookshop in Palo Alto only last year. However, the first-rate biography of Franklin by Carl van Doren (Putnam 1939) can still be found in Britain.

John Muir

John Muir is also very difficult to find in Britain, though he ranks with the very best writers on nature and travel. Most of his work is published in Boston by Houghton Mifflin. By far the best introduction is their anthology, *The Wilderness World of John Muir*, with comments by Edwin Way Teale.

Writing on Literature

Every generation, in every country, will approach writing in a different way, reflecting the attitudes prevalent in its society at the time. So every generation will also see different qualities or defects in the literature of the past. Your own enjoyment will be enriched by reading what outstanding writers have had to say about their contemporaries and their predecessors.

As a schoolboy in the early thirties I was greatly influenced by F.R. Leavis' *New Bearings in English Poetry* (Chatto & Windus,

1932); this rejected the spirit of the Georgian poets who dominated the twenties in favour of the later Yeats, T.S. Eliot, Ezra Pound and Hopkins. Leavis applied the same criteria in his later work — for example *The Common Pursuit*, and *Revaluations* (Penguin Books).

The poets themselves are even more stimulating. T.S. Eliot in *Selected Essays* (Faber & Faber), covers literature from the Greeks to the twentieth century, with a section on religious writing and even an essay on the music-hall singer Marie Lloyd!

W.H. Auden wrote brilliantly about everything, with a more eclectic taste reflecting the generation which lived through the last war. *The Dyer's Hand* and *Forewords and Afterwords* (Faber & Faber) range very widely — over music and opera as well as poetry and prose.

As I was writing this book early in 1992, many parts of the world were convulsed by conflicts over religion, nationalism and race. The poet and lecturer Tom Paulin has just produced a collection of essays, *Minotaur — Poetry and the Nation State* (Faber & Faber), in which he uses an Ulsterman's insight to examine these elements in many of the poets I have quoted — including Milton, Clare, Clough, Dickinson, Hopkins, Yeats and Robert Frost, as well as novelists from Dickens to D.H. Lawrence. It is well worth reading to discover once again how poetry can illuminate the problems of its time. And in an age when so many universities are dominated by unloving and humourless reductionists, it is good to find in Tom Paulin a Reader in Poetry who actually enjoys reading poetry!

ACKNOWLEDGEMENTS

I have made use in this book of parts of my earlier writings: *Healey's Eye* (Jonathan Cape, 1980), *The Woolfs and Politics* (*The Charleston Magazine*, September 1990), the 1990 Baggs Memorial Lecture on 'Happiness' (University of Birmingham), and 'Voices Recalled from a Cataclysm' (*The Times*, 23 July 1990).

The author and publishers would like to thank the following for permission to reproduce extracts from copyright material:

Faber & Faber Ltd for 'Lullaby', 'Musée des Beaux Arts', 'A Tribute to W. B. Yeats' from *Collected Poems* by W. H. Auden and for *Forewords and Afterwords* and *The Dyer's Hand* by W. H. Auden; Pan Books Ltd for *Murphy* by Samuel Beckett; Peters Fraser & Dunlop Group Ltd for 'The Pacifist' and 'Epitaph on the Politician Himself' from *Complete Verse* by Hilaire Belloc; John Murray (Publishers) Ltd for 'Mayday Song for North Oxford', 'Myfanwy at Oxford', 'Parliament Hill Fields' and 'In a Bath Teashop' from *Collected Poems* by John Betjeman; Quartet Books Ltd for *In Place of Fear* by Aneurin Bevan; Macmillan London Ltd for 'Timothy Winters' and 'Ward 14' from *Collected Poems 1951–1975* by Charles Causley; Faber & Faber Ltd for 'Bloody Men' and 'Men and Their Boring Arguments' by Wendy Cope; Penguin Books Ltd for *Nineteen Nineteen* by John Dos Passos; Penguin Books Ltd for *The Brothers Karamazov* by Fyodor Dostoevsky, translated by David Magarshack; Faber & Faber Ltd for 'Burnt

INDEX